Becoming Farah

A Life in Bombay, 1943 to 1986

Farah Rustom

DEDICATION

This book is dedicated to my lifelong friend Aubrey Stanley, who came out of retirement to inspire and help me complete my memoir, and came up with the evocative title, *Becoming Farah*.

And to Michael Anderson for his selfless dedication in offering his expertise as well countless hours of attention to the minutest details to publish this book, which otherwise would never have seen the light of day.

This book is therefore dedicated with all my heart both to Michael Anderson and Aubrey Stanley.

CONTENTS

Preface

Some of you may be wondering why you should read this memoir. As most of you have never heard of me, please allow me introduce myself.

I was born in November 1943 at the Parsi Lying-in Hospital (also known as Temulji's Lying-in Hospital) to middle-class parents. I grew up in a two-room, dilapidated flat on Wodehouse Road. Though the building teetered on the verge of collapse every monsoon, the location was excellent, just a block away from old Cuffe Parade with its lovely villas, which are all sadly gone now and replaced by skyscrapers. I spent my evenings walking on the elevated walkway by the sea, watching the sunset, memorizing my French verbs and vocabulary, and eating *bhel puri* before returning home.

I had a lonely childhood as I was an unwanted child, and my older brother was put in a boarding school when I was born, so he too hated me as he thought that my parents preferred me to him. The fact was that they simply could not afford to send both of us to boarding school, so they sent me to St. Mary's school, far from our house, where I received an excellent education. Unfortunately, none of my classmates lived close to me so I had no playmates.

I was born a boy and called Farokh. But inside, I have been a girl ever since I can remember.

So in addition to bearing the burden of being an unwanted child and being rejected by my brother, I was without playmates. I was even more lonely as my father was ashamed of me for being a "sissy."

I too was ashamed of myself for being a sissy and for feeling the way I did, so I buried myself in books and my studies and found comfort there.

I had one real passion, and that was the piano. Our Anglo-Indian neighbours across the street, the Borthwicks , had a piano with which I fell madly in love and when my mother went to visit them, Jerry Borthwick would pick me up and put me on the revolving piano stool, knowing that I would blissfully play one key at a time with a chubby little finger, listening to the golden tones.

1

I started writing this memoir as a series of emails to my friends, some of whom had known me all my life and had, like me, grown up in Bombay, (but most of whom are now scattered like me, around the world), as well as new ones from the New World and England. I called it an "Epistolary Memoir " and wrote like one possessed, as memories came flooding in, and ideas for the next chapter presented themselves even before I finished the one that I was typing.

Then one day it was complete, and to my amazement and immense gratitude, my school friend Aubrey Stanley came out of retirement and took all my letters and arranged them in book form.

And so, for the first time, I began to think of publishing my memoir. I had undergone a landmark transgender surgery (called a sex change operation in those days) at the Masina Hospital in 1976 which sent shock waves through Bombay and the Parsi community in particular. I was then thirty-two years old and was known to classical music lovers in the city for my courses in classical music appreciation at the Indo-American Society and Max Muller Bhavan, and for my recitals, thanks to my great teacher Madame Olga Craen. So yes, my love of the piano bore fruit and my dream of being a woman also came true, and the details of how all this came about are in this memoir.

While the Parsis gasped, they were also sophisticated enough to accept me as Farah and were very kind to me, though I am sure that there may have been a few juicy jokes behind my back, which is quite understandable under the circumstances.

While I was commended for my courage, thousands of people couldn't understand how such a transformation was possible, for I *looked* like a woman, a normal Parsi woman in a sari worn in the Gujarati style.

So I gave interviews to magazines and wrote articles explaining the intensive hormone therapy I received before the surgery, all of which I have detailed here. I received thousands of letters of appreciation as well as gratitude (from others in my shoes) from all over India.

Without intending to, I became famous and got to meet famous celebrities at cocktail parties to which I was invited. I got newspaper columns and became music as well as foreign film critic for Mid-Day..

I was also given a social column for the Daily and interviewed many famous Bollywood stars such as Deepti Naval, like Shabhana

Azmi, Nutan (on whose son Mohnish Behl I developed a crush), Om Puri, Shashi Kapoor, and Mithun Chakraborty. I had my photo taken with some of them and they are in the book.

From 1976 to 1986 I rode on the crest of a wave of popularity and in 1986 I left Bombay and never returned, so most of you will never have heard of me.

The sub-title of my memoir *Becoming Farah* is *A Life in Bombay, 1943 to 1986*, so I have chosen to end it there.

I hope that my story will bring hope and courage to all those who are struggling with intimate personal problems, to live their lives fearlessly and authentically, and thereby find the fulfilment in life that every human being deserves. For those of you who are simply looking for a good read, I hope that this book brings a few hours of pleasure and information, because isn't that what books are for?

Farah Rustom

A Word from the Editor

I came across Farah Rustom quite by chance in a Facebook group, in an exchange of comments on a subject about Bombay with which I happened to have a personal connection. An email correspondence ensued, and I eventually agreed to act as editor and help her publish her memoir. While I have until now focused primarily on my own work, I found this particular memoir to be of exceptional interest.

Bombay in the period covered here was a very special place, sophisticated, cosmopolitan and cultured, with many imposing public buildings and gracious bungalows. I was born and brought up there from 1949 to 1968, and unlike most of my European contemporaries was a full-time resident and went to school there as well. And while I am obviously familiar with many things that Farah mentions, especially relating to the Parsi community, my personal experiences overall could hardly have been more different.

Farokh / Farah is a Parsi, one of a tiny minority in India, Zoroastrians who fled from Persia over a millennium ago and who despite their lack of numbers, have had disproportionate impact on India and Bombay in particular, where most of them now live. Her descriptions give a unique and colourful insight into the life of Parsis of all classes, an ethnic group virtually unknown outside India.

And there is Bombay itself, the star of the show. Farah describes its many facets and the city's uneasy transition into the world of modern India, as well as her travels to the Himalayan Hill Stations she loved and her tour of Europe and year in Ethiopia.

And last but not least is Farah herself, with an impressive list of achievements personally, academically and musically, and the recipient of the very first successful transgender operation in India that transitioned her to the final female form she had always longed for. Along with many insightful and delightfully personal asides on people and other places in India, this is the altogether unique account of an extraordinary life in times that are already fading from our collective memory.

Michael Anderson
London, 2023
www.michaelanderson.org

1 - I Enter This Beautiful and Terrible World, Independence Day and Gandhi's Assassination, Mrs. Archer, My First Dress, and Daddy's Sola Hat

I was born in Bombay on the west coast of British India on the 14th of November 1943, the second of two children. My older brother was born in Bhusawal in central India, not far from Bhopal where the infamous poison gas leak by Union Carbide occurred in 1986. Bhusawal was a railway junction where trains from different parts of India intersected, and as my great-grandfather on my mother's side was an engine driver in the railways under the British, my mother was born there.

A month before my brother was due my father took her from Bombay to Bhusawal, as it was the custom for a woman to deliver her first child in her mother's house. Mummy's labour was long and arduous, lasting over twelve hours. The midwife kept asking my grandmother, "Shall I put a cut?" But my grandmother asked her to wait until she finally gave in.

"Oh, Mummy, it must have been so painful!" I exclaimed as my mother told me this over lunch one day when I was a young woman.

"I was in so much pain that I did not even feel the cut," she replied. This cut, though, would lead to the prolapse of her uterus in middle age, as happens in all such cases. Fortunately, the sister of a classmate of mine in Elphinstone College was a gynaecologist and had her private clinic just a couple of blocks from our house. She did a superb job of surgically repairing the damage, and Mummy was fine after that. (It was the impending surgery that triggered her to tell me about my brother's birth). But I digress.

When it was my turn to arrive, Mummy decided to have me at the Parsi Lying-in Hospital across the street from the Cathedral and John Canon School in downtown Bombay.

Her water broke at 2.30 am and Daddy ran to fetch a taxi. As we lived on a quiet residential street, he thought he'd have to run a mile before he could find a taxi at that hour. But as he came out of the building, a taxi miraculously appeared out of nowhere and he immediately flagged it down. Three hours later I opened my eyes to this world for the first time.

"You gave me no trouble at all, as you were my second child." It was the first nice thing my mother had ever said to me (I was in my twenties at the time). It was, unfortunately, also the last.

When I was two days old, I was taken from the maternity hospital to our flat at 61 Wodehouse Road in Colaba, at the southern tip of Bombay. Our building was just half a mile from the cantonment area which was reserved for the army, after which the island disappeared into the sea. It was a dilapidated old building, and it was an eyesore on beautiful Wodehouse Road. When I was older I remember that I was always ashamed of it, because everyone I knew lived in far better buildings and people were shocked when they saw the humble circumstances in which I was living when they first came to my place.

As Mummy did not want to have anything to do with me, because I was an unwanted child that she could not abort, Daddy used to bottle-feed me. He told me that I insisted on holding the bottle myself and that when it was empty, I would fling it away. Daddy, and our servant Namdev who was then only seventeen years old, would stand on either side of my cradle ready to catch the glass bottle as I flung it.

I was never far from the sea. Our view of the Arabian Sea was blocked by the fancy bungalows of Cuffe Parade. These were upscale bungalows built on land reclaimed from the sea in the 1920s. They had elaborate turrets and towers and domes, somewhat like the fantastic pavilion at Brighton.

Namdev used to carry me in his arms and walk me on Cuffe Parade on hot, somnolent afternoons. He would walk to the end of a jetty that jutted out into the sea. There was a mangrove swamp on one side of it, and I used to watch the water snakes and crabs and crustaceans that swam in its clear waters with fascination, from the safety of his arms. One day, he picked a magnolia flower from the garden of one of the bungalows at Cuffe Parade and I gazed into its yellow chalice with rapture, inhaling its intoxicating fragrance,

There was an elevated walkway across the quiet street from the bungalows, with benches on which one could sit and watch the sun set into the Arabian Sea, as that part of the Indian Ocean that washes the west coast of India is called. Growing up, I would sit on one of those benches watching the sun melt into the sea and memorizing my French verbs and vocabulary. There was a man who would walk up and down with a basket around his neck selling shelled peanuts, with a small pot of coal placed atop the peanuts to keep them warm. He would fill a small paper cone made from old newspapers and sell the peanuts for a couple of annas (back then a rupee comprised 16 annas). At dusk, I would always buy one of these and munch on the peanuts before going home, which was only a block away.

A special treat would be to walk to the southern tip of the walkway, near the mangrove swamp, where a man sold *bhel puri*, a hot-sweet mouth-watering snack of rice and tamarind sauce which I ate out of a soggy old newspaper plate mopping up the remnants with a hot puri, while sitting on the tip of the jetty which was lapped by waves even at low tide. The jetty was old, gnarled and encrusted with limpets and there were large openings in it at periodic intervals through which one could see the sea water swirling below at high tide. I was always afraid of falling through one of those cracks.

BEST (Bombay Electric Supply and Transport Company) double-decker buses would lumber past our home every twenty minutes and the first bus at 7 a.m. acted as an alarm clock for my day. But no buses were allowed on Cuffe Parade which was quiet and almost devoid of traffic, except for the occasional Dodge or a Cadillac that would emerge from a bungalow garage.

(2)

One of my earliest memories is of the very first Independence Day on 15th August 1947, when I was three years and nine months old. I vividly remember being in my father's arms with jubilant crowds all around and an open truck carrying sailors going by, and one of them putting the new Indian flag in my tiny hand, calling out "Baby!" I was wearing a *jhabloo,* a sequined dress that little Parsi boys wore for their first four or five years, and he naturally took me for a girl.

Another vivid memory is of the day five months later when Gandhi was shot, in January 1948. It was evening, and my parents had left for a walk on Cuffe Parade, leaving me at home with the teenage servants and I was startled when they returned just five minutes later. Daddy looked pale and visibly shaken, and Mummy had her usual frown on her face. Daddy immediately switched on our old RCA radio and started listening intently. When I was old enough to understand, Daddy told me that as he and my mother reached the corner of our building, the owner of the little bookstall, who was closing his shop, said to my father, "Where are you going, Mr. Rustom?"

"We are going to Cuffe Parade," said Daddy calmly.

"Go home!" shouted Jamnadas, "Gandhi has been shot!"

My parents instantly turned around and returned home.

Rivers of blood had flowed in Punjab and in Bengal just a few months earlier because of the Partition, and though there had been no bloodshed in Bombay, my parents rightly feared that Gandhi's assassination would set off bloody Hindu-Muslim riots across the length and breadth of India.

The nation heaved a sigh of relief when it learned that the assassin had been a Hindu. Had it been a Muslim, the massacre, looting, burning, and rioting would have been unimaginable and the whole of India would have become an inferno.

But the partition did bring an influx of Hindu refugees from Sindh, which was now in Pakistan, into Bombay. This enterprising business community first lived in refugee camps in Chembur in North Bombay. But they soon prospered and started snapping up flats (apartments) in South Bombay where we lived. They came up with the concept of condominiums, which they called "ownership basis flats." Soon high rises began to spring up on every vacant lot and Colaba became crowded and prohibitively expensive.

In a word, Independence and the abrupt departure of the British swiftly changed the world into which I was born. In a surge of patriotism, it was even suggested that schools should no longer teach in English!!! This was vehemently opposed by all educated Indians, the Parsis and Catholics taking the lead. Fortunately, wiser counsels prevailed.

(3)

When I was four years old I was sent to Mrs. Laly's Montessori School, where I didn't learn a thing. It was run by a Parsi lady in her spacious apartment behind the Gateway of India. My brother, who was five years older than I and a born artist, had taught me how to draw a duck and the teachers always asked me to draw a duck on the blackboard and it made me feel proud and happy.

After a short lunch break when we ate the sandwiches that we had brought from home, we all stood up and said, 'Good Afternoon Aunty,' as all the teachers were Parsis. To my five-year-old ears, it sounded like "Khoda Taari Punty."

So, when Daddy asked me what I had learned in school I said, "Khoda Taari Punty" even though I didn't have a clue what it meant. Daddy laughed till he cried!

A year later, my mother sent me to be privately tutored by a retired Anglo-Indian school mistress, Mrs. Archer. She was very white and to me looked totally English. Her husband, Mr. Archer, had lost a leg in the First World War. He walked with a crutch and smoked a pipe with the other hand. He was friendly and would stand around chatting with the local shopkeepers and the fruit stall guy and others. Everyone liked him.

Mrs. Archer was a beautiful, white-haired woman in her sixties or seventies, of average height and build. She wore cotton dresses and looked every inch the school mistress.

The Archers lived just around the corner from our house, so I used to go for my lessons by myself. Their flat was on the ground floor, with stone steps leading up to it and Mrs. Archer had flowerpots bathed in sunshine on either side of them. She also had cats which stared at me, and of whom I was afraid. This was because there were feral cats in the narrow alley which ran alongside our apartment, and they fed on the large rats or bandicoots which sometimes even made it into our second-floor apartment, to my utter horror and revulsion. These cats would sometimes get into fierce fights with one another, and during the day, when I looked down at them, they stared back at me with myopic eyes. That is how I developed a lifelong aversion to cats.

I spent enchanting hours with Mrs. Archer and soon became proficient in speaking, reading, and writing English. She was a teacher belonging to the old school, and when she said "Spell 'beautiful,'" and I started "b-u," and she said, "Stretch out your hand." Whack came the cane down on my chubby little hand and soon it was swollen black and blue with fierce welts on it.

But I liked her nonetheless and spent many happy hours with her, reading the stories and poems in The Radiant Way, looking at elementary Geography books and black and white photos of Tibetans and Native Americans and the Empire State Building. I loved the watercolours in the Radiant Way, depicting English flowers, and barefoot English children frolicking on the beach running hand in hand, their hair flying in the sea breeze, and Grace Darling and her father in a boat on a stormy sea going to rescue the victims of a shipwreck.

All this was meant to prepare me for the entrance exam for St. Mary's High School. The school had classes from kindergarten all the way to the Senior Cambridge "A" level exams. The Indian government discontinued these exams in 1960, so I was very fortunate that my class — the class of 1959 — was the last class to do the Senior Cambridge Exam. Our question papers came from England and our answer papers were mailed to England to be corrected.

Even though I was only six years old, my mother wanted me to be admitted into the third standard, and Mrs. Archer did her best to prepare me for it in one year. I still remember my entrance exam in St. Mary's conducted by Mrs. Lobo. She decided that I should be placed in the second standard.

This sent my mother into a rage against Mrs. Archer. I can't remember what she said to her, of course, but I remember Mrs. Archer returning to her the dress piece that my mother had given to her before my test. And so I lost a beloved teacher - my first - thanks to my mother. She would eventually fight with all the neighbours, one after the other, leaving me isolated as a child.

(4)

Looking back, I can see that the neighbours loved me, because who doesn't love children? They gave me little tokens of their love. Framroze Uncle next door would tie a Cadbury's chocolate to his walking stick and call my name. I would run as fast as my little legs could carry me and grab the chocolate at the end of the extended stick (from his balcony) with eager hands. Goola Aunty downstairs knitted a "baby suit" for me. And when I came down the stairs wearing a waist-length wig and a dress for a school play, she was the first to say, "Oh, how pretty he looks! He should have been born a girl!" My heart said a fervent *Amen!* I was six years old, in my first year in St. Mary's and desperately unhappy that I wasn't a girl. It was the first time I played a girl's role in our all-boy's school, but not the last. All the way through school I would be given the girl's role and would have been outraged if I had been given any other. So, everyone, the teachers included, was aware of my femininity.

Goola Aunty had been the first to voice it. Thirty years later, when I was Farah and walking by a clothes store near my house, Soona Aunty, who lived across the street from us and was Goola Aunty's sister, came running out of the store calling "Farah! Farah!" and took me into the store to see Goola Aunty who had come for a brief visit from America where she was staying with her only son who had emigrated there. Goola Aunty was delighted to see me as Farah, and I gave her a warm hug! I don't know if she remembered the words she had spoken when I was six, but she must have realized that I had grown up to be the woman I was always meant to be.

(5)

In 1960, when I was sixteen, the Bombay I had grown up in began to change. It would never be the same again. It began with convoys of trucks loaded with dirt, rocks, and rubble, which descended on Cuffe Parade and began to push the sea back. In just a couple of years, the first high-rise was built on the reclaimed land and over the years, there was another and another while the trucks kept coming and pushing the sea further and further back. The beautiful bungalows of Cuffe Parade were demolished one by one, replaced by towering high rises. Finally, even the elevated walkway with its benches where I had spent many happy hours as a child, was demolished in order to widen the road for traffic, but fortunately, this happened after I left Bombay.

Another childhood memory is sitting in a lawn chair in the members' enclosure of the WIFA (Western India Football Association), blissfully sipping lemonade, while Daddy would jump from his chair and shout "Goal!" He was an avid football fan and I still remember the soft thud of the football as it was kicked, and the warm breeze coming from Back Bay.

Daddy always wore a white suit and a sola hat. When I grew up, I would watch from my balcony to see him getting off the bus and I would run downstairs to take his heavy briefcase from him as he came home, hot and exhausted after going all day from business to business, to request them to advertise in the Bombay Samachar, of which he was Advertising Manager.

When I was in college, I persuaded Daddy to trade his coat and tie for the popular "bush shirt" — a light coat with pockets, worn with only a cotton vest under it to soak up perspiration. Daddy loved it, and from that day onwards, he proudly carried his fountain pen in his top left pocket. But he continued to wear his beloved hat. When he died in 1986 he must have been the last Indian to hang up his sola hat on our hat and coat stand, thirty-nine years after the British left.

2 - St. Mary's School, Friends, Puberty

My first year at St. Mary's in 1951 when I was seven, was uneventful except for the first day. During the long recess at 1 A.M, I stepped out onto the playing field beside the Skating Hall to eat my lunch. Lunch was a plain egg sandwich, rather unimaginative: two full-boiled eggs between two slices of bread – no butter, no mayonnaise or ketchup – no nothing. But I was not old enough to know any better, and it was something to eat (thanks to my father, I never knew a day's hunger growing up). I had noticed a number of huge kites soaring in the glaringly bright sky, which were new birds to me as there were none in Colaba where I lived. Suddenly one of them swooped down and snatched the sandwich from my hand as I was about to take a bite, leaving a gash on my forefinger that swiftly began to fill with blood.

I learned very quickly never to eat on the playing field. I also learned to hate kites. I have always hated pain or injury in any form. But that did not stop me from running on the barren and gritty playing field and bruising my knee again and again. That meant a trip to the Infirmary, where the kindly brother Pardo made me sit on a high table and dabbed my knee with a cotton pad dipped in Iodine. Ouch! How I wish he had chosen the gentler Mercurochrome which we used at home!

St. Mary's was founded in 1864 by the Jesuits as a boarding school for orphaned Anglo-Indian boys. The priests devoted themselves body and soul to the education of the boys, including extracurricular student activities such as athletics, sports and music etc. *Mens sana in corpore sano* was their creed.

Sometime later they started admitting non-Catholic day scholars for a fee. The well-to-do Parsis, Hindus and Muslims had not failed to notice the school's growing reputation and what an excellent education it provided. There was a rickety old school bus that came around puttering at twenty miles an hour and picked me up at 8.30 every morning. It took an hour to get me to school, stopping to pick up students and making a detour to fashionable Marine Drive as it drove through the downtown Fort area with its magnificent Neo-

Gothic nineteenth-century structures, and through the native Muslim sector (Mohammed Ali Road) where women in black burkas dodged the traffic, clutching a child with one hand and carrying a baby in the other, and finally to the Portuguese Roman Catholic part of the city, Byculla, where St. Mary's was situated. It was at the foot of Nesbit Bridge, under which great historic trains like the Frontier Mail started their journeys across the length and breadth of the subcontinent.

In later years I would see my Alma Mater from the window of the Frontier Mail (which had once carried mail from England to homesick Englishmen at the frontier in Peshawar, on the border of Afghanistan) on my way to my beloved Himalayan hill stations and not give it a second thought. Little did I know then that there would come a time when I would dream of standing on Nesbit Bridge and looking down on the stone buildings of my school with their Gothic ecclesiastical windows, only to wake up under an alien sky on the other side of the world.

This dream recurred until 2001 when I got my first computer and long-lost friends began to find me on the internet. One of them was Aubrey, my classmate in St. Mary's since 1951. He sent me precious photographs of our school and our classmates for which I was beyond grateful. I was ecstatic! My oldest friend in the world and I still email each other from time to time.

It is yet one more achievement of the Jesuits that generations of St. Marians to this very day are passionately attached to our Alma Mater, though, of course, they did not know it while they were there.

From 1952, when I was in the third standard, I started standing first in class. This was because my mother had told me that if I did not stand first in class, she would not let me into the house. Even back then, when I was but eight years old, I did not believe that she would carry out her threat. But I strove with all my might to stand first in class because this was what she wanted. And I would do anything in the world to win her love and to get even one drop of love from her.

But I also enjoyed studying. There was nothing else to do and I loved books. Both my parents would go out in the evening, leaving me alone with the teenage servants. A very large, dark room separated me from the kitchen, and a long open passage led from there to the servant's room. I was afraid to cross that dark room, so I sat alone in the living room doing my homework with Queen

Victoria, dressed all in black, glaring down at me with her "we are not amused" look. A large portrait of her hung on the wall and I began to take an intense dislike to it. When I became a teenager, I traded it for the Coronation Portrait of King George V and Queen Mary, which was much pleasanter. My parents did not mind at all.

Mummy kept bothering the principal, Father Rebot, to give me a 'double promotion'. He finally agreed, just to get rid of her. But it ruined my math forever. I did, however, do my Senior Cambridge exam at the age of sixteen, and got an aggregate of one (the highest) in English Language, English Literature, French, Scripture, and History.

Returning to St. Mary's, it wasn't just academics. There were elocution competitions, inter-house dramatic competitions, music competitions, and visual instruction during which we were shown documentaries. Distinguished speakers were also invited to come and speak to us. One of them was Gurudayal Malik, a Sikh with a long, white beard. He had been a follower of Gandhi and told us that after he became a barrister he returned to India and went to Gandhi's ashram and offered him his services.

"Very well, go and clean the toilets," said Gandhi.

"What! I am a barrister! I have come to offer you my legal services for free and you are asking me to clean toilets!"

"I am a barrister too," replied the half-naked Gandhi calmly. "If you cannot clean a toilet properly, you are not even as good as the untouchables (whom he renamed Children of God) who perform that humble task!"

I started winning competitions in elocution, first with a simple poem when I was in the third standard (Three Blind Men and the Elephant) and graduating to Shakespeare (Portia's Speech, Hamlet's soliloquy) but I was not given any instruction to help me understand the depth of meaning and beauty in these words.

We had annual prize distributions with a stage constructed overnight on the playfield. We sat beside our proud parents as the stars came out one by one overhead and went up to the stage to collect our prizes which were in the form of books. The prizes were for getting the highest marks in any subject. Once Cardinal Gracias came to hand out the prizes, splendid in his Cardinal's robe, and the Catholic boys went down on one knee and kissed his ring. I envied them. I, being a mere Parsi (Zoroastrian) who was not allowed the privilege. The Cardinal graciously shook our hand instead.

There were also Parent-Teacher socials on the terrace of the new school building built in the 1930s and inaugurated by Lord Linlithgow who later became the Viceroy of India and announced that India was at war with Germany.

Each student sat at a little table with his parents and the masters, teachers and priests circulated among them sitting at each table for five minutes. My heart stopped (I was about ten) when the very handsome Spanish priest, Father Iscla, came and sat with us. He had never smiled when I said "Good morning, Father," on the playfield. But he was very gracious that evening.

The mother of one of my classmates, Nozer Dubash, who was a glamorous divorcee and looked like Ava Gardner, showed up in a dress. A couple of years later she was shot dead by a jealous lover, in a murder-suicide. When my parents told me about it, I expressed my condolences to Nozer who quietly shed tears. He did not come to school by the school bus, but in a chauffeur-driven Dodge. His grandmother looked after him, and after we finished school, we would sit in the same Dodge in front of the sea on Back Bay, and chat while the chauffeur patiently waited to drop me home.

There was a school magazine which carried photographs of every class, with the teachers and masters sitting on chairs while we stood above them in three ascending rows. There was the school calendar in which we wrote our homework assignments, along with the beautiful merit cards with Gothic lettering that I had won for standing first in various subjects, and the special general proficiency cards that I received for standing first in class, and of which I was so proud!

All dust now in a landfill somewhere in Bombay. But how I wish I could have had them with me now!

(2)

Mummy would go round the corner to visit Dolly Aunty who was a cheerful woman and at whose place there was a gathering of ladies every evening. Dolly Aunty had a gay servant called Krishna who lined his eyes with kohl and used her red nail polish, much to the amusement of the ladies. Barefoot and dressed in a simple cotton shirt and shorts, he would simper and act and say things that he knew would make them laugh. When they asked him "How is your husband?" he would make a dismissive gesture with a flick of his wrist and say, "He's dead!" The ladies would roar with laughter because this meant that he and his partner had broken up. This happened every week!

Poor Daddy had a serious gambling addiction and was out playing cards with his friends, or, if it was Sunday, at the racecourse. I can never forget how Daddy, even after he had lost all his money at the racecourse, would come home with a sweet for me in his coat pocket and give it to me with a trembling hand, unshed tears in his eyes. My heart ached for him, and it breaks my heart even today as I type these words!

But this also meant that creditors would come to our house and tell my mother in front of me, "If I don't get my money by next month, I will take the piano." You can imagine how afraid that made me feel!

On a happier note, neighbouring children would drop by to play without announcement, especially during the summer holidays. One of them was Farrokh Bulsara who, I am led to believe, become one of the most famous rock singers of all time after he moved to England where he headed the rock band Queen and sang under the name, Freddie Mercury. He was a couple of years younger than me, easy-going, friendly, a good mimic, and brilliant at checkers. He defeated me every single time.

Farrokh lived in Royal Terrace, diagonally across the street. That was an Art Deco building built in the 1930s, with Venetian tiles covering the floors as opposed to our dilapidated wooden structure with stone floors built-in 1870. I was always afraid that it would come tumbling down in the next monsoon, or go up in flames, and I was heartily ashamed of our building which was an eyesore on Wodehouse Road. This feeling was exacerbated by my mother who always talked of moving to a better building, which of course we never could as Bombay had become prohibitively expensive, and we were protected by the Rent Act. To move to a better flat, we would have had to give hundreds of thousands of rupees to the prospective landlord before we could sign a rental lease.

(**3**)

Moving on in time, when we became teenagers, my classmates began to secretly hit on me. During the dress rehearsal of a Spanish dance in which I was the girl, my partner, a handsome Punjabi boy, whispered in my ear, "I wish you were a girl!"

"So do I", I whispered back.

The first sex change operation in the world had just been performed and Christine Jorgenson's name was known around the world. Her photograph even appeared on the front page of the Times of India. So, some of the boys suggested that I should have a sex change operation. But how could I? These were performed only in the West. I would have loved to go to London and Paris even as a low-budget tourist, but my parents simply did not have that kind of money. How on earth was I to pay for surgery and hospitalization in the expensive West?

There was no hope of that, and I resigned myself to being an effeminate gay, which I was not. I was a girl trapped in a boy's body. It would be many years before I would tell the world - and show the world - who I really was. But by then, I was thirty and had lost out forever on being sweet sixteen. In a word, I became a young woman but lost out on being a young girl.

I developed crushes on the handsome sportsmen in my class, especially on the school captain, who proudly carried the school flag in marchpasts on the playground, presided over by our drill master, Mr. Pardiwala, who loved Nazi style mass drills and made us do a terrifying Tarzan Jump, standing on a "high horse" and holding a thick rope with a large hook and jumping. I just couldn't do it and Mr. Pardiwala exempted me from the drill class, to my great relief. Vincent, the school captain, never even looked at me. I was the geek of the class, with disfiguring glasses. Decades later, when Aubrey brought us all together with his wonderful website on St. Mary's, I emailed Vincent who was then in Florida. I told him about the crush I had on him in school.

"Oh why didn't you tell me then!" he emailed back. But how could I? He never even looked at me! Ha! Ha!

I also developed a teenage girl crush on Father Selwyn, a very handsome priest just out of the Seminary. He was our Moral Science teacher. (The Catholic students took Catechism while we non-Catholics took the Moral Science class). I wrote him a letter of appreciation when I finished school, and to one other priest, Father

Mascarenhas, who was the opposite of him in looks. Father Mascherenas wrote back saying that while he knew that I appreciated him, he had not expected a written expression of it.

Father Selwyn wrote back with musical notation, saying, "If you were a girl, I would ask you never to B flat, sometimes B sharp, always B natural. But since you are a boy, I say to you, live only for others and you will ever be amazingly happy!" I am glad to say that in the years that followed, I took his advice to both sexes.

Just before I came to America in 1986, I wrote to Father Selwyn asking him if we could meet so that I could say goodbye. By then I had been Farah for ten years and was a normal young Parsi woman in saris and sometimes in a dress. Father Selwyn knew this, of course, because I had been in all the society magazines (an inevitable consequence of my "change"). I constantly explained in interviews that nothing had really changed and that the inner Farah had been fortunate enough to emerge and my outward self now conformed with my inner self.

Father Selwyn kindly agreed to meet me at the Sea Lounge at the Taj Mahal Hotel. Even though priests had stopped wearing cassocks by then - which I hated! - Father Selwyn came wearing a cassock, and a large crucifix on his chest. We chatted over tea. I told him that I hoped I would find a man in America who would love me enough to marry me. That, of course, was impossible in India. "But I am forty years old now, Father!"

"So much the better," he replied, "it will eliminate the playboys who want you only for sex."

Dear Father Selwyn - perfect to the last!

3 - Daddy and My Brother

My paternal grandfather came from Iran to India in the 1890s to work for a distant relative who owned a restaurant in Poona, the summer residence of the Governor of Bombay, situated at an altitude of two thousand feet. The altitude, and the surrounding mountains, which culminated in the resort town of Mahabaleshwar at 4,500 feet, the highest point in Bombay State, protected it from the extreme heat and humidity of Bombay. My great-grandfather had a small fruit orchard in Isfahan in Northern Iran, but he also had many sons, and the property was too small to be divided. So, my grandfather had to launch out on his own. By dint of hard work he came to own his own little tea shop, and Indian readers will easily recognise the famous "Irani restaurant." There were two kinds - the first was patronised by the working class and the second provided rich meals and was patronised by the middle class and the rich. My grandfather's was of the first kind.

Among the second kind was Cafe Britannia in Bombay. All Irani cafe owners were loyal to the British and had a portrait of the King and of the prophet Zoroaster on their walls, and had names like Cafe Royal, King George etc. The owner of Cafe Britannia was such a passionate lover of the royal family that he wrote several letters to the Queen. So, in 2016, when Prince William and the Duchess of Cambridge came to India, they visited Cafe Britannia. The 93-year-old owner was beside himself with joy. Their visit didn't come a day too soon, because the dear old man passed away six months later.

Needless to say, Cafe Britannia was very upscale compared to my grandfather's little tea shop. He would get up at 4 A.M. to prepare "chai" and open the cafe in time for the day labourers before they went in search of work. These poor men fortified themselves for a hard day's work with a cup of tea and a "bun maska" (a loaf of bread with butter). My father loved to help him to open the place, and when he said this to some of our elegant friends, my mother would scowl at him and shame him in front of me afterwards. She had never heard of the dignity of labour.

My grandfather followed his father's example and had eleven

children. My father was the tenth. Fortunately, my grandfather, Merwanji Irani, sent my father to a superb Jesuit school in Poona - St. Vincent's - and Daddy grew up speaking perfect English. He was more into sports than academics and was on the school's lawn hockey team. But on one occasion he recited Gray's "Elegy Written in a Country Churchyard" from the stage of the school hall on Parents' Day. His eldest sister, Perin Aunty, who adored him, wept tears of joy.

When I was little, Perin Aunty, who had heart trouble, would call out 'Jehangir!' from below our balcony when she came to see him. When I ran to the balcony she would ask, "Is your father at home?" and if I said "No," she would say "Then I'm not coming. I'm going to Dolly Aunty's place." She disliked my mother.

Perin Aunty looked exactly like the Queen Mother in the film *Heat and Dust* right down to the eyes heavily lined with kohl and a long cigarette holder with a cigarette in it. Her only son married a German, Hannah, and settled in England. Perin Aunty went to join him, and her husband died of a heart attack during their voyage to England. He was buried at sea.

On one of her visits to Bombay, she begged my parents to let her take me to England with her.

"He will have a much better future there."

But they refused. I was their old age insurance.

I was eager to go and was bitterly disappointed. How different my life would have been if they had thought of me rather than of themselves and let me go!

When Daddy finished school at 18 he went to Bombay to live with his eldest brother, Rustom Uncle, who was the manager of a liquor store. He soon got a job with The Sporting Times, owned by an Englishman named Collins, who had decided to stay on in independent India. Rustom Uncle's wife, Sarah Aunty, who was so obese that she found it difficult to even lift her feet to walk, was very fond of Daddy, and set out to look for a wife for him when he was 25. Through a Parsi marriage broker, she heard of my mother. The broker grossly exaggerated my mother's dowry, and Daddy, already enmeshed in his gambling addiction, was tempted.

But first, a little about my mother. I have already mentioned that she was born in Central India in Bhusawal, a railway junction near Bhopal. She went to a railway school for Anglo-Indian children of railway officers (my grandfather was a boiler inspector with the Peninsular and Central Railway) and her schoolmistress was a beautiful but strict Englishwoman. I still have her photo.

Mummy was betrothed to her cousin (my grandmother's sister's son) who, when he went to study in England, fell in love with an English girl and married her instead of my mother. This sent my mother into a rage (she was twenty-one then). My great aunt was so mortified that she offered my mother the stocks and shares and jewels that would have been hers had her son married her. Mummy took them without a moment's hesitation. It was a substantial sum in those days.

My mother's father had died young. He wore three-piece suits, complete with a watch chain and swagger stick, and sported a military moustache even though he was a railway man. He died at 42 of a massive heart attack. Mummy told me that she remembered the note he had sent with a servant to the resident railway doctor, Dr. Rishworth, an Englishman, requesting him to come and see him as he was not feeling well. By the time the doctor got there, my grandfather was dead.

After his death my grandmother, who spoke very little English, went to Bombay despite that, to get a probate of his will from the Bombay High Court as she knew it would be contested by her elder brother-in-law, who had been disinherited.

She then built herself a three-story house on Station Road, where her son (my mother's brother) Kersi Uncle, opened his radio and electronics shop on the ground floor. She had sent both her children to boarding school in Poona and that is perhaps where my mother got the idea of sending my brother to boarding school. The only reason I was not sent too was that my parents could not afford to send both of us to boarding school.

My grandmother was also anxious to get both her children married as soon as possible. So she hired the marriage broker who found my father in Bombay. At 25, my father was a dapper and handsome young man in shark skin suits and a solar hat, and Mummy liked his photos. He went to Bhusawal and met her. He also suggested his beautiful niece, Homai Aunty, marry my mother's brother, Kersi Uncle. He had been led to believe that my grandmother had much more money that she really did.

Homai Aunty was very beautiful, and Kersi Uncle agreed to marry her. So, my grandmother arranged a double wedding for both her children at Cama Hall in Bombay, paying all the wedding expenses. She also gave my father a gold watch that he cherished to the end of his days and proudly wore it on his wrist for the rest of his life. I remember him winding it up every morning and I miss real watches in these days of battery powered and digital watches!

Unfortunately, they did not hire a wedding photographer, so there are no photos of my parent's wedding or of their wedding reception.

Soon my brother was born. I have already written about his birth in my very first chapter. He was named Merwan after my paternal grandfather who had asked all his sons to name their first-born son after him. The pet name for Merwan is Mehli, so my brother was called Mehli while growing up. When he moved to America, he changed it to Mel.

After he was born my mother had two pregnancies, both of which she aborted. My father took her to a midwife who secretly performed the abortions, as in British India abortions were illegal. Both times my mother bled heavily, so that when she got pregnant with me, she just did not have the courage to have a third abortion. So, she had me.

She told me when I grew up: "I just couldn't get rid of you!" She told me that with a vicious look.

"You were determined to be born!"

She thought I was the same soul that she had twice aborted, who kept returning to her womb.

It was only then that I understood her ruthless rejection of me from the day I was born.

As a child, I felt her rejection so deeply that one day I ran to the balcony on my chubby little legs (I may have been six years old) threatening to jump off the balcony and hoping that she would try and stop me.

She did not.

Instead, it was the teenage Namdev who ran after me shouting "Baba! Baba!" and grabbed me.

The death wish has always stayed with me, and the wound has never healed. Much later, when I was in New York, I tried to heal my inner child. I bought a gorgeous doll from the Lebanese sidewalk sellers on West Fourteenth Street (descendants of the ubiquitous Phoenicians).

She opened and closed her blue eyes and said "Mummy" and was the symbol of my inner child, but also a wish fulfilment because when I was little and my parents were shopping in the local shops at Grant Road, I saw a cheap doll for sale on a roadside stall. I asked my parents for it, and they refused - they said that they couldn't afford it. Buying myself this gorgeous doll also healed at least that wound.

One winter evening when it was already dark at 5 P.M., I had to go to a meeting for adult children of dysfunctional families. I laid the doll on my bed (she always closed her eyes in the horizontal position) and covered her tenderly with a blanket, telling her that I would be back soon. I lived in a tiny studio apartment, and it was very lonely. I bent down to kiss her on the forehead, and as soon as I did that, an emotional pain such as I had never felt before surged through me. It was like a physical pain that started in the soles of my feet and welled up and went right to the top of my head, where it exploded.

I was stunned. What was that? Where did it come from? I sat down, feeling too shaken to remain standing. After a while I understood. My mother had refused to pick me up when I cried for her from my cradle, and the memory of this pain had welled up. So, you see, we forget nothing, and we carry all that pain within us through life. How sad is this!

But it was not just me that my mother did not want. Looking back, I am certain that even my brother did not get much love during the five years before I was born and my arrival was the death blow for him, because he was sent off to boarding school after I was born.

The truth of the matter is that my mother simply did not want to be bothered with children.

It is this third most significant relationship of my life that is the saddest for me. Growing up, I hardly knew my brother because he was at boarding school. But when he came home for the summer vacation, he was my hero! But he would not speak to me. His rejection came on top of my mother's rejection, and he was my only sibling and I adored him, even as I loved my mother. My parents encouraged this behaviour rather than discouraged it because they had been told that if the brothers are close, they will both leave you and settle abroad. By dividing us, they felt that even if one left, the other would stay. This was a time after Independence when Anglo-Indians and Parsis were emigrating to the West in a mass exodus.

And why did they not want us to settle abroad? Because we were their old age insurance.

One incident is seared into my memory. Rustom Uncle had given my brother and me a mechanical toy with springs that made cars dash across a wooden board. Never having had any toys, it was a magical thing for me. My brother let me watch him play with it but would not allow me to touch it. He was about ten years old at the time, and he took it with him to boarding school. Because manual labour and porters were cheap, he always went with a large, iron trunk and I watched the trunk being carried down the stairs with the toy in it.

Six months passed and my brother returned. The trunk was carried up the stairs and I thought the toy would be in it. Instead, my brother came up the stairs and smiled straight at me. In his hand was the coveted toy. It was broken.

His hatred of me had already become toxic. But, of course, I could not understand that then. I was heartbroken.

As against this, there are happy memories too, and I shall end this chapter with them.

My parents would visit Rustom Uncle and Sarah Aunty about once a year. They lived in a large flat on the third floor of Temple Terrace on Gwalior Tank. The Gwalior Tank Parsis were what would be described in England as the lower middle class. (The upper middle class Parsis lived at Cuffe Parade, Bandra and Juhu, and the rich on Malabar Hill, Cumballa Hill, Worli Hill and Worli Sea Face.)

Their flat had a large, covered balcony with cane chairs and armchairs covered with mattresses and cushions. It ran the length of the small living room (called drawing rooms in Bombay) and the master bedroom which had its own bath. A long corridor stretched from the drawing room, with a number of rooms on one side, all in a row. Then came the kitchen, the bathroom, the servant's room, and the servant's bathroom.

How I wished we could have lived in a flat like that, where I could proudly have invited my friends!

The sad thing is that Daddy did move into a smaller but equally nice flat at Gwalior Tank. But it was at the back of the building and Mummy did not like the peace and quiet, so Dolly Aunty's father found the flat in the dilapidated building on Wodehouse Road, always teetering on the verge of collapse (the floor trembled when we walked), and riddled with rats and cockroaches, where I spent the first forty-two years of my life.

Sarah Aunty would take us to the dining room where there was a large dining table covered with black glass and groaning with delicious food. How I enjoyed it! Then they would drop us home in their 1940s Studebaker. Rustom Uncle took the wheel and Daddy sat beside him.

Mummy and Sarah Aunty sat at the back while I stood by the door with my head just making it above the door. I remember Roshan Aunty saying fondly, "Look how his eyes are sparkling like diamonds!"

No doubt I was very happy, and the lights of the passing cars added to the sparkle in my eyes.

We had black and white sepia prints of my brother and I sitting atop an elephant in the Zoo (The Victoria and Albert Botanical Gardens) and of us sitting on a bench at Cuffe Parade. My brother and I both had Greek profiles and I was a plump, pleasant-looking little boy until I broke my nose and got a Roman profile (ugh) and turned into a lanky, gangly teenager with hideous glasses (ugh again).

How I wish I still had those childhood photos!

But I gave them to my brother when he came to see my parents on one of his visits from Long Island because I knew I could not have children and I wanted the photos to remain in the Rustom family.

Now I can never have them back. Not even copies!

Let the last memory be of my beloved brother and brother alone.

It is of him, about ten years old, in the garden of the Prince of Wales Museum, not far from our house, sketching the Indo-Saracenic Neo-Gothic museum building, while I played on the lawn nearby and Daddy watched over us.

4 - The Towers of Silence, my First Book

In 1951 when I was seven years old, my maternal grandmother came to visit us after having a terrible row with her daughter-in-law Homai, Daddy's niece. This did little to endear her in Daddy's eyes as he was very fond of his niece. Moreover, a couple of years earlier, when Mr. Collins, Daddy's English employer, began to think of returning to England, my grandmother had said to my mother, "Oh no, he will be a burden on us," - meaning my father.

Daddy, who had a great work ethic, was mortally wounded by the remark.

I remember as though it were yesterday, my father ripping up the Times of India which he was reading when my mother informed him that my grandmother would be arriving. My grandmother loved to travel (a trait that I inherited with a vengeance), and shortly after she was widowed, in addition to building herself the three-story house on Station Road, had taken her children with her, and gone on extended visits to her brothers in Karachi (then a part of British India) and Darjeeling. She gave her sisters-in-law gifts of gold jewellery to sweeten her visit.

A studio photo taken of her in Ahmedabad (travel again!) in 1917 shows her with my one-year-old mother sitting on a table covered with a printed tablecloth, wearing a richly embroidered dress, and grandmother in a "gara" - a sari hand embroidered with silk thread in China and very popular with Parsis (I still have it with me), and a long-sleeved blouse trimmed with lace. She looks very Edwardian. She is looking straight at the camera, and her face is sad.

She was 63 when she arrived on her visit. On her second day she insisted on bathing me herself (pouring warm water on me with a mug, from a brass bucket). Shortly after that she had a stroke. In less than a week she died.

The doctor said that she had died of a concussion. As she was going down the stairs of her house in Bhusawal, she banged her head against a low beam in her haste to catch the train to Bombay.

When my mother asked her shortly before she died, if she wanted anything, her last words were, "I want peace."

Her body was taken to the Towers of Silence atop Malabar Hill where the remains of deceased Parsis were devoured by vultures.

When the East India Company leased the seven islands of Bombay from Charles II, who had received them as a marriage dowry from the Portuguese in 1661 for his wife, Catherine of Braganza, and they built a fort overlooking the main island's magnificent, deep natural harbour. Soon the Parsis from Surat, where the British had first set foot on Indian soil in 1600, petitioned the East India Company for permission to settle in Bombay (Portuguese for Beautiful Bay). They had been trading with the British ever since their arrival in 1600 and providing them with necessities etc.

The Parsis then asked the East India Company for permission to build a Tower of Silence atop Malabar Hill. Malabar Hill was then part of a separate island and regarded as outside the city.

But what is a Parsi?

After the Muslim conquest of Persia, the Zoroastrian descendants of the Achaemenid Empire were regarded as heretics. In 800 A.D. the high priest and a few important families took the sacred fire which had been kept perpetually burning (there was a legend that Zoroaster had descended from a hill carrying the flame in his hand) and crossed the Arabian Sea to the west coast of India. They landed in Surat, (where the British arrived eight hundred years later) and sought asylum. The king refused. So, the high priest asked for a full glass of milk and some jaggery (sugar) and dissolved the jaggery in the milk. The jaggery made the milk sweeter but the glass did not overflow. The king was impressed and granted them asylum.

The local people called them Parsis - People from Persia.

The Parsis would not cremate their dead because they worshipped fire as a symbol of God. They did not want to pollute the earth with burial. So, the only alternative was to be devoured by vultures.

Grandmother's body was wrapped in a cotton sheet and placed on a marble slab in a bungalow on the tower complex, a heavily wooded area atop the hill. Next to her was an urn with fire fed by sandalwood. Priests in white robes and masks sat beside it and cantillated prayers in the ancient Zend language for three days and nights, while Mummy and I slept in an adjoining room with the door open.

On the fourth morning, four priests came and stood by the body and chanted prayers at the top of their voices. Then a sweet dog was brought and shown the body, and the priests clapped twice to drive away all evil spirits. A dog's eyes are supposed to be so holy that no evil spirits can remain in their presence! (I heartily agree). Then the ladies (the men waited outside under an open shelter) reverentially touched the ground in front of the corpse. They were all dressed in plain white saris with no ornate borders, and the saris were drawn over their heads. Any make-up or jewellery of any kind was strictly forbidden.

Then two pallbearers came with a litter and carried the body out of the bungalow and started walking towards the tower. The men followed in pairs, dressed in long white coats with ribbons and a tall, round Parsi hat, holding one end of a handkerchief between them. As I was a boy, I went with my father, holding one end of the handkerchief while he held the other. We arrived at the tower which soared above us and was surrounded by ancient trees. I could see vultures perched atop it, covering the entire circumference. The pallbearers went in through a low door, while a priest handed each of us a special prayer for the dead. We started to read the prayer aloud. (It was printed in Gujarati as well as the Roman alphabet). As soon as the pallbearers came out (they had removed the sheet that had covered the body when they were in the tower) and the vultures heard the door slam, they swooped down.

We continued to pray as they stripped the body down to a bare skeleton. It is said to take only a few minutes. The vultures often had to wait for days for a body to arrive.

After the funeral, my mother accused me of killing her mother! Why? Because my grandmother had collapsed shortly after giving me a bath (which I had not asked for). She ignored the fact that her mother had died of a concussion as a result of a head injury.

(2)

Then there was the time when my parents went to visit my grandmother's house in Bhusawal, which deserted because Homai Aunty had taken her son Sam and returned to her mother's house in Poona forever. She was not fond of her husband, Kersi Uncle, who was too different from her - quiet, soft-spoken and courteous, while she was fiery and impetuous and not well educated.

Kersi Uncle had also been sent to a boarding school! The famous

Barnes School, where, like all good schools in India, education was entirely in English from Kindergarten up. My uncle remained celibate for the rest of his life, consoling himself by going for long drives in his Morris Minor (the English car, and not the Indian-made Ambassador which would be modelled on it later on). Cars were his passion, and there is an old sepia print of Daddy and him standing with one foot on the footboard of the car, Daddy with his bowler hat in his hand, and both in well-tailored white suits), and perhaps also visiting dancing girls (Mummy once said that he used to do so in the company of the Maharaja of Sangli whose son was later with me in St. Mary's by pure coincidence).

I enjoyed the train journey to Bhusawal and distinctly remember the house that grandmother had built, which was now deserted except for Kersi Uncle, who had gone off on one of his motor car trips. I remember sleeping beside my father in a room on the roof (evocatively called a *barsati* in India - "Rain Room") and the great trains passing by at night blowing their mighty whistles, redolent of vast spaces being traversed across the length and breadth of the sub-continent.

There was a detached bathroom on the roof which had a pipe over which one had to directly sit. I was terrified of that big, black, gaping hole as I was afraid that my little body would fall into it !

We returned to Bombay with the framed portrait of my grandmother taken in 1917.

Less intense memories of childhood are visits to Beroj Aunty's beautiful bungalow in Jogeshwari, then a distant suburb of Bombay. Beroj Aunty was my grandmother's younger sister. She was childless, and not the mother of the cousin to whom my mother had been betrothed, (the one who married an English girl instead of her). She lived with her husband Dhanjisa Uncle, who was a successful broker, in a beautiful bungalow with a rose garden in which I used to love to walk while my parents visited upstairs. There were roses of all hues and varieties tended by a friendly gardener, and there were flowering bushes, including the Night Queen, whose flowers would open only after sunset and exude an intoxicating fragrance.

Upstairs, on the covered balcony with marble floors, a small clock delicately tinkled the quarter hours with Westminster chimes, quietly chiming her uneventful life away. She resembled Lady Catherine de Bourgh in the BBC version of Pride and Prejudice. My poor parents hoped that she would include my mother in her will.

She did not.

She was probably aware of the purpose of these visits, which entailed an hour's ride each way on the local train.

But I loved her bungalow, and her garden even more. It was situated in Malcolm Baug (Garden), named after a former British Governor of Bombay. It was only for Parsis and was dotted with bungalows in a peaceful, sylvan setting - the diametrical opposite of downtown Bombay where the hardest thing to find was a tree.

It had once been covered with tropical vegetation which was cut down to make room for apartment buildings and slums, and later the apartment buildings were demolished to make room for skyscrapers. Indeed, there were only two trees that I could see from the balcony: a coconut tree and a mango tree. The mango tree was home to a flock of rambunctious, screeching parrots as green as the serrano peppers they loved, which a man who lived in the building next to the tree left for them on his balcony.

A year after my grandmother's death I got measles. In India, when a child gets measles, it is believed to be possessed by a Goddess who loves the child and wants him or her for herself. So, in addition to the medicine I took, a Hindu priest was sent for. He lit a few incense sticks and waved them over me and prayed to the Goddess of Measles, begging her to spare me, and she did.

But what I remember most is the visit of Piroja Aunty from next door (with whom, needless to say, Mummy quarrelled from time to time). I still remember the cool touch of her hand on my fevered forehead as she too prayed for me. More about her later.

Another memory from around this time is a trip to Apollo Bunder with my mother. *Bunder* means "Dock" in Marathi, so the name is a hybrid, meaning Apollo Dock. As Bombay was a number of islands separated by creeks through which the sea swept at high tide, there were a number of jetties or docks, from where people took sailboats manned by local fishermen (the original inhabitants of the islands) to go from one island to the next. Colaba, where we lived, was the island immediately south of the main island, which was known as the Fort. Apollo Bunder was a short half-mile walk from our house, and just before the monsoon, Mummy would buy a coconut and a garland of flowers to throw into the sea to appease the God Neptune.

All this may confuse the Western reader to whom it was just explained that we were Zoroastrians, followers of an ancient Persian religion - indeed the first monotheistic religion in the world, pre-dating Moses. All this made no difference to my mother. She subscribed to a number of superstitions: Hindu, Muslim, and even some Zoroastrian superstitions. But my mother was not alone in this. It is the charm of India that religious beliefs overlap. Muslims adopt Hindu customs and beliefs, as do Parsis and Christians. This softens the edge of prejudice and bigotry.

I was once sitting in the back of a taxi which had the Hindu god Ganesh on the dashboard, so I assumed that the driver was a Hindu. But when we passed a Church, he reverentially made the sign of the Cross and when we passed a Mosque, he placed one hand on his head and the other on his heart and bowed.

I was confused, so I asked him, "Are you a Hindu, a Muslim or a Christian?"

"I am everything, madam," he replied. "Who knows who is right? Better to be on the safe side!" and waggled his head.

I smiled. The world would have been a better place if everyone had been like him. History would not have been a long record of religious wars and Catholics killing Protestants and Sunnis killing Shias, Christians killing Jews and Muslims killing Hindus and vice versa, in all cases.

Anyway, returning to Apollo Dock! There was my mother making her offering to Neptune when little urchins dived into the waves and salvaged the coconut to re-sell to the coconut seller for half the price. Mummy yelled at them, and they laughed.

After that, she decided to take me for a boat ride on one of the launches that took off from the Gateway of India, opposite the grand Taj Mahal Hotel, and made a short run around the lighthouse. I must admit this was nice of her. Perhaps she wanted to take the boat ride herself too? I loved the salt spray on my face and the breeze cooled by the waves and seagulls soaring around us.

But while getting into, as well as getting out of the launch, Mummy missed the stone steps and would have fallen into the murky waters of the harbour. Only the boatman's tight grip on her arm, and his grabbing her with the other saved her from a watery grave.

Ever since then, I became passionately and fiercely protective of my mother. She was small and delicate and inspired protectiveness even by her very appearance, which was weak and fragile. It was hard to see the will of iron behind it and the rage that fuelled her delicate frame.

One last childhood memory. Daddy decided to go to Lonavala with my brother for one summer vacation. Lonavala was a modest "Hill Station" at an altitude of two thousand feet, halfway between Bombay and Poona. It was the poor man's hill station, with hotels for the lower middle class, accordingly. Many of these were run by Parsis. One of them, run by a doughty Parsi lady, said "Kick Out Time" (instead of "Check Out Time") in the notice posted at the reception desk.

Since he was not going to take me along, Daddy gave me money to rent a book from Jamnadas' bookstall on the corner of our building (the same Jamnadas who asked my parents to "Go home!" when Gandhi was shot). I chose a book called *Shadow, the Sheepdog*. It was beautifully illustrated with scenes of the English countryside. I fell in love with Enid Blyton and devoured her books before I graduated to more serious reading.

Daddy had a wonderful time with my brother and came home elated, also refreshed by the (comparatively) cool air.

Mummy, meanwhile, was unusually nice and relaxed, telling me the story of the Ramayana (the Hindu epic) at bedtime.

My brother's hobby was stamp collecting, and when he started getting duplicate stamps he made another album especially for me, with my name on it. I brought that album with me when I left home in 1986. As I came by air, I could only bring twenty kilos with me and could bring nothing except my clothes, photographs, and a couple of books. I included this stamp album as one of my most precious possessions because to me it betokened - and still does - that my brother had a spark of fraternal feeling for me.

5 - My Navjote, Home Routines, Goodbye to Childhood

When I was eleven years old, I was initiated into the Zoroastrian faith in a ceremony called Navjote. For this, my mother sent me to a priest at a fire temple in a Parsi Colony for middle-class Parsis, built by the munificent Wadias (a ship-building and mercantile family that had been indispensable to the East India Company). It was less than half a mile from our house and the Colony itself, called Cusrow Baug (Garden) after Cusrow Wadia who endowed it, was an oasis of peace and quiet and beauty in the midst of a very busy Colaba Causeway. But I was not happy on the porch of the fire temple, where a very bored young priest who obviously hated what he had to do, made me memorise my prayers. The feeling was mutual.

I didn't understand a word that I was saying, and it was only decades later when I looked them up on the internet, that I learned that they said, "Blessed is the righteous man who is pure in thought, word, and deed, and praised virtue and charity and the Creator, Ahura Mazda (the good twin, as opposed to the evil twin, Ahriman, or Satan). Both were born from the womb of eternity and our good or bad thoughts, words and deeds strengthen either one or the other.

My parents gave a rather extravagant (for our humble means) reception on the lawns of the Colaba Fire Temple which was actually situated in the military cantonment half a mile from our building on the other side from Cusrow Baug. It was beautifully situated as it had a scenic view of the entrance to the harbour, with the Sahyadri hills as a backdrop, and being in the cantonment, was away from the hustle and bustle of Colaba. It was the obvious choice, as it was so close to our home.

My brother had just finished boarding school and come home a tall and very handsome seventeen-year-old of whom my father was mightily proud. Was I jealous of my father's love for him? No, not at all, as I loved my brother very much and was as proud of him as my father was. But he would not speak to me and treated me like dirt. This broke my heart and made me feel locked out of both my father's as well as my brother's love. My mother's love, as you already know, was non-existent, and by now I was resigned to the fact. Not all the standing first in class to win her love had made the least difference. It did, however, help me later in life, and for that I am most grateful.

Unfortunately, this complete rejection by the three most significant people in my life instilled in me a lifelong hunger for love. I sought from others the love that I, in the normal course of things, would have received from them. I have always been grateful for even one drop of love. Perhaps this is not a bad thing. Fortunately, the springs of love in my heart never dried up. I was never embittered, and I love people both high and low.

Is it better to love than to be loved? I wonder about that. Someone said that it is far better to be loved than to love. Ha! Ha! I think that maybe they were on to something! On the other hand, the poet Auden expressed a more Christian feeling:

"If love must always unequal be,
Then let the more loving one be me."

And I am reminded of Father Selwyn who wrote in my little autograph book with the plastic cover and coloured pages, "Live only for others, and you will ever be amazingly happy!"

So then, all this may have happened for a reason - to make me a better, kinder, more understanding person.

On the morning of my Navjote a group of Parsi ladies came singing religious songs even before they reached the foot of the stairs and sat on a carpet in our drawing room and sang for nearly an hour. I didn't understand a word, but it was meant to bring a blessing on the house. I was embarrassed that the poor coolies who were sitting downstairs, waiting for work and saw all this fuss being made over me. I also felt a little lost amidst all this celebration, as no one took the least notice of me.

The reception that evening was all that my eleven-year-old heart could desire! There were about two hundred guests, comprising an equal number of lower middle-class and well-to-do. The latter wore beautifully embroidered silk and brocade saris and were dripping with diamonds, emeralds and rubies collected from the bank, especially for that day. My mother had to be content with a gold necklace and gold bangles. Beroj Aunty (alias Lady Catherine de Bourgh) was there in splendour, having driven all the way from Jogeshwari in her chauffeur-driven car.

Before the Navjote I was taken into the fire temple and forced to sip cow's urine from a cup of leaves. I fiercely resisted, only touching it with my lips as the priest kept insisting. Then I sat on a flower-bedecked stage on the lawn before all the assembled guests as the priests prayed over me and made me a Zoroastrian. I donned the white muslin undershirt signifying a pure heart and tied the sacred thread three times around my waist, signifying Good Thoughts, Good Words, and Good Deeds. (Manashni, Gavashni, Kubashni.)

Then came the fun part!

Nelly Aunty (a Parsi) and her band regaled the guests. Nelly Aunty herself cheerfully played the accordion and was accompanied by a small but excellent Anglo-Indian band, and the "crooner" was also an Anglo-Indian.

My brother was much loved by one and all at the reception, and rightly so, not just for his good looks, but because he was a wonderful and friendly host along with my parents, while I sat nearby, blissfully sipping Mangola from a straw and admiring him. His own Navjote had been far less splendid, and it is to his credit that he did not begrudge me that!

Then came the part that everyone was waiting for - the dinner! Long tables covered with white tablecloths were lined up near the rocky seafront. We dined under the stars, as experienced waiters hired by the caterer slammed banana leaves in front of each person and slapped slices of pomfret fish on them, served in a delicious white sauce, spicy, but not hot. Then came chicken in a rich gravy that tasted every bit as good as it smelled. It was followed by juicy mutton cooked in rice and golden lentils and finally, a cone-shaped pistachio ice cream called "kulfi."

It was a feast to die for and is served at all Parsi weddings and Navjotes. I hereby declare that Indian food is the most delicious in the world and that among Indian foods, Parsi food is the best! I hear a chorus of heartfelt Amens not only from the Parsi community but even thousands of my fellow Indians who love Parsi food.

My parents came and shook hands with each guest during the dinner, and they, in turn, handed them sealed envelopes with their names and good wishes, containing a cash gift, each according to their means. An eminently sensible custom that went towards defraying at least part of the cost of the reception and the banquet.

After my Navjote, Daddy wrote thank you notes to each of them in his beautiful calligraphy, of which he was justly proud.

(2)

At home, we did not eat quite as well. Mummy did not want to be bothered to decide each day's meals and ordered "tiffin" lunch and dinner which was prepaid by the month. It contained two dishes for each meal and rice was cooked at home. We also cooked breakfast at home which consisted of a fried egg and a slice of bread and a cup of tea.

The servants got only tea for breakfast but as the tiffin was very little, they did not get a slice of fish or a piece of mutton or whatever other treat arrived in the tiffin, with their rice. Instead, they ate it with curry which they themselves cooked.

At 5.30 in the morning, while the servants were still asleep in their room, the milkman rang the doorbell and Daddy got up and took the milk and boiled it. He then made a cup of tea, while the newspaper man brought the Times of India. The doorbell never stopped ringing from dawn to dusk. No one is lonely in India as they are in the Western world. As Mother Theresa said, "The disease of the Western world is loneliness."

Daddy read the newspaper on the balcony while I lay in bed with my eyes closed, reluctant to open them and get up. As I heard the teaspoon tinkling against the sides of his cup as he dissolved the sugar in his tea, I felt that all was right with the world, and I was safe.

Till today, the morning ritual of making tea and reading the newspaper is sacred to me. It is also a silent tribute to my dear father.

After boiling the milk, Daddy would skim the cream from the top and save it on a plate. Mummy made sure he ate it because he was the breadwinner. But Daddy would give me a teaspoon and I would eat it with jam as honey was too expensive, and a luxury. How blessed I am that I can afford it today. That is surely one of the blessings of having been born in the lower middle class to struggling parents - that I can appreciate every single blessing that comes my way!

It was an altogether different story for our teenage servants who were separated from their parents and had to get up early each morning to wash other people's dishes, sweep someone else's floor, and dust someone else's furniture. That is why I have never been able to feel sorry for myself, having grown up in an India teeming with poverty, and having seen what I have seen.

Once, the rent collector came and demanded the previous month's rent.

"But I have already paid it!" said my mother, turning pale.

"Show me the receipt!" he demanded.

She couldn't find it.

So I started a file in which I started collecting each month's rent receipts. I did the same with the phone bills and the electricity bills. This was the beginning of my co-dependency, as the adult-child relationship between my mother and me was reversed, and I became the caretaker, and she, the child.

My mother encouraged this by comparing me to my great-grandfather, the engine driver, who settled his family in Bhusawal, married the girl he loved, and bought her a casket full of gold, jewels, and a home which included their own well and a water buffalo that provided fresh milk each day, and a man who looked after it. My great-grandmother loved grapes from Kabul and made homemade wine, and until I left home, I used to drink wine from her little wine glass.

But this comparison with my great-grandfather was intoxicating for a twelve-year-old and I became an incurable caretaker. But caretaking also means controlling, which is the downside of caretaking, and which turns caretaking into co-dependency. I attended three years of co-dependent anonymous meetings in New York before I could cure myself of it.

Meanwhile, my brother formed his own band in which he stood in front and played the accordion! With his good looks and charm, he was loved by the Parsi ladies who invited him to play at their parties. While he never became as famous as Nelly Aunty, he enjoyed it, and it was more a hobby for him than a source of income.

(3)

When I was fifteen, my parents were invited to the Navjote of Sir Dinshaw Petit's daughter in Petit Hall. He was a Baronet, and Petit Hall was famed for its grandeur. I was eagerly looking forward to the evening, but Mummy refused to give me my embroidered Parsi cap which she kept locked in her steel Godrej cupboard and wanted me to wear the plain one instead. When I threatened not to go, she shrugged and said, while powdering her face, "Don't come, then."

My parents drove off in a taxi, and I walked for hours with the crowds on the seafront at Marine Drive, walking all the way to Chowpatty Beach four miles away, and back, as I had no money. When I returned home, Mummy gloated about the splendours of Petit Hall. But I didn't care. A new life had begun for me, independent of my parents.

6 - The Piano, My First Student, Madame Olga Craen

Soon after my Navjote, the Piano entered my life. I was surrounded by pianos. Just across the street, the Borthwicks had a beautiful upright. In the same building, Soona Aunty (Aunty Gold) had a beautiful Blüthner on which I could hear her daughter practising. And in the building next door was Jeroo, and I could hear her playing too. Also across the street was a German who typed late into the night (perhaps he was a writer). Then he would play recorded piano music. I was enchanted by Chopin's Waltz in C sharp minor, which tugged at my soul and summoned me out of bed, but as I was only four or five years old, I was afraid to go to the balcony alone, and I would drag Daddy (next to whom I slept) out of bed and we would quietly stand on the balcony while I listened, entranced, to the music. It was the first piece of classical music that I fell in love with.

Professor Friedrich Niecks has written that "one cannot help but believe in the immortality of the soul." It seems to have been heaven-sent into my life at that tender age when neither of my parents listened to classical music.

Mummy used to visit Mrs. Borthwick and take me along. Her son Jerry was a passionate amateur photographer. He took a photo of me in which I look about three or four, seated on the revolving piano stool with a cushion on it, a chubby forefinger putting down a key. I was looking solemnly at the camera, and later on my student Josh commented that I looked very sad. That was because I had cried and begged of Mummy to take me to Mrs. Borthwick's piano. I could think of no greater happiness than sitting at that divine instrument, putting one ivory key down at a time, and listening to the golden sound. Jerry used to lift me up and put me on the piano stool.

As far back as I can remember, I used to beg of my mother to get me a piano, but she said, 'Who do you think you are? A princess! That you want to play the piano?!'

No doubt my parents were hurting for money, and so I had to wait till I was eleven before I could start taking piano lessons, and this happened quite by chance. Mummy sent me to Mrs. Mowdawala in the next building to give her the Parsi newspaper which listed Parsi deaths, funerals etc. I gazed lovingly at her piano and her 18-year-old daughter Jeroo offered to teach me for free. And so I started piano lessons! I worked furiously to make up for lost time and made rapid progress. Within six months, Jeroo prepared me for the first-grade exam of the Trinity College of Music, London, which I passed with Honours.

Here I must pause to explain that we in India were very fortunate, that as we were a leading member of the British Commonwealth of Nations, the Trinity College used to send its examiners to India once a year to assess piano students at all levels, and the examiner would travel all over India, including the boarding schools in the hill stations, to assess the candidates who were mostly Anglo-Indian or Parsi. A year later I did grade 5, skipping grades 2,3, and 4, and once again passed with Honours. By now, my parents, seeing that I was doing so well, rented a piano from Bayne and Company.

I shall never forget the day when the piano arrived! I used to dream that there was a piano in the house, and was ecstatic, only to wake up and find to my dismay that there was none. The piano arrived on the heads of six coolies who were special piano carriers. I must deplore this practice! Even though it helped them to earn a living, I wish that pianos in India had been transported by truck as they are in more affluent countries, the coolies then transferring them from the truck into the house. It must have been harrowing for them to carry it on their heads for a mile and a half over hot streets and then up our stairs! I was a child and innocently unaware of this. In fact, I waited on my balcony and was thrilled when I saw them coming down the street. Of course, I started playing on it as soon as the coolies left! The next day, Mr. Bayne, very dapper in a white, sharkskin suit (I have no idea why they were called that) came and tuned it.

Jeroo got married and I had to start taking lessons from our school music teacher, Miss Saldanha. She was a lovely woman who lived in a flat in Byculla, near our school. This meant that I had to take the bus on Sundays, and after a forty-five-minute ride, walk down a quiet street to reach her flat which was tucked away some distance off the main road. I liked Miss Saldanha and enjoyed the long ride on the upper deck of the BEST bus, and also felt grown up doing it all by myself. The lessons pretty much took up my whole Sunday afternoons and I played the piano both before and after the lesson. I cannot recall her actually instructing me, as, because of my zeal and my ambition, I pretty much learned the pieces on my own. She did teach me the fingering of scales which by now I had to play for four octaves and taught me theory up to the fourth-grade exam. I passed the sixth grade "Senior" piano ("Practical") exam with honours, in which I played my beloved C sharp minor Chopin waltz. I skipped the seventh grade and did my higher local for which I was pretty much self-taught. Unfortunately, I missed Honours by two marks and passed only with Merit. My mother picked up the phone and berated Miss Saldanha! Miss Saldanha asked to speak to me, and said, simply, "Please find another teacher. I'm sorry, I can't teach you."

And so, I lost another beloved teacher, years after my mother did the same thing to Mrs. Archer. Meanwhile, my father had bought me a four-legged grand for three hundred rupees. In terms of the cost of living, it was the same for him as $300 would be for an American then. It was very old and had only one pedal and the rod that connected it to the piano kept breaking. The ivory keys had turned brown with age, and some were cracked and others simply not there and my fingers played on wooden keys. This was all my father could afford and I don't blame him. But I disliked the piano, even though I practised and played a lot on it.

(2)

Immediately after I appeared for my Senior Cambridge school exam at the age of 16, in December 1959, Daddy got me started on my teaching career.

Daddy used to wait every morning at the bus stop opposite our house with a youngish woman called Miss Butler. She was a light-skinned Anglo-Indian and could easily have passed for an Englishwoman who had lost the roses in her cheeks thanks to Bombay's debilitating climate. She liked him, as all women did, for his obvious fondness for them and his old-world chivalry.

Daddy used to brag about me excelling at school (I had no idea he was doing that), so one day she said to him, "I have a 13-year-old nephew who hates school. I wonder if Farokh would tutor him and prepare him for his matriculation exam?"

So, she came to see me. I told her that I could teach everything except math and science. It was agreed that he would come for an hour every morning five days a week.

"And how much will you charge?"

"Charge?"

"Why, yes, of course, you will be working. You must be paid for the work you do!"

"I don't know," I said honestly.

"Would sixty rupees a month be all right?"

"Why yes, of course!"

And so started my teaching career! I will be everlastingly grateful to my beloved father for this. For this, and for putting me in St. Mary's, and for making sure that I never went hungry even for a day while growing up.

David was a gangly 13-year-old, a couple of inches taller than me. He was extremely shy, and I grew very fond of him (inside me was Farah, whom he could not see, and had no idea, existed). The last school he had been sent to was the excellent boarding school at the hill station of Mount Abu in the princely state of Rajasthan. But that too didn't work.

David was intelligent and a good student, and I was a strict teacher (I knew no other way because that was all that I had seen) and scrupulously corrected his homework every day and explained things as often as required and in as many different ways as I could. I also had a passion for teaching. Earlier on, I had tried to teach the alphabet to my servants so that they would learn English. But they told my mother, "Tell baba to stop teaching us, or we will run away!"

Fortunately, David and I were a good fit.

He even asked his doting aunt if I would give him piano lessons, so lo and behold, he also became my first piano student!

Miss Butler told me privately that "You are the first teacher he's liked."

Less than a year into his lessons, he left with his whole family for Australia under the special provision that Lord Mountbatten had made for Anglo-Indians in 1947. Most of the Anglo-Indians emmigrated to England, Canada or Australia in the decade following Independence. Today there are still a few hundred thousand Anglo-Indians living in India, descendants of those who remained, and they are recognised as unique in the Indian Constitution.

The term Anglo-Indian first appeared in the Government of India Act, 1935. In the present context, Article 366(2) of the Constitution of India states: "An Anglo-Indian means a person whose father or any of whose other male progenitors in the male line is or was of European descent but who is domiciled within the territory of India and is or was born within such territory of parents habitually resident therein and not established there for temporary purposes only..."

While writing this memoir, I have realised that I am practically an Anglo-Indian myself, in addition to being a Parsi, so close has been my lifelong association with them.

Seven years went by, and I was teaching courses at the Indo-American Society in French and in music appreciation. (Here I am jumping the gun. More about that later). When I got home, Mummy told me that David was visiting from Australia and staying with relatives and waited one hour to see me. He left no contact info, or if he did, Mummy, with her practised sadism, did not give it to me. I kept hoping and praying he would come again.

He went back to Australia, and despite internet searches for him in every possible way that I could think of (including putting postings on Anglo-Indian websites), I have never been able to find him.

There is always an ache in my heart when I think of him because he has no idea how much he did for me. Nor does Miss Butler, who must be now in a far more beautiful world than this. David must be 74, a grandfather for sure - perhaps even a great-grandfather. And that must be my solace. If only he could know how fondly I remember because I know that he too must remember me. Why? Because those of us who leave home never forget our years in India.

(3)

I had to wait six months before college started in June. I started walking deep into the military cantonment not far from my house, all the way to the point where the peninsula of Bombay with its teeming millions, disappeared into the sea. I loved the cantonment for its ancient trees, its old bungalows for English colonels with servants' quarters behind them. One day I came upon an old English cemetery covered with weeds and broken tombstones with dates on them - 1803 to 1827. How young they died in Bombay, "where but two monsoons are the life of a man." I took long walks on the sea wall along the golf course, which ended in Ducksbury Point, and stood there thinking "until life itself to nothingness doth sink." There was no one there, as the cantonment was a restricted area.

I did not choose to be alone. I just was alone ...

On those evenings when I did not go for a walk, I would give imaginary recitals at home, playing every piece in my repertoire, and getting up and bowing after each piece, as I saw the concert pianists doing, while the servants were baking "chapatis" on a coal stove in the kitchen. By then I had become very proficient at sight reading.

Speaking of recitals, Bombay had a large number of classical music lovers, and for decades the Bombay Madrigal Singers Association used to invite some of the greatest pianists in the world. I don't know why they called themselves that because the organisers never sang a madrigal in their lives. Another organisation that invited artists was more elitist. Led by some of the richest Parsi ladies in Bombay, it was called the Time and Talents Club. Years later one of those ladies most graciously told me, "We have the time, and you have the talent" - because they also sponsored local artists and arranged for me to get master classes from visiting artists.

During the six-month period between school and college, I also sought more students. The sister of a boy who was with me in school and who tutored just for play money, passed all her students on to me when she got tired of teaching. One of them was a darling little six-year-old called Shakeel with eyelashes to die for. His parents owned the posh Bombay Hotel, and his mother was a real beauty. Shakeel was a little dynamo and a very bright child. I was hired to help him do better at school. One summer his parents took him to Kashmir, so I asked him to write five sentences on Kashmir.

The very first sentence was "In Kashmir, I played with the snow."

He asked me where was the most snow, so I said Antarctica. He started pestering his parents to take him to Antarctica in winter! In order to make him behave himself at home (his mother complained that he wouldn't listen to her), I told him about Medusa and the Unenines who could be summoned to punish naughty little boys. At first, he was afraid, but soon saw through me, and would say to me with a twinkle in his eyes, "Please don't call the Unenene!"

By the time college started, I was making enough to pay my own college fees which were extremely affordable and nothing like the unconscionable fees charged by American universities. So, I was no longer a burden on my father as far as education was concerned.

For four precious years, when my brother went to the Sir Jamshedji Jeejeebhoy School of Art (its first principal was Rudyard Kipling's father), he was at home with us. He slept in the front room with Daddy, and I slept in the back room with Mummy.

The piano and his drawing board were in the same room and though he never spoke to me, he laughed once at the end of a Mozart Sonata and said, "You can always know when a Mozart Sonata ends" (because of the repeated perfect cadence). I was thrilled that he addressed me! I, in turn, listened to the Elvis Presley songs he listened to on the radio on Voice of America while I was doing my homework in the same room.

My parents, meanwhile, wanted him to marry into a rich Parsi family. There was a beautiful and very fair Anglo-Indian girl who lived next to the Borthwicks across the street from us. She and Mel used to gaze at each other from the balcony. My mother made quite a scene.

Meanwhile, an old Parsi lady wanted someone to play on her Steinway grand, and someone suggested me. I used to love playing on Mrs. Nanavaty's piano! She was not related to the handsome Commander Nanavati who in 1959 had shot his beautiful English wife's Sindhi lover, resulting in a sensational trial. He became Bombay's hero, and poor Sylvia, his wife, was booed and called names as she came to the court to give testimony. In a surprising verdict, the jury declared Nanavati not guilty on September 23, 1959, but the verdict was declared "perverse" by the judge. The case was then referred to the Bombay High Court. On March 11, 1960, the HC found Nanavati guilty of killing Ahuja and sentenced him to life in prison. He was granted parole on health grounds in 1963 and moved to a hill resort. In 1964, new Bombay Governor and Jawaharlal Nehru's sister Vijayalakshmi Pandit pardoned Nanavati. Having reconciled, Nanavati and Sylvia emigrated to Canada with their three children in 1968, to live out the rest of their lives far from the bloody shadow of the infamous case. Nanavati died in July 2003.

My imaginary concerts turned to reality when I asked if I could give a private concert in Mrs. Nanavaty's spacious living room. She offered to rent folding chairs and about fifty guests attended. I gave a full recital, playing Bach, Mozart, Chopin, Brahms, and Debussy. The recital was a success and a local piano teacher, Mota Aunty, whose son was a gifted pianist and a friend of mine, went to my mother and said: "Your son is so talented! Please send him to Olga. He deserves to study with Olga. I myself will take him to Olga!"

My mother could not care less, because by then I was making enough from tutoring to pay the fees of Madame Olga Craen, Bombay's most famous and finest piano teacher.

She had studied at the Royal Academy of Music in London and also at the Paris Conservatoire. She settled in Bombay with her Belgian husband Jules Craen, who was a conductor, and they were Bombay's power couple in classical music. Madame Olga Craen played the Emperor Concerto and Rachmaninov Second and the Schumann and Tschaikovsky Concertos with the Bombay Philharmonic Orchestra, under her husband's baton. Just before, during and after the War years, she was the darling of Bombay's music lovers and all the rich Parsis sent their children to her.

In 1960, when I was still sixteen, Mota Aunty took me to Olga. She received me in all her glory in a shiny raw silk dress, filling the armchair in which she sat - a true dowager. After I played some Mozart she said, "You don't pedal so much in Mozart. You are very musical, but you have no technique! For six months you will only play Czerny's Art of Finger Dexterity! I charge forty rupees a lesson and you pay each month's fee in advance. I also get one month off each year with fees. If I miss a lesson, I don't get paid, but if you miss a lesson, I get paid." And so, Olga turned me into a pianist.

Two months into my lessons, Mota Aunty's son Phiroze, who had studied with Olga since the age of eight, said to me, "If you weren't my friend, I would hate you. Since you started, she says to me at every lesson: "You play like a bloody machine! Now look at Farokh! He is a musician!"

"And she says to me," I replied, "Lift your fingers! Attack!! Butter fingers!!!" (While the metronome ticked relentlessly).

She never praised her students to their faces. I have followed the opposite approach for six decades - offering gentle encouragement every step of the way.

There was another fallout from playing on dear Mrs. Nanavaty's piano. Sir Dinshaw Petit told his manager that he wanted someone to play on his Bösendorfer concert grand. Mrs. Nanavaty's son, whom the manager contacted, recommended me! So, one morning I took the bus for the long ride to Petit Hall on Nepean Sea Road. It commanded the sea, with a huge lawn going down to the rocky sea face. The manager took me into the vast hall filled with chandeliers and fretted and carved teak wood furniture.

"Where is the piano?" I asked eagerly.

The manager smiled with justifiable pride and pointed to the other end of the hall.

"It's there."

The vast hall dwarfed even a concert grand piano!

And so I became a regular visitor at Petit Hall, where my mother had refused to take me while she went to Sir Dinshaw Petit's daughter's Navjote!

I gradually mustered the courage to walk around the house and came upon the French room. It had French furniture from the eighteenth and nineteenth centuries and a Pleyel grand piano with an ornately carved cabinet. I eagerly sat down to play it, but it was not only completely out of tune, it also had a soundboard that was cracked. Simply dusting a grand piano every day is not enough. Above all, it must be played! And tuned at least twice a year.

Under Olga's tutelage I did my Licentiate in piano performance in 1962, and in 1965 I did my Fellowship exam. One normally succeeds in this exam on the second or third attempt and Olga kept saying, "You'll never pass!"

As I had graduated from Elphinstone College the previous year, I had plenty of time and practised five hours a day. Three hours between breakfast and lunch and two in the afternoon. In the evenings I taught. I had to give a full concert comprising all the styles from Bach to the twentieth century. I played Bach's Italian Concerto, Beethoven's Appassionata, Chopin's Ballade in G Minor, Debusy's Undine, Liszt's Campanella (as an obligatory Etude by Chopin or one of Liszt's Grand Studies of Transcendental Execution) and Bartok's Allegro Barbaro. At least three of the pieces had to be played from Allegero Barbaro.

I appeared for my exam and waited weeks for the report to come from London. When it arrived, I opened it with my heart thumping in my ears. Here's what the report said: *"This exceptionally gifted candidate played his challenging program with remarkable strength and unfailing accuracy. Both technically and musically, his performance, completely from memory, was masterly."*

And this is a good note on which to end this chapter.

7 - My Brother Leaves Home, Elphinstone College, I see North India for the First Time

In February 1961 my brother moved to New York. He was 22 and I was 17. Sponsored by the prominent Parsi industrialist Sohrab Godrej and a wealthy Gujarati businessman, Virendra Seth, he got a job with an advertising agency in New York and went on a work visa. He rented an apartment in the North Bronx and started sending my parents post cards which said, "Greetings from the land of milk and honey."

I think that they were meant for me rather than them!

Soon he met an Irish American girl whom he married and who made him an American citizen, much to my parents' chagrin. Her father was a doorman in a residential building and wrote to my parents saying, "We too would have liked our daughter to marry an American, but she loves your son, and we like him." To no avail. My mother was adamant, and that her father was a doorman gave her even more ammunition against her.

But I explained to my parents that they would marry each other anyway and that they should not ruin their relationship with her. My father immediately wrote to her, warmly welcoming her into the family. But my mother remained intransigent.

He had gone to New York by ship with Messageries Maritimes, taking all his most cherished possessions with him, among them his accordion, in which he smuggled three hundred dollars which he had bought on the black market. At the time, the Indian government, still led by Nehru and his faith in Fabian socialism which he had espoused at Cambridge, did not allow more than $75 to be taken out of the country.

I could not go to Ballard Pier to see him off, as I was in the middle of my terminal exams for First Year Arts at Elphinstone College and had a three-hour exam that morning. My mother was enraged that he was going and pretended to faint on the ship.

That evening she was sitting on her bed looking furious, and I knew how bad she was feeling, as she knew in the marrow of her bones that Mel would never come back. So, to make her feel better, I said, "Don't worry, Mummy, he will be back in a year as he promised."

She gave me a venomous look and said, "Don't think that just because he's gone, I will love you."

I knew only too well that she didn't love him either, that he too, like me, was just her old age insurance. What shocked me was the revelation that she was only too aware of my lifelong hunger for her love, and she had knowingly withheld it from me. It was then that I saw her sadism clearly for the first time.

(2)

To go back a year, I entered Elphinstone College in 1960. It was the oldest and most prestigious college in Bombay, and as it was also just a mile from my house, it was a natural choice. I had looked forward to walking over Wodehouse Bridge on Back Bay, to get there. But alas, Wodehouse Bridge had been pulled down to make room for Railway officers' flats. Fortunately, the abandoned Wellington Mews, where horses were stabled, still stood and was a beloved reminder of the Raj era.

When I went for admission, Principal Banerjee read my Senior Cambridge report with an approving smile and said,

"Well, young man, what can I do for you?"

My mother wanted me to become a doctor or an engineer where the money was, so even though I abhorred math and science, I said,

"Sir, I would like to be admitted to First Year Science."

"WHAT??!! You have got distinctions in English Language, English Literature and French and Scripture and History, and a mere pass in Mathematics and Physics, and you want me to admit you to First Year Science? I will do no such thing! But if you want me to admit you to First Year Arts, I will be happy to do so."

"Then, sir, I will be most grateful if you would admit me to First Year Arts," I said with relief and joy because that is what I had wanted in the first place!

When I went home and told my mother, she, like Queen Victoria, was not amused. I realised that God had saved me from immolating myself in order to please my mother. What I did not know is he would not save me the next two times.

My first day at Elphinstone College was a shock. Established by the great scholar, Mountstuart Elphinstone, it was the first college to be affiliated with Bombay University, which was established immediately after the Indian mutiny of 1857 with the goal of imparting the same education to Indians as that provided by universities in England. It had always been a government college and in the Humanities, at least, the professors had mostly been Englishmen or Indians with degrees from English universities.

But now it was thirteen years since the British had left and I entered a classroom of a hundred and fifty students, mostly girls (boys went for science) prattling away in Marathi and Gujarati. They were from vernacular schools and had studied English only in high school.

I was in shock. But gradually those of us who had studied in Jesuit or Anglo-Scottish schools met one another, and we formed an elite clique, disassociating ourselves completely from the vast majority whom we contemptuously called "The Vernaculars."

Looking back after sixty years, I can see that this was both snobbish and unkind, but in our defence, we were just 17.

In our group, there was a girl from the historic La Martiniere school in Calcutta, who tried to speak with a posh accent. During roll call, she would say that her number was 140, which she pronounced "one foot hay." I never learned what her name was, because we all called her "one foot hay" and whenever she walked towards us, one of us would say "Here comes one-foot hay." The only one who wasn't in on the joke was her.

Among others in our group was a gay boy called Nanoo Pamnani whose father was a prominent doctor. He had been to the Anglo-Scottish Cathedral School, Bombay's most expensive. He was high-spirited and full of fun and sought my friendship. We had many laughs together. He was very popular with the girls who were too innocent to know that he was gay or that I was transgendered.

This created a serious problem for me with a girl called Anita Bilani, both of whose parents were doctors and had just bought a building not far from my house in a superb location. To-day that building must be worth a king's ransom. She went aggressively for me, inviting me to her flat to listen to the LP of "My Fair Lady" which had just come out. At a college event, she asked me if I would accompany her on the piano if she sang "Come Back to Sorrento," which I did. The College very kindly rented a grand piano for the occasion.

She asked me if I would take her to the college social. I felt cornered. How could she know that I was not a boy, but a girl just like her - only, in the wrong body? How could she know that I too was attracted to boys, just as she was, and not to girls?

Being thrust into the role of a boy was abhorrent to me. For the first time, I became acutely aware of the fact that not only was I trapped in the wrong body, but that I was living a lie!

Less traumatic memories are of chatting with friends in the college canteen. This was run by a South Indian contractor, so on my first day when I asked the waiter what they served, he rattled off "Batata Wada, Masala Dosa etc." These were entirely foreign words to me as I had never had South Indian food. I had expected to choose between mutton sandwiches or cucumber sandwiches. Another shock!

Fortunately, behind the college there was a tiny "Milk Bar" which served hot chocolate and sandwiches and pudding! In those days I could eat to my heart's content because I was not just slim, I was skinny. It was only when I started taking female hormones that I started to gain weight for the first time in my life and joined the rest of mankind (or at least that portion of mankind that has money to eat) in its everlasting struggle to lose weight.

Our history professor was an ex-army officer, Professor Naik. He sported a military moustache with the ends twirled up and was a most lovable man, and was the heartthrob of all the girls (including me). Unfortunately, he lectured on Ancient Indian History, which we all found a crashing bore. His own passion was the French Revolution, and he would sometimes ask us, "Do you want me to talk about Ancient India or the French Revolution?" And we would all chorus "The French Revolution!"

During one lecture, Nanoo and I were continually whispering and giggling, not realising that Professor Naik was noticing us. He suddenly stopped and said, "Mr. Rustom, can you repeat what I have just said?"

As I had been listening to him with half an ear, I repeated every word that he had said in his lecture. He was delighted and said, "From now on you have my permission to talk throughout my lectures."

To the chagrin of all the girls (including myself), he soon got married. Less than two years later his young wife succumbed to breast cancer! Professor Naik was devastated and shed tears on the podium and told us that it was a love marriage. "She was from another caste, and a strict vegetarian, and yet she chopped meat and cooked meat and chicken for me!" We all loved Professor Naik not just for his looks, but also for his humanity. He was totally sincere.

When the Count of Urbino, a great Renaissance scholar, was asked, "What is the greatest quality that a man can possess?" he replied without a moment's hesitation, "Essere humano."

"To be human!"

Professor Naik was human.

As are also all true artists.

Years later, (in 1976), when I became Farah and was interviewed by the prestigious "Imprint" magazine, I mentioned that in Elphinstone College I had had a crush on a young professor. Lo and behold, a few days after the interview was published, the phone rang - it was Professor Naik!

"Am I right in thinking that the professor in question was me?" he asked with his typical honesty.

"Yes, sir."

We went out to dinner to catch up on the intervening years and had a very happy evening. In the course of our conversation, he told me that after he was prematurely widowed, Dr. Shroff, a Parsi spinster, told him, "You must get married again, Naik! You are too young to remain single."

"She told me this! I was thinking, 'But what about you, dear madam? It is so sad that you are still single'."

This brings me to Professor Shroff. Having been educated by masters and Jesuit priests, lady professors were a new experience for me. She had been to Oxford, and she was brilliant!

Her appearance worked against her because her cheeks were covered with pimples. She wore cat's eyeglasses and bright red lipstick. She also had a screechy voice. But she was inspiring! She went way beyond the first-year poetry syllabus in Advanced English (not required of the Vernaculars!) with Keat's Eve of St. Agnes, Milton's L'Allegro, Il Penseroso and Lycidas, and Tennyson's Mort d'Arthur.

Her commentaries were brilliant, and I furiously took notes.

One day she walked into class and without any preliminaries, read out the whole of Coleridge's Rime of the Ancient Mariner and left without a word. I was enthralled!

I went home and immediately sought it out in my Oxford Book of English Verse and walked up and down my living room, reading it aloud as she had, until, one day I had it by heart.

In years to come, I would thrill to Richard Burton reciting it on an audio YouTube recording.

I will be eternally grateful to her for always going beyond the call of duty - beyond the syllabus and beyond what we were required to know. I have followed the same principle as a piano teacher, talking about the composers and the great pianists to my students and refusing to merely confine myself to the piece in front of them.

I am grateful to Miss Shroff for one more thing. One day she stopped me in the corridor: "Farokh! Come here! Do you mind if I ask you a personal question?"

"No, Dr. Shroff."

"How much does your father earn?"

I blushed. "Six hundred rupees a month."

"WHAT?! Come to my office at once!"

She made me fill out forms for a scholarship and a few days later the Times of India carried a paragraph on the third page, which said, "The Bhabha Memorial Scholarship for gifted students has been awarded to Farokh Rustom of Elphinstone College." It was an award granted each year to only one student out of all the students at Bombay University.

I was amazed that some people actually read that paragraph! And they all said the same thing, "I would never have associated limited means with you." For some reason, my persona never proclaimed "lower middle-class" though I never tried to hide the fact.

All the students in my clique were rich and gave parties in their beautiful homes, and they invited me though I could never give a party myself. Not only that, but they also even arranged among themselves, to pick me up and drop me home, though I had done nothing to deserve it.

For that, I shall always be grateful, even though I hated having to dance with girls, as well as sit through the smooching that went on when the lights were dimmed.

In St. Mary's I'd had a crush on a boy one year senior to me, Mansoor Laljee. (How many silent crushes! Another price to pay for being born trans-gendered - unrequited love is the norm). He was handsome and athletic as well as brilliant and very popular with all his classmates. I cannot remember how I got to know him in school as he was one year senior to me. After doing his Senior Cambridge he went to St. Xavier's College and so he did not have the shock that I had on my first day in Elphinstone College with all the vernaculars, as St. Xavier's was a Jesuit College and very much like St. Mary's. Years later I would lecture there on classical music.

In his second year, Mansoor was transferred from St. Xavier's to Elphinstone College. I cannot remember why. Perhaps I didn't even care to ask. I was just so happy to see him again! The funny thing was that he bore a noticeable resemblance to me. That is to say, he looked like how I would have looked if I'd had a Greek nose instead of an aquiline nose after it broke, and if I were less skinny and above all, if I were manly and athletic.

The girls noticed the resemblance at once. One of them joked, "How come you are down there in the quadrangle and up here at the same time!" At one of the above-mentioned parties, when the lights were dimmed, Mansoor came and sat next to me where I was sitting alone on a couch (I could pretend to dance with a girl - but smooching was unthinkable!) and reached out and held my hand for a couple of minutes. Nothing was said. And this is the only romantic moment I had in my four years in college.

Mansoor went to England after graduating and disappeared from my life. I have done multiple searches for him on the internet, including on the St. Mary's alumni website, just for old times' sake, but there was no trace of him. I am sure he has lived a normal life - had a successful career, married, and had children and grandchildren. I am happy for him, and grateful for that wordless memory that he has given me. Clearly, he had seen into my heart, and he silently acknowledged it. Thank you, Mansoor.

(3)

A couple of more things need to be mentioned.

One was a college trip to North India in 1962. It was organised by Lala Tours, and because I was tutoring, I could afford to go on it. A compartment had been reserved for us and Dr. Shroff came along as a chaperone. She switched from the conventional sari to the duffel skirts she had worn at Oxford, for comfort and convenience.

Among the girls was a plump, pink Parsi girl called Ruby Vevaina whose mother owned the famous Donne's Institute for rich kids. It was a Mecca for well-to-do Kindergartners who eventually went on to the Doon School in Dehra Doon in the Himalayan foothills, a boarding school for boys where princes and other rich boys went.

In 1967 when I was in Addis Ababa, I met an American Peace Corps worker who'd just had a baby boy and asked me where he could be schooled if she worked in India, "Oh, you could send him to the Donne's Institute, and then to the Doon School" I said to her. "My poor, little boy," she cried, "first he has to go to the Dunce Institute and then to the Doom School!" I split my sides laughing.

Two memories of the North India tour stand out: In Delhi, when we were at the historic Red Fort, we hired a handsome tour guide to whom I listened attentively while my rich friends chatted among themselves. I asked him, "Who came first? Shah Jahan or Jehangir?"

"I'm surprised that you are in college and don't even know that much!" he said with the usual Indian frankness.

I shamefacedly tried to explain to him that I had only studied the history of England and European history in school as I had done my Senior Cambridge.

The other memory is of when were in Chandigarh. The rich clique asked Dr. Shroff if they could be dropped off by the tour bus at Kwality's restaurant, where they wanted to have lunch. They had invited me to join them, but I had declined saying that I was keen on seeing the sights.

"We haven't travelled one thousand miles to have lunch at Kwality's which you can also have in Bombay," she shrieked.

They apologised, but she was beside herself and insisted that they get off at Kwality's.

We went on to see Raj Bhavan, the residence of the Governor of Punjab. It had a huge garden with the most beautiful flowers, and as we were walking among them, a guard ordered us to keep our distance from the house.

"It's all right, you can approach," said an old man.

"But we don't want to disturb the Governor," said Dr. Shroff.

"I am the Governor" said the old man and invited us all to tea at the palatial residence where we were served on a silver tea service by bearers in colourful uniforms and turbans, a legacy of the Raj era. He took a keen interest in our tour and asked us many questions about Elphinstone College.

When the rich clique re-joined us from Kwality's, Dr. Shroff triumphantly told them, "While you were having lunch at Kwality's we had tea with the Governor of Punjab!"

I shall end on yet another happy note. There was a rich Vernacular in my class called Parimal Shah who lived just a block away from my house and who hooked up with me to improve his English. We would go every night to Napoli restaurant to have a Cappuccino, and occasionally he would treat me to dinner at an expensive restaurant so that I could teach him how to eat with a fork and knife. Nanoo did not approve of my friendship with him, but I couldn't care less. After he learned to drive, he would take along a couple of his friends and me for long drives into the country, all the way to Khopoli, at the foot of the Western Ghàts (mountains), where we would have lunch at a restaurant that served the most delicious Indian meals, before returning home. Years later, it was his sister, Dr. Sudha Seth, a superb gynaecologist, who operated on my mother for her prolapsed uterus, in her private nursing home.

8 - More Students and Mrs. Archer re-enters my Life

This chapter will be a counterpoint to the previous one, like a two-part Invention of Bach. (Except that in music the two voices can sing simultaneously, but here they can only sing one at a time.)

I shall re-trace my years in Elphinstone College (1960 to 1964) but write about my life during the hours that I was not in college. I was in college only from 11 a.m. to 3 pm, so I had a parallel life that I lived during the remaining hours.

Daddy had a well-to-do Parsi friend, Temhurus Parekh, with whom he used to sit and chat at Band Stand most evenings. The Band Stand was about a mile from our house, and during the Raj days, a military band used to play there on Sunday evenings, while the English took the sea breeze wafting in from Back Bay, and promenaded or sat on benches on a lawn, to listen.

When I was a child, children would take pony rides around the Band Stand, and Daddy took me for a couple of rides that I clearly remember. The pony men ran barefoot, holding on to the children. The ponies were stabled in the Wellington Mews, at the side of Wodehouse Bridge. Wodehouse Bridge was torn down in 1960, but Wellington Mews remained. Shortly after I left India in 1986, the Mews were also demolished, as were the livelihoods of the poor men who trotted their ponies around the Band Stand.

Temhurus Uncle had a beautiful daughter, whom he adored, but she was in tears because she was not allowed to marry the man she loved as he was deemed unsuitable. He wanted her to have a distraction and asked Daddy if I would give her piano lessons. As we lived very close to their building, I used to go there once a week to teach her.

Temhurus Uncle not only paid me but also had a ceiling fan installed in our living room. Just imagine, we had lived all those years in a city where the temperature went up to thirty degrees Celsius and more, for months on end, without even a fan!

In summer Daddy would have his bed moved to the balcony, and as I always slept beside him, I got to sleep on the balcony too. It didn't bother him that people in the building opposite could see him, as he was an early riser, and in India life is lived in the open. As I was a child, I was not at all self-conscious.

I remember those sultry nights with Jerry Borthwick across the road, playing his mouth organ on his balcony, and mornings before dawn when I could hear the milkman's gradual approach as he rang doorbell after doorbell before he finally rang ours. I would hear the crows begin to caw soon after the crack of dawn, and later the sparrows would begin to twitter. Finally, the joyous, screeching flock of parrots that roosted in the mango tree would fly to get their breakfast of serrano peppers from the balcony next door.

I could also hear the bell marking the changing of the guard at the military installation next door, called I.N.S. Hamla where military trucks were parked and Radio Engineering cadets lived in barracks. One night, in the small hours at about one or two a.m. I heard the chanting of male voices approaching from I.N.S. Hamla. Daddy and I got up to look and we watched, sitting in bed, as a troop of soldiers carrying flaming torches did a rhythmic dance, moving forward in unison.

We realised that it was in celebration of one of their festivals, unknown to us. It was surreal.

It was in the same I.N.S. Hamla, next door to us, that the sailors had mutinied in 1946 because they did not like their breakfast. Some historians believe that this little revolt made the British feel that they could no longer hold on to India any longer, as they had promised Gandhi independence in exchange for Indian support during the war, and the Quit India movement was in full swing.

How sad! Our dilapidated old building, an eyesore on Wodehouse Road, next to a small military installation that proved to be the death knell of the Raj!

After Mr. Parekh installed a ceiling fan in our living room, I installed one in the back room, and as the rooms were huge I finally ended up installing three ceiling fans in each room and last but not the least, one in the servants' room.

How they loved it! During the afternoon siesta when they had no work, they would switch on the fan and lie down under it. To my horror, Mummy started going to their room and switching it off!! When I discovered that she was doing that, I had a terrible row with her, as I was paying the electricity bill and so the servants using the fan did not cost my parents anything.

"You don't know how to keep servants," she scoffed.

"And who do you think you are?! A bloody maharani?"

My mother never raised her voice. She could say the most awful things in a voice that only I could hear (or my father, if she was berating him). Daddy said nothing, but I gave her as good as I got.

It did not serve me well, as I became too outspoken, and the habit of always speaking my mind made me suffer many losses, both personal as well as financial.

The damage she thereby did continues to this day, though she is long gone. I am too frank for my own good.

Mr. Parekh's tenants, the Sophers, had a twelve year-old son who was very talented in music. His name was Eric and Mrs. Sopher asked Mr. Parekh to ask if I would tutor her son. Eric made swift progress, and it was a joy to teach him. He played a student version of Liszt's Second Hungarian Rhapsody at a school concert in the Sir Cowasjee Jehangir Hall which has wonderful acoustics and two balconies. Mrs. Sopher shed tears of pride and joy and her heart swelled as the hall was filled with the sound of her son's piano playing.

Eric went to the posh Cathedral and John Connon school, and like all rich kids, was somewhat spoiled. So Mrs. Sopher asked me if I would also tutor him in school subjects and I said yes, everything except math and science.

Immediately his grades started going up and Mrs. Sopher became very fond of me. I used to teach Eric on their huge, covered, fourth floor balcony. It was totally different from our ramshackle wooden balcony, the floor of which sloped towards the sidewalk below, and which looked as though it would collapse in a heap any day. This balcony was made of concrete and on the floor, there were Venetian tiles. The balcony overlooked a small, gated park with a beautiful, wrought iron fence and beyond that stretched Garden Road, with art deco buildings on either side.

Mrs. Sopher would have tea sent in on a trolley with sandwiches and Indian snacks for both Eric and me, and I used to really look forward to those evenings on the balcony. Mrs. Sopher, a real Earth Mother type with a huge bosom, would stand on the balcony in a printed cotton frock and smoke as we ate.

She gave me my first hundred rupee note, and I was thrilled.

It was one of the last of the huge hundred-rupee notes printed in the Raj era, and Mrs. Sopher told me, "You are so lucky that you've had to work for it. Not like this son of a bitch who gets everything and takes it for granted."

"Mrs. Sopher!" I joked, "why are you calling yourself a bitch?"

She ignored my remark and went on, "When I was your age, I was poor, just like you. I went to typing school and became a secretary. I got a job where I met his (Eric's) father. He was my boss's son. We fell in love and got married."

One evening I was roundly scolding Eric. He was 13 and I was 18. He calmly told me, "You are too big for your boots."

I couldn't help laughing, because I knew that he was repeating what Mrs. Sopher must often have told him.

This idyll ended when they emigrated to England in 1964.

The last I heard of them from a mutual friend was that Eric's older sister, a beautiful girl, died of food poisoning in England less than a year after they left.

I have made futile searches for Eric Sopher on the internet. He must be in his seventies to-day. To me, he is eternally thirteen.

(2)

Do you remember Mrs. Archer, who prepared me for the entrance exam to St. Mary's when I was six years old, and with whom my mother fought? That story, at least, has a happy ending.

On my short walk to the Sophers' home, I had to pass Mrs. Archer's. She lived on the ground floor, and one evening I saw her standing at her window. I stopped below her window and said, "Good evening, Mrs. Archer."

She could not recognise me as an 18-year-old, but I told her who I was and thanked her warmly for all that she's done for me, and for the beautiful memories. Neither of us mentioned my mother, but we started chatting regularly after that - me on the sidewalk, looking up at her (which was appropriate), while she stood at her window.

One evening she gave me a book. It was by Sigmund Spaeth, and was called *Stories Behind the World's Greatest Music.*

I brought it with me to America in 1986, even though I came by air and could bring very little, because it was this book that inspired me to evolve my own style of teaching music appreciation!

9 - Music Appreciation, Mr. Krishnan, and the Indo-American Society

In 1962, when I was 18, three boys a couple of years senior to me at Elphinstone College asked me to teach them something about European classical music. They would soon be going to England to continue their studies and they felt that they should acquaint themselves with Western classical music before they did so.

Caveh Munshi was going to the London School of Economics, and Nitin Desai to Oxford. The third, Kumar Shani, was not going abroad, but asked if he could join them.

I was thrilled. Kumar had perfect Greek features, and a slight limp due to polio, which was very attractive. He was soft-spoken and aristocratic, and smoked, which made him look very grown up to me. He eventually became a distinguished maker of low-budget art films (as opposed to the Bollywood melodramas-cum-musicals). I had a crush on him. (One more secret crush that I had to keep to myself!) I would watch him from the third-floor corridor of the college as he limped his way through the quadrangle below, to the college canteen (cafeteria).

I invited the three of them to come to my house once a week and had to figure out what to do. It occurred to me that instead of introducing them to the different periods and styles (Baroque, Classical, Romantic etc.), and the different forms (Sonata, Symphony, Concerto etc.), that I should start by introducing them to program music.

So, on their first visit, I played them Long Playing records of Rimsky-Korsakov's Scheherazade, pointing out the beauty, intensity and yearning in the violin theme that represented Scheherazade as she starts her haunting tale (The Sea and Sinbad's Ship) before the orchestral music unfolds. Then The Storm at Sea etc.

They enjoyed this. Then I introduced them to Mussorgsky's Pictures at an Exhibition describing each painting and telling them the touching story of the genesis of this work (the premature death of Mussorgsky's painter friend, Hartmann) and some biographical information about the two composers - Rimsky-Korsakov was a naval officer and Mussorgsky was a dipsomaniac.

They lapped it all up and came back week after week as I gradually introduced them to Beethoven's Emperor Concerto, taking the opportunity to explain how a Concerto differed from a Symphony, then Mozart's tragic D Minor Piano Concerto where I explained the difference between Major and Minor, and finally the austere and sublime Bach Concertos where I explained the difference between the Baroque and Classical styles, and also added that Scheherazade and Pictures at an Exhibition were products of the Romantic period.

Gradually they relaxed and started asking questions which I was only too happy to answer.

They came every week for six months. I gradually introduced them to piano solos (which I played myself and which delighted them), and then Chamber Music (The Brahms Violin and Piano Sonata in D Minor, Brahms' Cello Sonata in D Minor - here I introduced them to the special sound of each instrument and its emotional qualities - then Piano Trios etc.). And, of course, to the lives of the composers, to humanise them, and bring down their marble busts from their marble pedestals and strip off the snobbery surrounding the names of these most humans of men!

Of course, I did not charge them. But they helped to evolve my own way of introducing laymen to classical music, and for this, I shall always be grateful to them.

(2)

Fast forward to 1966.

I was teaching English to a young man called Paul (he was a Sindhi, and his name was really Paal) and one day he said to me, "You should approach the Indo-American Society and ask them if you could teach one of their English language courses. You will make a lot more money than you can only by tutoring."

So off I went and met the Executive Secretary, Mr. N. Krishnan. He turned out to be a south Indian gentleman of the old school, tall, pleasant looking, courteous. He agreed to hire me.

One day, Paul - to whom my debt knows no bounds - brought me several typed sheets and asked me to read them. To my dismay, they said that the central government in Delhi was using machines to influence and control our brains, etc. etc. I was only 22 and had never

70

met a schizophrenic before. Indeed, I didn't even know the word back then. So, my immediate reaction was, "Oh, my God! Paul is mad!"

At the next lesson, Paul asked me if I had read the pages he'd given me.

"Yes."

"Well, what do you think?"

"Paul, you know that that's crazy. Delhi is not sending electronic rays to control our brains."

Of course, this was the absolute worst way to respond to a suffering schizophrenic, but God forgive me, I did not know any better back then.

I never saw dear Paul again.

May his soul rest in peace, for he has surely passed on by now. May his soul be in a very beautiful place, freed at last from the brain that tormented him!

The next day, when I was having tea with my boss, Mr. Krishnan, he asked me wide-eyed:

"Did Paul give you some printed material to read?"

"Yes, he did."

"My God, the poor fellow is mad!"

He too hadn't heard of schizophrenia.

Thanks to Paul, though, but for whom I would never have met Mr. Krishnan, I was able to ask Mr. Krishnan if I could conduct a course in Western classical Music Appreciation.

This was a market that had never been tapped before, but Mr. Krishnan (dear Mr. Krishnan!) agreed to take the chance. I would be allowed to use one of the air-conditioned classrooms. They would buy a record changer on which I could play my LP's. They would pay the advertising costs. They would keep forty percent of the fees and I would get sixty percent.

I had nothing to lose. They did.

My worst fears were realised when only six people enrolled for my twelve lecture courses. I humbly apologised to Mr. Krishnan. This would not even cover a fraction of their cost!

"But look who's enrolled!" replied Mr. Krishnan. "The Maharaja and Maharani of Cooch Behar, The former Chief Presidency Magistrate (an Englishman who stayed on in India), Mr. Yahya Jhaveri the diamond merchant." And two others whom I can't recall.

"These people will now enroll enrol for other courses at the Indo-American Society."

He was incredibly noble and encouraging. My lectures were much appreciated, and at the end of the first lecture, Mr. Jhaveri came up to me as I was putting my LPs in my bag, and said, "How are you going home?"

This was a common question in India because only a tiny fraction of the millions of Bombayites could afford a car. A car, in fact, was a significant status symbol.

"Oh, I'll just take the bus from across the road."

"No. I'll drop you home."

On the way, he told me, "You are very good. But you must advertise. Nobody knows you exist."

Eventually, he hired me to tutor his very spoilt little boy who simply didn't want to study. But I enjoyed going to his penthouse in a newly constructed high rise (Sagar Sangeet / "Sea Song") just a block from my house and with a stunning view of the harbour.

The large rooms, with marble floors, over which his bejewelled, young wife pranced barefoot, were all air-conditioned. She was the most cheerful and happy young woman, and Mr. Jhaveri himself was a most amiable young man, descended from generations of jewellers going back to Mughal times. They were the nicest, happiest couple I have ever met and I recall them fondly.

Subsequent music appreciation courses got larger classes as word spread, and the Indo-American Society was at last able to make a profit in return for the huge risk they took in providing me with a platform.

In 2001, fifteen years after I came to America, and finally learned to use a computer and make Google searches, I searched for Mr. Krishnan, so I could write and thank him for all that he had done for me.

Unfortunately, the first words I found were "the late Mr. N. Krishnan of the Indo-American Society ..."

10 - Olga's Student Recitals, Buji, and Katy Chinoy

To continue rambling through my late teens ...

Madame Olga Craen used to have one student recital a year, at which not all her students played, only the best.

Her only concession was to allow just one intermediate-level student to begin with a Clementi Sonatina or a Bach Two-Part Invention. Then came the remaining five or six of us - in our late teens or early twenties, and what we played included a Chopin Ballade or Scherzo or Sonata, Schumann's Toccata, Mendelssohn's Variations Serieuses, Beethoven's Tempest Sonata, Bach's Chromatic Fantasia and Fugue, and other staples of the concert pianist's repertoire.

The audience did not comprise just adoring parents and supportive friends. All of Bombay's concert goers were invited in the form of announcements in the newspapers under "Today's Events."

About three or four hundred music lovers showed up!

Invitations were sent to the music critics of the city's leading English language newspapers including the Times of India, the Bombay Gazette, the Indian Express, the Evening News, etc.

We were all compelled to play by heart!

The magnificent Crystal Room in Bombay's historic five-star Taj Mahal Palace Hotel was booked as the venue.

All this required money, so a committee was set up to get advertisements for a printed concert program. The ads just said, "With Best wishes from Air India," or "With Best wishes from Tata Chemicals" etc.

A committee member was also appointed to check with concert organisers if any famous international artist was scheduled to give a performance on the same evening. And also, to send special invitations to VIPs, including the advertisers, the city's prominent citizens, the consulates of foreign countries, etc. for whom the first ten rows were reserved.

You can easily imagine how intimidating this would all be!

I slept fitfully for weeks before each recital. Although I practised diligently and was well prepared, what killed me was the thought of a memory failure! If only Olga had let us have the music in front of us! In years to come, I have made a point never to insist that my students play in recitals from memory, even though I always encourage them to memorise and to try and play at lessons at least, from memory.

Olga would have at least three rehearsals before the recital. The first two were at her apartment. We would all squeeze into her modest living room and play on her Austrian Brasted grand piano, while the rest of us squeezed onto the sofas or sat on the floor. Olga almost never said anything at these rehearsals. But we all got to know one another as a result and became friends and visited one another, and talked about music, and played for each other, and listened to one another's LPs and laughed and joked about Olga and imitated her temper tantrums.

The third and last rehearsal was in the Crystal Room on the morning of the recital, and then Olga would spring to life!

We could never walk onto the stage fast enough.

"Faster!" she screamed, until we all but sprinted onto the stage.

Our bows were not good enough. And on one occasion that I shall never forget when Roshan Suntoke played the opening phrase of the first movement of Chopin's great Sonata in B Minor ("that sublime song of all suffering," as Liszt called it), Olga made her stop repeatedly and play it either slower or faster.

"Too slow!" she would scream. Or "Stop! Too fast!"

Poor Roshan Suntoke was a nervous wreck, and she still had to play 38 pages of the most difficult piano solo music ever written! Four long and difficult movements - three of them fearsomely difficult - and she was stuck on the first phrase of the first movement.

Why Olga did that, I shall never know.

But the fruit of these concerts was sweet indeed.

The next morning, we woke up to fulsome praise. One critic started his review by saying, "By now Madame Olga Craen's annual student recitals have become an institution in Bombay and are eagerly looked forward to by the city's musical cognoscenti."

Every piano teacher in Bombay was in the audience and some of them told me, "The trouble is that all of you talented ones go to Olga, and the rest come to us!"

(2)

I also came to the attention of Bombay's aristocratic music lovers and some of the guests staying at the Taj Mahal Hotel who were also welcome to the recital. One of them happened to be the newly arrived manager of the Bank of America whose wife asked me if I taught and became my student.

Among the cognoscenti was a great Parsi music lover, Buji Chinoy. He had three grand pianos in his fourteen-room penthouse A Steinwey, a Bechstein and a Blüthner. The rooms were filled with priceless Ming vases and jade and ivory carvings. He asked me if I would teach his boys.

The Chinoys had four boys, but the youngest, Jimmy, was only two years old.

Every Sunday afternoon I would catch the C route bus from my house to Chowpatty Beach and enjoy the drive along the sea from the upper deck, along Marine Drive. Then I would climb up the steep Siri Road with its ancient trees and increasingly beautiful views of the Bay, to Chinoy Towers atop Malabar Hill. There were four three-bedroom luxury apartments on each floor. The Chinoy penthouse on the fourteenth floor occupied the space of all four apartments, and eight-year-old Neville used to ride his two-wheel scooter all over the fourteen rooms.

After I had taught two of the boys, their mother, Katy, would say, "Farokh, you must be tired. Have some tea!"

We would all assemble at her huge dining table covered with black glass and have Earl Grey Tea flavoured with spearmint and sweetened with honey, in addition to cakes, scones, sandwiches and more. Oh, how I looked forward to those English teas!

Years later, when I was Farah and was accompanied by my teenage servant Anthony to cocktail parties to which I was invited as a critic and a social columnist, and Anthony was sitting with a bunch of servants in a secluded corner of the banquet hall, I stashed his plate with goodies from the buffet table - chicken biryani, tandoori chicken, fried pomfrets, lobster etc. and told him "Eat your fill, Anthony, You won't get such food at home!"

Unfortunately, the Prince of Bikaner happened to be passing by, and heard me!

He laughed heartily, and said, "Farah, I love you! Come, sit. Talk to me."

And so, we shared a glass of champagne and some laughter together.

I never forgot those days when I so enjoyed those teas and snacks at Mrs. Sopher's and the Chinoys and how much pleasure they had given me, because when I went home from St. Mary's I just got a raisin bun and a cup of tea, and I looked forward even to that humble treat with pleasure each day.

In 1967 when I was in Ethiopia, Neville Chinoy, who was by then twelve years old, played for Zubin Mehta, the world-renowned Parsi conductor who arranged a full scholarship for him at the Curtis Institute of Music in Philadelphia.

In 1974, after I had returned from Ethiopia, I went to see Neville who was in Bombay for his summer vacation. I was afraid that he would be stuck up now and be haughty with me. To my surprise and delight, he came right up to me where I was sitting on the couch and gave me a peck on the cheek. This meant a lot, as I was still Farokh. He, Buji, and I sat and chatted. I asked Neville how he liked Curtis. I expected him to rave.

Instead, he said, "I would rather not go back. I miss home. I wish I didn't have to go back!"

I looked at Buji, and because I had been very homesick in Ethiopia and knew what homesickness felt like, pleaded for Neville.

But Buji said, "Oh, he has to go back! He can't play chamber music here! He can't play concertos here! He can't make the right contacts here!"

And so, Neville got on the long flight to America. On the connection from Athens to Rome, his flight TWA 841 crashed into the Ionian Sea killing all passengers in a suspected act of terrorism.

"I should have listened to you," wept Buji when I went to pay my condolences. "I just want my baby back! I don't care if he never becomes a concert pianist!"

"But how could you have known, Buji! You just wanted the best for him!"

Katy was numb with tranquillizers. But when I said that I had dreamt of Neville and he was playing on a magnificent grand piano, she asked at once, "How did he look?"

"Very happy" I replied honestly.

She burst into sobs. After drying her tears, she said very softly, "Thank you."

Olga's most gifted student had been Hilla Khurshedji. She was indeed superb but stuck up and standoffish and never made friends with any of us. Her parents were insufferable, talking about "My Hilla! My Hilla!" all the time.

Hilla won the Ravel competition in Paris and married and settled in London. At the age of thirty-two, she went up to the tenth floor of Harrod's and plunged to her death. She left her purse by the window. It had her money, her house keys, her car keys, her driver's license, her bank book - everything. But there was no suicide note.

By then I was Farah and went to her sky funeral at the Towers of Silence (her body had been flown from London). The two bereaved mothers, Hilla's mother and Katy Chinoy were sitting side by side. I was wearing the plain white sari drawn over my head and no make-up and no jewellery, as required at funerals, and as I shook hands with them and said how sorry I was, they both looked puzzled, as I did not resemble any of the aristocratic Parsi ladies they knew. Then suddenly it dawned on both of them at the same time:

"Farah!" smiled Katy.

And even Hilla's mother could not help smiling, though she had just lost her gifted daughter to suicide.

11 - Escape from Raj Bhavan, My first Hill Stations

I was still in my late teens and owing to my outward appearance and false identity as Farokh, I could only visit those of my classmates who were living in boys' hostels.

One of them was Dago Tschering from Bhutan. He was tall and masculine and had a deep Mongolian voice. As his hostel was on C Road, just off Marine Drive, we used to take walks by the sea and watch the sunset from Nariman Point. We would walk hand in hand, as is the custom with Indian boys. I loved the feel of his calloused manly palm, against my soft, feminine palm. In fact, he remarked on it, to my delight.

"Your hand feels like a girl's."

He also liked the perfume I regularly wore - it was called Kanta perfume. It was lovely, and not too expensive.

But we were not lovers - not even remotely so. He was not inclined that way, and when we sat close together on the rocks at Nariman Point watching the sunset, I longed for him to kiss me. But he didn't.

I wouldn't wish to be trans-gendered on anyone. It has its own unique brand of endless emotional pain and unfulfilled longing.

Then one day, Dago sought me out in the hallway at Elphinstone College. We were not in the same class, as he was in the Science section. He looked distressed. He had just been summoned to the principal's office and told that the King of Bhutan, who was paying for his education, wanted him transferred to the Indian Administrative Service College in Simla.

We were both distraught.

He went. We exchanged a few letters, and then he was sent to the Bhutanese legation in New York. We still wrote, but our correspondence soon died.

I have never been good at saying goodbye. I have always hated it. And in letting Dago go by not staying in touch, I was following a pattern that would plague me all my life.

Dago eventually served as Home Minister of Bhutan, and later Ambassador to Japan, as I learned from the internet decades later.

For some reason, I did not even try to contact him. When I saw his photo with a well-trimmed beard, smoking a pipe, and forty pounds heavier, he did not even remotely resemble the boy that I had loved, and who, perhaps, had loved me.

Then there was Kulachandra Khwaiarakpam from Manipur, famed for its Manipuri dances, from India's easternmost state of Assam.

I met him in the hostel after Dago left, and because of his Mongolian features and manliness, instantly took to him. We too went on walks by sea. One day I decided to show him a part of Bombay he had never seen - posh Nepean Sea Road, on the other side of Malabar Hill from Marine Drive.

It was low tide and we stepped on the rocks and kept walking towards the tip of Malabar Hill. The high rises disappeared, and, to my surprise and delight, the tip of Malabar Hill appeared untouched by the progress of time. We climbed the hill and came upon a beautiful nineteenth-century bungalow.

That is when it hit me!

We were in Raj Bhavan - the Governor's residence!

We beat a hasty retreat down the hill, back down to the rocks and made it back to Nepean Sea Road just as the incoming tide covered the rocks we had been walking on.

The gated entrance to Raj Bhavan was from Walkeshwar Road and an armed guard was always on duty. It never occurred to them that there would be someone stupid enough to climb up from the sea!

At some time in the past, only the Parsi Tower of Silence stood atop Malabar Hill. Over the years as it was being developed, the Governor of Bombay decided to live on the western edge of the hill, and the rich started building bungalows there, and peacocks roamed in their large and lush gardens. It was paradise.

Then came Independence, and the bungalows were torn down one by one to make room for high rises (including Chinoy Towers) and the lush gardens with their ancient trees were replaced by concrete parking lots.

With Independence began the overcrowding and excessive urbanization of beautiful Bombay!

I cannot swim. And the tide coming in and covering the rocks over which Kulachandra and I had beaten a hasty retreat just minutes before, reminds me of my lonely walks at Ducksbury Point in the military cantonment next to my house in early 1960, when I had six months off between school and college.

It afforded a clear view of Prong's Reef Lighthouse built atop some high rocks. I had read that one could walk to it at low tide, and was sixteen, lonely and romantic. So, one evening, when the tide was out, I decided to walk to it. I jumped off the wall and started walking towards the lighthouse. But the further I got from land, and the nearer I got to the lighthouse, which now loomed large, I noticed that there were deep puddles of water rapidly forming between the rocks and that the tide had turned and was coming in fast.

Suddenly I heard a voice come out of thin air. It was a male voice, and it said, "Go back! Go back!"

No human being was in sight.

I felt the fear of God and started running back, slipping, falling, and bruising my legs. I made it back to the wall when the waves were almost lapping against the wall.

What was that voice that I heard, that saved my life?

Was it my Guardian Angel?

I have always wondered about it and kept it in my heart. Till today I have told no one about it.

(2)

I shall now digress to write about my passionate love affair with India's Hill Stations.

I started with the humblest, when I was eleven and had just started playing the piano, and still in St. Mary's. Mummy joined a five-day trip by the Irani Ladies Zoroastrian Association. (Daddy was called an Irani as his father had come from Iran, whereas the Parsis had been in Bombay for generations and made vast fortunes. The Iranis only owned tea shops and were looked down upon by the Parsis).

As my mother was a Parsi, and quarrelsome to boot, the Irani ladies did not like her and called her "Our Enemy" behind her back. Mummy knew it and told me so herself. But they couldn't very well refuse to let her join them on the trip.

Mummy took me along.

Matheran, atop a two-thousand-foot mountain, was discovered by the English District Collector, John Mallet.

He inquired from the locals what was atop the mountain.

"They replied in Marathi, "Mathe Raan ahe." ("Up there, there is just a forest.")

Mr. Mallet took it to be the name of the place and christened it Matheran.

At 2000 feet and heavily forested with millions of Acai Berry trees, it was cooler than the steaming plains below and just forty miles from Bombay.

Mallet built himself a vacation house up there.

Soon others followed, including enterprising Parsis who built hotels, and before long Matheran became a Hill Station.

Tigers prowled the mountain and as with Malabar Hill in Bombay, were all killed off.

I fell in love with the place.

By then a narrow gauge "toy train" took vacationers up the mountain.

Matheran was the middle-class family's hill station. There was no motor-able road up to it in my time and years later I climbed up to it because there was a footpath leading to the top. It was the off-season because it was the monsoon and the hotels were empty, so I spent a night up there and came down the next day.

On the way down I saw a snake by the side of the road and went up to it to get a closer look because of my myopic eyes. But it slithered away.

When I told my students and friends about it, they were furious.

"You fool! The whole world runs away from snakes, but you go towards one!"

Ouch! That's me.

In 1962 I got the opportunity to visit Bombay State's most upscale Hill Station. At 4,500 feet it was more than twice the height of Matheran and cooler. The English built bungalows there to get away from the sweltering heat of Bombay (it was 120 miles from the city), and they even had fireplaces built so that at Christmas it would feel like home, even though the temperature did not drop below ten degrees.

It was posh compared to Matheran and there was a lake where one could go boating.

It came about like this:

Our neighbours, the Barias (they lived a block away) hosted an American high school girl for a month while their high school son spent a month with her parents in America. Her name was Nancy and the Barias wanted to show her Mahabaleshwar. They asked me along to keep her company.

Nancy was friendly and outgoing, and she was joined by another American girl in the same program, Tracy. If anything, Tracy was even more friendly and bright and enthusiastic about everything. They secretly told me that they thought that the Barias were snobs. They were not used to their British ways and strict etiquette.

While I liked both of them and had absolutely nothing against them, I felt rather queasy pretending to be a boy. I think they both picked up on the fact that I did not have the least interest in either of them or probably thought that I was gay.

I liked getting away from everyone and going for a walk by myself whenever I could. One day a chauffeur-driven car slowed down and pulled up beside me and from the back seat a beautiful and elegant woman addressed me: "Farokh! What are you doing in Mahabaleshwar?"

It was the Maharani of Sangli whose son Vijay had been with me in St. Mary's. I told her about my hosts and the American girls, and she invited me to tea and asked me to bring them all along.

The Barias were impressed, and the American girls were thrilled to bits that they were going to meet a Queen!

The day after our visit to the Maharani, a Bollywood star moved into the rooms next to ours at the Fountain Hotel. When I told them that he was the famous actor, Mahmood, the girls grabbed their autograph books and knocked on his door. (Yes, those were still the days of autograph books. Remember them? With plastic covers and coloured pages?). Mahmood was very friendly to them, and unbeknown to us, invited Tracy (who was not staying with the Barias) when she was in Bombay, to his home.

Before we knew it, she had married him and become his second wife. (Under Muslim law he was allowed four wives).

In the years that followed I would occasionally see her photo with Mahmood in film magazines. She was demurely dressed in a sari and looked very beautiful. So, miraculously, the marriage was a success.

12 - Jer Jussawala, and My First Wrong Turn in Life

Soon after I started my courses on music appreciation at the Indo-American Society, a remarkable woman entered my life. Her name was Jer Jussawala, and even though a Parsi, she was also a Theosophist.

This is how I met her. I was contacted by the Nalanda Cultural Club to give a lecture recital. It was in the home of two Parsi spinsters in the suburb of Bombay called Bandra. They were two dainty little sparrows, straight out of a Victorian novel. They were both elderly and fragile, soft-spoken, and elegant, and being with them, you would think that Queen Victoria was still on the throne.

They lived in genteel poverty, in an old bungalow belonging to a more gracious time.

The moving spirit behind the Nalanda Club was Jer Jussawala and she rented a large room in their bungalow to host lectures and cultural events.

After my recital, in which I remember I played, among other things, Bach's Chromatic Fantasia and Fugue, Jer came up to me with a radiant smile and not only complimented me but invited me to her bungalow on Juhu beach so we could talk.

I took the local train and bus to Juhu beach and arrived at her spacious bungalow which had once belonged to Annie Besant who had written many books on Theosophy and personally met Madame Blavatsky, the founder of the Theosophical Society which believes in universal brotherhood and the equality of all religions.

Jer was then about fifty, and a dedicated spirit. She was warm and vibrant and friendly and full of enthusiasm. Her bungalow was large and airy and dominated the sea with its octagonal balcony, scattered with chintz-covered sofas and armchairs. It was in the Theosophical Colony, which I later discovered she owned, as well as Jussawala Wadi next to it. Together they comprised the last remaining bungalows in Juhu, and among her tenants was a Bollywood star. But also, a seamstress who was widowed, and to whom Jer charged rent far below the market rate, even though she had to pay tax on what the bungalow would have fetched had she rented it at the market rate.

She kept open house, and when convent schools organised picnics to Juhu, the nuns told the girls, "If you have any problem, call Jer Jussawala."

She had Indian as well as international house guests and left them alone to enjoy the beach and spend their day as they wished while joining them at her table at mealtimes.

She kept receiving fabulous offers for her land (so that the old bungalows could be torn down and luxury high rises built on the prized location) but she considered herself a trustee of the land and refused all the offers which would have made her richer than Croesus.

"Not while I'm alive!" she said stoutly.

Jer inducted me into the Round Table, the junior branch of the Theosophical Society and asked me to play at their monthly prayer meetings in which we all sat in a circle and each person would recite a prayer from their religion while the rest respectfully listened. Christian, Jewish, Hindu, Muslim, Zoroastrian, Jain, and other payers were all said.

She also organised holiday camps, so thanks to her I got to visit the beautiful city of Hyderabad ("where North and South India meet," as Nehru so beautifully put it) with its excellent zoo and the Salar Jung Museum which housed the collection of the famed Nawab which included everything from coloured chandeliers to books, mechanical toys, clocks, paintings, antiques, musical instruments - everything.

One unforgettable camp was at her bungalow in Deolali, in the hills of the Western Ghats.

Here I must pause to add that she had a mother who was about 80, and because she had a skin condition that robbed her skin of pigment, she looked like the Queen Mother. Not that Jer was not light-skinned, like most Parsis, but she dressed unselfconsciously in flower print cotton dresses, or saris with ethnic colours and prints, while her mother (whom we all called "Fuiji" "Father's Sister") dressed regally in embroidered silk saris and diamond and emerald broaches befitting her status in life. She was a sight to behold as she stood regally at the top of the stairs, welcoming guests to her house!

Her mother was still alive, and she was a hundred years old - nearly blind, almost totally deaf, and suffering from Alzheimer's. She had a maid whose only job was to look after her. All day she would rest or sleep against cushions on a sofa on the huge balcony with its marble floor, lulled by sea breezes, and the maid would hold her hand and help her to the dining table where she dined with whoever was present, which often included guests.

She was hilariously funny.

Jer had recruited me to give recitals to raise money for the camps, and she had a huge invitation list of the elite of Bombay. Part of my job was to address and stamp the envelopes and send off the printed invitations to all the people in her guestbook. As with Olga's recitals, I was blessed in that these house concerts brought me to the attention of even more distinguished people, among them being the personal physician to the President of India (who told me that as I was playing he felt the presence of Gandharvas and Apsaras - celestial musicians and dancers to the gods) and the famed Bharat Natyam dancer Rukmini Devi Arundale who made this ancient classical temple dance respectable by bringing it out of the realm of the "devadasis" - temple dancers who were also prostituted - and bringing it onto the international stage, and into the lives of the daughters of the rich and privileged.

On a humorous note, hundred-year-old grandma, who was out of it, would suddenly speak loudly while I was in the middle of a Chopin waltz or a Liszt etude. The bee in her bonnet was "If Beethoven was deaf, how could he compose?" She always forgot my answer and kept asking.

Also, when her eighty-year-old son arrived and said, "Hello mother," she would ask him, "Who are you?"

"I am your son, Jamshed," he would shout into her ear.

"Who?" "Where do you live?" "What is your name?"

I was too young not to find this hilariously funny. It would be decades before I would begin to understand the sadness of Alzheimer's.

Jer used to joke that it was an entirely female household.

The only male servant was the chauffeur. All the rest, from the cook down, were maids. "Even the dog is female" she laughed.

Despite her wealth and talent, she was not married, and one day, as we were driving to downtown Bombay, she told me the reason. It was heart-breaking!

As a young girl, she had fallen for a handsome and famed south

Indian dancer. She almost eloped with him but was caught in the nick of time. Then she fell in love with an Englishman who told her that he was gay. The third time she fell in love with a married man.

"And in case you are wondering if I am a virgin or not, the answer is that I am."

Poor Jer! By then she knew all about me. I had confided in her that I was transgendered. She explained it (perhaps to herself) by saying that I was born a woman in my last few incarnations, and being born a boy this time was a shock. Her unconditional acceptance meant the world to me!

But before I forget, the camp at Jer's bungalow in Deolali:-

During the Second World War Bombayites feared an attack by the Japanese from the sea. And so, Jer's father bought a large bungalow at the hill station of Deolali, atop a hill, and while he was at it, he bought the hill as well. This was supposed to be a safe haven in case of Japanese occupation.

Jer refused to have it electrified as she preferred to maintain the ambience of lamplight in this rural setting. The lamps had lampshades in beautiful colours. We all slept in its many bedrooms, two or three to a room, in large wooden beds with mosquito nets, and enjoyed hiking in the mountains all around, at the comfortable altitude of two thousand five hundred feet.

The meals were provided by the priest's wife in the local fire temple, and they were as delicious as the meals at a Parsi wedding or Navjote.

Jer told me a hilarious story about the hill atop which the house was built. They had allowed the "mali" (gardener) who looked after the property when they were not there, to grow rice for himself and his family on a couple of acres. Under a new law in post-Independence India, absentee landlords could lose their land.

So, Jer went to Deolali (which is two hundred miles inland from Bombay) with her lawyer to see the local official.

"Are you the heir?" he asked Jer.

Unfortunately, he pronounced "heir" as "here."

So, Jer thought that he was saying, "Are you the here?"

"Oh, yes" she replied," we are regularly here."

"No, no madame. I ask you, are you the here - "h-e-i-r! here?"

"Oh, heir!" cried Jer. "Oh yes, I'm the heir."

"Is it pronounced air?" asked the official, abashed.

I laughed till I cried!

Jer and I both shared a passion for the monsoon. Despite the age difference of twenty-six years between us, we had become very close, as I even helped her with the publication of the Round Table Magazine and wrote an article for each issue (not learned, just moral). The camp in Deolali was during the monsoon when the hills were covered with a carpet of green.

As you already know, I had developed a passion for hill stations. So, when I returned from Ethiopia (more about that later) I went for a few days to Panchgani, which, at four thousand feet, was near the town of Poona where Daddy had grown up. I walked the hills singing "Beautiful Dreamer" and other songs and was blissfully happy sitting on the balcony outside my room at the Prospect Hotel in the dusk, imagined the tall and straight Eucalyptus trees that are a special feature of Panchgani, were really pine trees. But of course, to experience pine trees I would have to go to a Himalayan hill station at least seven thousand feet.

After about four days I began to wish for a piano.

I asked the proprietor, Mr. Irani, where I could find one, and he told me that there was one at St. Joseph's Convent, just up the hill.

Off I went. But the piano was locked. I was told that I would have to get permission from the music teacher, and one of the students kindly went to fetch her.

A young nun arrived and said, "We do not allow outsiders to play on our piano, but since you have come all this way, you can play for a few minutes," and unlocked the piano.

I started playing Chopin's Waltz in C sharp minor and she exclaimed, "Oh my! Do you mind if I sit and listen?"

She was beaming from ear to ear.

She then asked me if I would listen to her students and give them some tips, and also give a concert at the school and I said "Of course!"

I was delighted, as I loved Panchgani and looked forward to the prospect of going back after a month when the monsoon would be in full swing. I had gone in the second week of June, just before the arrival of the monsoon, when the heat and the humidity in Bombay are fearsome, and one's skin erupts in "prickly heat" for which the only relief is cold showers (actually, pouring water with a mug on oneself from a bucket) followed by a dusting of talcum powder.

When I told Jer (I occasionally spent a day at her bungalow) about my impending recital, her mother asked,

"How are you going?"

"Oh. I'll take the train to Poona, and then the bus up the mountain to Panchgani."

"No you won't," she replied. "We will take you."

"Oh, you don't have to do that!"

"You'll be our excuse to take a vacation" explained Jer. Her mother loved the monsoon as much as we did and so fond was she of travel that she had bags perpetually packed and ready so that she could travel at a moment's notice.

So, I returned in state to St. Joseph's in style, in a huge Packard.

By then the monsoon had arrived and Panchgani was Heaven!

St. Joseph's is a girls' school, and the head monitor was put in charge of me. I asked her if there was a green room near the stage where I could be alone by myself for a few minutes before I stepped onto the stage.

"We do have a room," she replied, "but it's not green."

"Oh, it doesn't have to be green," I reassured her with a big smile.

There were other drives into the country during subsequent monsoons with Jer and her mother and a couple who were their tenants.

My debt to Jer is incalculable as she was also a superb speaker and on one occasion when she gave a speech, a Supreme Court judge who was the guest of honour, said, "I have heard the finest lawyers in India appear before me, but never have I heard a speaker so good as Miss Jussawala! She spoke straight from her heart!"

I am certain that I picked up this quality from her, and she unknowingly enhanced the quality of my lectures!

And then there was the voyage to the Portuguese-Catholic enclave of Goa along with Jer and her mother, getting a bit high on cashew feni (a speciality of Goa) on the deck of the ship, watching the Indian coastline go by, and sleeping under the stars with the sea breeze wafting over us. Yes, there were many times when I was very near heaven in the company of that noble and glorious woman.

When I left Bombay in 1986, twenty years after meeting her, I think that my greatest loss was losing her. She used to sing songs in Spanish, French and English and I had the pleasure of accompanying her. Though she expressed regret that she would lose her accompanist, she was still big-hearted enough to give me a handsome cash gift "to tide you over during your first few months in New York."

She visited America after her mother died at the classic Parsi age of 101. The Parsi blessing is always "May you live to be a hundred and one!" So did her grandmother, who died peacefully between lunch and afternoon tea on the balcony sofa. When her maid went to wake her up for tea, she was gone.

Jer had repeatedly received invitations to visit from Round Table members who had settled in America. But she would not go because she was afraid that her mother would pass away while she was gone. They took Jer to Yosemite and Niagara Falls.

I (at a much humbler level) showed Jer Central Park, which she loved!

"I don't know what I have done to receive so much kindness," she said, referring to the trips they had arranged for her.

"My dear Jer, I'm afraid that your good deeds have finally caught up with you!"

Like all givers, she was uncomfortable when she was at the receiving end.

Upon returning to Bombay, she wrote that she fondly remembered "the polar bears, god's innocent creatures, frolicking in the sunshine." She was referring to the little zoo in Central Park where we watched two polar bears playing with a large ball in their pool which even had a small waterfall.

We continued to occasionally talk long distance on the phone, but I was surprised that she took more and more time to recognise me! I later learned from a friend that she was in the early stages of Alzheimer's and trying to cover it up. I could not bear to call her after that! As you already know, I am not good at saying goodbye. She died a few years later at the age of 88. A mutual friend, Pesi Padshah, who continued to visit her, wrote to me that in her last days, she would sit on a sofa on her balcony, smiling her gentle, affectionate smile.

On 16th August 2018, when she would have turned a hundred and one, I was sitting on my balcony and thinking about her. Where was she? Had some part of her, which we call the soul, survived her death?

One day it was in the middle of a drought where I now live and there had not been a cloud in the sky for weeks. Suddenly, out of nowhere, a grey cloud appeared overhead, a gentle breeze sprang up and a few drops of rain, wafted by the breeze, fell on my cheek even though my balcony is covered. Then, just as suddenly as it had appeared, the cloud vanished, and the blinding sunshine returned.

I was filled with gratitude to God.

I have absolutely no doubt that it was a greeting from Jer.

She was smiling her beautiful smile and saying, "Yes, my soul has survived my death! And I can see you on your balcony, and I know that you are thinking of me."

I pray that I meet her again in a better world than this when my time comes, and I too reach the end of my journey here on earth.

(2)

In 1963, when I was 18, and completed my second (sophomore) year at Elphinstone College, I had to choose a Major for my B.A. (Hons.) degree.

This is when I made the first major mistake of my life!

I chose Political Science, in which I had no particular interest, over English Literature, which I adored, because I was supposed to be a boy and that is what boys did - either Politics or Economics, according to the common belief in Bombay at the time.

My mother applauded this decision.

"What will you do with English Literature? Become a college professor? Hrmph!"

College professors are not well paid in India.

And what she wanted was that I should get a high paid job not only in order to give her a more comfortable life, but also to raise her social status.

As you may recall from a previous chapter, I had already bought her a fridge, installed ceiling fans and paid the electricity and telephone bills, as well as the servants' salaries from my income as a tutor.

In once again trying to please her at the cost of not being true to myself, my downward spiral in life began!

Until now I had had a golden academic record. Being interested neither in my Political Science textbooks nor in the professors who taught us, I graduated with a qualification that would be of no earthly use to me.

I was supposed to seek a job as a Junior Executive in a large corporation. Imagine me! A junior Executive in a tie and carrying a briefcase! Ha! Ha!

So, I didn't even try for a job but continued being just a self-employed tutor.

After I graduated with what was to me a useless degree, Professor Mehroo Jussawala (no relation to Jer Jussawala, although they knew each other socially) signed up for a private course in music appreciation, for which she came to my place twice a week. Her father was a prosperous solicitor (attorney) and she had grown up privileged. She lived in a large flat (apartment) atop Cumballa Hill with her father, drove an expensive car (which she would not be able to afford on her salary as a college professor) and moved in the highest circles.

I remember one occasion when I received an unexpected call late in the evening from a Parsi lady living in one of the last remaining bungalows atop Malabar Hill, asking me if I would go over and play the piano at her party (which was going on when she called!)

I entered a large living room where a number of men in tuxedos and women in priceless jewels sitting on sofas scattered across the room or standing with champagne glasses in their hands, and conversing in soft, refined voices.

One woman sitting on the sofa nearest the door visibly started when she saw me enter carrying my music books. Then she burst into a huge smile and said proudly, "That's my student, Farokh!"

It was Professor Jussawala, dressed as I had never seen her in college. wearing a priceless sari and a glittering diamond and emerald necklace. It was then I realised how rich she was.

After a delicious buffet dinner (of which I partook heartily) the gentlemen actually retired to smoke cigars!

It was the 1960's and the Parsis were still defiantly keeping Victorian English traditions alive!

During her music appreciation sessions, I told Professor Jussawala about the horrible mistake I had made in choosing Political Science over English Literature, and she suggested that I could enrol myself for a master's degree in English Literature, while she would tutor me in all that I had missed for my bachelor's degree (Greek Tragedy, the Dithyramb etc.).

I was overjoyed!

But to do this (that is, enrol for a master's in English Literature without having a bachelor's degree in the subject) I would need to get the permission of the university's Head of the Department of English, Professor Banerjee).

This was the same Professor Banerjee who had saved me four years earlier from committing academic suicide by trying to enrol in the science section of Elphinstone College. But this time, to my stunned disbelief, he was harsh and unyielding, despite my telling him what Professor Jussawala was doing for me!

"I cannot permit that! You must go back and do a bachelor's degree in English Literature first!" he insisted.

He had a point, but I was young, foolish, and brash and could not bear the thought of being with younger classmates.

This was my second huge mistake!

Looking back to 1964 from 2021 - or, at my twenty-year-old self from my seventy-seven-year-old self - I bitterly regret not going back and spending two years getting a bachelor's degree in English Literature.

Had I had the wisdom and the humility to do so, the course of my whole life would have been different!

I would now have been a retired professor of English Literature from Bombay University, having done my whole life what I loved doing, and in addition to a secure salary and benefits, I could still have continued to give piano lessons and lecture on music appreciation in my free time!

Certainly, I would have been writing this memoir in Bombay and not in in the USA.

But would the university have been allowed to keep me when I became Farah in 1976?

That must remain a matter for conjecture.

Perhaps I would have had to file a lawsuit to keep my job!

But that is all speculation.

One cannot live one's life with "what ifs!"

Still, I cannot emphasize enough to young people, that the choices we make in youth determine the course of our whole lives!

Continuing with the story of Professor Mehroo Jussawala, when Arthur Rubinstein came to perform in Bombay in 1966, she asked me if I would be going to the concert.

I told her that regretfully I would not, as all the tickets had been sold out and only a few of the most expensive seats were left.

"But that is nonsense!" she cried. " But you must go! My father and I will take you with us!"

So, I found myself sitting next to the chauffeur while she and her father sat in the back seat of their air-conditioned car, on our way to the concert!

Professor Jussawala joked with her father, "Oh. Papa! I've lost one ticket! I only have two!"

"Just give me mine," replied the wily old solicitor without missing a beat.

Rubinstein was 78 at the time and pink as a rose.

I shall never forget with what strength and power, with what a full, rounded tone, totally free of all harshness of attack, he played Chopin's great Sonata in B Flat Minor!

On page 573 of the second volume of his autobiography ("My Many Years"), he wrote:

"The concert in Bombay, the only one that I have given in India, was the crown of the whole tour (which included Hong Kong, Tokyo and Sydney). Nowhere was I received with more enthusiasm by the public and in a more gracious and hospitable a manner by the local organisers."

I am also beholden to Professor Jussawala introducing me to her young neighbour Pesi Padashah (also a Parsi) who had studied in England and spoke with a polished British accent. The three of us went to the movies together, one of which was "Zorba, the Greek" with Alan Bates, the famed English actor, in his first film role.

In 1969, after I had returned from Ethiopia, Pesi honoured me by bringing over the girl to whom he was secretly engaged, Zarin, who was a BOAC air hostess, as they were then called. "I was dying to tell someone," she smiled.

About three years ago I tracked Pesi down on the internet. He was then ninety years old! God had blessed him with good health and a superb memory, and he had not lost either his kindness or his cheerfulness. Just a couple of days ago I received an email from him in response to my chapter on Jer Jussawala (which I had emailed him). He also had known Jer very well. He called it "another breathtakingly heartwarming heart-warming chapter" - perhaps because it had so much to do with dear Jer.

The story of Professor Mehroo Jussawala has a sad ending. I learned from the internet that she was brutally stabbed to death in her bed when she was living by herself, after the death of her father. She was an elegant and cultured woman and an excellent professor of whom I cherish many fond memories during a difficult period in my life.

After I graduated from Elphinstone College in 1964 with a degree in Political Science, which was of no use to me, a neighbour who was a Chartered Account (certified accountant) offered to get me apprenticed with the firm of Bhiki Bilimoria, the second most prestigious firm of chartered accountants in Bombay, where he worked.

Mummy was all for it, as chartered accountants were very well paid.

So, I decided to give it a shot. As always, I wanted to please her and win her approval and love.

It was a waste of two years of my life. As I did not have a degree in accountancy, it was bound to fail. And it did. But I continued to tutor and enjoyed that aspect of my life at least.

I even applied for the job of Purser (airline steward) with Air India, because of my longing to see London, Paris, Rome, and New York.

I passed the written exams, the medical test and the first interview.

But just before the second and final interview, my mother persuaded me not to take the job.

I cannot say what her motive was, as I planned to resign in a couple of years anyway after seeing the world.

It may have been simply because she knew that it would make me very happy.

But I cannot put the whole blame on her because I was 21, and still letting her influence me and run my life.

In 1966, thanks to my schizophrenic student Paul (God bless his soul) I started teaching at the Indo-American Society and was earning good money for the first time in my life.

In addition to my courses in music appreciation, I was also teaching English classes and had a kind and wonderful boss, Mr. N. Krishnan, who never interfered with my teaching, and with whom I enjoyed having tea in his office, between classes.

For those who are not familiar with India, I must explain that all over the country there are little tea stalls in business districts that send boys with cups of tea to the surrounding offices.

So having tea both at home as well as at work is as much of a ritual in India as it is in England!

Some of my students even wrote appreciative letters to me, which I proudly showed to my boss Mr. Krishnan during our tea sessions.

Mr. Krishnan read the first one with a happy smile and immediately asked, "Have you replied to it?"

"Not yet. But I will thank the student for it."

"That is not enough! You must always reply to every appreciative letter you receive!"

A great life lesson for which I am beholden to Mr. Krishnan!

13 - My Year in Addis Ababa and Christopher Hudson

In June of 1967, the honorary Consul for Ethiopia called me to say that the Bulgarian government had offered to build a music school in Ethiopia and the Ethiopian Ministry of Education was looking for music teachers. Their free school system, financed by Emperor Haile Selassie, was run entirely by teachers from India and they were now looking for music teachers for the music school.

So, I agreed to be Head of the Piano Department.

I was 23 years old, had never been abroad and was happy when this opportunity to do so at no cost to myself came along.

So, when the job offer from Ethiopia came up, I accepted.

Unfortunately, the offer from Ethiopia came at a time when things were finally going well in my life, and it was foolish of me to interrupt my success at the Indo-American Society at this crucial moment in my life.

But Destiny called.

And so off I went to Addis Ababa, the capital of Ethiopia.

The principal of the music school was, of course, an Ethiopian who played the violin and also had some knowledge of conducting. He knew nothing of classical music but prided himself on being a composer (based on Ethiopian folk tunes) and was an extremely ambitious young man with a very good opinion of himself.

He and I clashed from the start, as he would not allow me to teach music appreciation and history to my piano students ("waste of time" he said), forbade exams, (called assessments these days) etc. etc.

I certainly don't wish to dredge up all the conflicts I had with him after a lapse of several decades.

So let it rest.

But as always, the Lord sent compensations.

The first came in the form of young, American Peace Corps workers.

The Peace Corps was a wonderful organisation started by President Kennedy (who had just been assassinated a year earlier, to my eternal sorrow). One of them was Carol Irwin, a graduate of the Eastman School of Music.

She approached the music school looking for an accompanist.

I had applied for and been given the post of Head of the Department of Piano Playing - a great honour for a mere 23-year-old. But it turned out that I was the whole piano department!

I enjoyed accompanying her, and she introduced me to, among others, the Last Four Songs by Richard Strauss and Mahler's Das Lied von der Erde (The Song of the Earth).

As Jer Jussawala sang only Operatic arias and Spanish songs by De Falla and English folk songs, this opened up a new world of music for me.

Carol lived with her husband, Lee Irwin, who later joined the State Department and visited Bombay twice. On his second visit, he told me that he and Carol were divorced.

Then there was Barbara Breznay, a remarkably likeable young woman who took private piano lessons from me through the music school. She was an artist and did a large pencil sketch of Schubert at the age of sixteen, from a tiny print in a music book. I had it framed when I returned to Bombay the following year (1968) and it was still on my living room wall in 1986, eighteen years later, when I left Bombay for the last time.

Internet searches for both Carol and Barbara failed to bring them up. How I wish I could have sent them a fair greeting after decades!

Barbara had a very handsome husband, George.

As we were all friends, I used to talk about everything close to my heart, one of which was vitamin therapy.

One evening, when I was having dinner at their house, George asked me, "Should I take my vitamins before, or after dinner:"

"After. Why do you ask?"

"Because you are so sure about every damn thing!" he laughed with hearty American humour.

Addis Ababa was only five degrees above the equator, but it was on a plateau eight thousand feet high. So, there were occasional hailstorms. As I had not yet seen snow (which I longed to see), the grass covered with hail stones was the closest I had yet come to seeing snow, even though I knew that it was entirely different.

One evening, as all the Peace Corps workers and I (they just included me in their gatherings as though it were the most natural thing in the world!) were sipping wine just after sunset, and the lawn outside was covered with hailstones, one of them, David Klein, remarked, "Who'd ever think we were only five degrees above the Equator!"

It turned out that David was a classical guitarist, and I was thrilled when he played Bach's Prelude in C Minor (from the Six Little Preludes) most beautifully on the guitar.

I was rhapsodic!

His friends began to tease him, telling him they had no idea he was so great!

David was Jewish, so he was the odd one out.

In 1986, (eighteen years later) when I moved to New York, David flew from Chicago to New York to come and see me, "Because I want to meet Farah!" he wrote.

A sad memory is of the day when Bobby Kennedy was assassinated. My Peace Corps friends were devastated, and so was I.

"Why go back to America?" they asked. bitterly. "For what? To eat hamburgers?"

When I arrived in Addis, the Ministry put me up in a hotel. As hotels go, it was decent enough. But I was appalled when I went to lunch in the dining room and received a tasteless meal with a thin slice of beef and a salt and pepper shaker which I was expected to use, and a bottle of mustard that I was supposed to squeeze on. With a palate accustomed to the most delicious food on earth, I was outraged at their idea of European food.

So, when an opportunity arose to move in with three Indian teachers into a spacious bungalow with a beautiful rose garden, I jumped at it.

I rented a piano to practice, and they started to complain.

So, I moved my piano into the home of an English professor and singer, Christopher, about whom more later.

One night, I dreamed that I was on the Titanic, and it was sinking. I woke up with a pounding heart.

Addis was four hours behind Bombay, and it was just before dawn when I woke up with my heart pounding, so it must have been about 1 A.M. in Bombay.

A few days later I received a letter from my father who informed me that there had been an earthquake in Bombay at the very moment that I dreamt that I was drowning on the Titanic!

My parents heard the cupboards shaking and woke up in the darkness wondering what that sound was. Suddenly my father realised the trembling, and cried to my mother, "It is an earthquake!"

Fortunately, it stopped and by God's grace our dilapidated building survived even the earthquake!

But I marvel at how my parents' terror was communicated to me in a dream at the very moment when they were feeling it!

Another memory of my nights in Addis is of the lions calling in the dead of night. Not far from where I lived was a public garden with a large cage in which there were many lions, both male and female. This was because Emperor Haile Selassie called himself "The Lion of Judah" (whatever that means). That used to frighten me, and I once had a nightmare in which I was walking on a deserted street in the dead of night and a male lion was walking straight towards me, its eyes fixed on me. I woke up to hear the lions calling.

Talking of Haile Selassie, his niece came to me for piano lessons at the music college. The principal himself introduced her to me with great deference.

She spoke more French than English, as she had been educated in Paris, and had fabulous rings on her fingers. A woman of great elegance and charm, she took a few lessons and vanished.

One day the principal called a truce with me. He had written a simple piano concerto in honour of the emperor's birthday, and he needed me to play the piano part. Mr. Nimeczech, the Czech violinist from the violin department and a few local musicians (including a Greek and an Italian) comprised the small orchestra. Ato Ashenafy conducted, and the rehearsals were fun.

He received a courtesy invitation from the palace to perform the concerto for the emperor. So off we all went, Ato Ashenafy bursting with pride.

After the performance, we were presented to Haile Selassie. He was a little man and stood on a stool to shake hands with us as we were presented to him. He was poker-faced and hardly made eye contact and did not show the least interest in us.

But we did not care. We were enjoying the champagne. Suddenly, I thought I saw a male lion walk by the door which lead into the next big room.

I felt as though my nightmare had turned into reality!

"Perhaps I am drunk," I said to Mr. Nimeczech, "but I think I just saw a lion walk by the door."

"Don't worry," he replied," it is an old, toothless lion, heavily drugged."

Perhaps just like his master?

Decades later I learned that Haile Selassie is revered by a cult called Rastafarians, and when I mentioned that distant evening in a conversation, one man went into raptures and said, "You shook hands with Haile Selassie? Oh, may I please shake the hand that touched his hand!"

Truth is always stranger than fiction.

I didn't do much teaching in Addis. My students were pleasant enough teenagers in rags who'd never seen a piano. They had joined the music school because they thought they wouldn't have to study. The practice rooms with the Russian, upright Poctob pianos (which were not bad) remained empty. The students often rioted, during which time the schools were closed.

So I had a lot of time on my hands, much of which I spent with my English friend Christopher whom I accompanied when he sang Lieder by Schubert, Schumann, and Brahms.

Christopher was a graduate of Oxford, just four years older than I, and like so many Oxonians in the 1960's he had to look for employment abroad.

He was a professor of English Literature at the university, tall and very handsome.

He looked like Benedict Cumberbatch, who could be his son!

He kindly agreed to let me keep my (rented) piano at his place and most graciously gave me the key to his house so I could practice even when he was not at home - an honour for which I was deeply grateful.

We had a great gift for friendship, and we did a lot of fun things together, like going out for a beer, or for lunch, or just driving around in the countryside around Addis.

He had a Volkswagen bug, and because of his height, he had to slouch when he was at the wheel because his head touched the roof.

I remember one occasion when we were driving, and I started reciting the first Chorus from Henry V. It was only eight years since I'd done my Senior Cambridge, and I remembered most of it.

Christopher started to recite it with me. At one point I had to stop, and he was able to continue.

He flushed with pleasure and said, "I knew I could out-quote you! I knew I could out-quote you!"

It is one of my many happy memories of him.

Others are of our rehearsals at his place, after which he would sit in his armchair and smoke his pipe, and I would sit on the rug beside his chair, and we would talk about everything under the sun.

He spoke in his mellifluous baritone voice, which modulated like music, and with a posh but not affected accent.

In fact, he was the quintessential Englishman!

He was the man of my dreams - in fact, a man beyond my wildest dreams.

Needless to say, I fell hopelessly in love with him.

One evening, when he was sitting in his armchair after a rehearsal, peacefully smoking his pipe and sipping his port and the hailstones covered his lawn, and I was sitting on the rug beside him, I told him of my love and my longing, painfully aware that I was in the wrong body.

He didn't say a word, and I started talking of other things to cover my shame and my embarrassment and pretended that nothing had been said that should not have been said.

But the next day, to my surprise, he said, "You know Farokh, I have thought deeply about what you said yesterday, and there's no future in it. There's just no future in it."

He was the first and the last man in my life not to take advantage of the love that I felt for him. Others just used my love for them to gratify their lust and dropped me after a few months, to get on with their lives.

What I did not know then, but learned more than half a century later, was that Christopher is also a devout Christian, and was even awarded an O.B. E. in the 1970s for establishing an Anglican Church in Saudi Arabia, where he was then teaching.

When I returned to India, I buried Christopher deep in my heart. In 1976, when I became Farah, I wrote to let him know. He had given me a book of poems when I left, and at my request, had written his address in England in it.

When I did not hear back from him, I assumed that he had not received my letter, and buried him still deeper in my heart.

But at the beginning of this century, when I discovered that I could reconnect with old friends on the internet, I made several fruitless searches for him.

Each time I remembered him with an ever-growing sense of loss and longing, and then two years ago, after yet one more search, I saw his name in my inbox!

It was fifty-two years since we had last seen each other.

Imagine my joy when I read that he not only remembered me but that he too cherished fond memories of me and our recitals and mutual friends and our time together.

We have been exchanging emails since then and he continues to be my mentor in English literature, pointing me to books I hadn't read, and that he knew I would like. We discovered that we are both film buffs and love the same kind of films.

To my joy, I also discovered that his family has a long history with India, his ancestors having served in the India of the Raj, in senior military and civilian capacities.

One of his ancestors was Aide de Camp to Lord Curzon, India's greatest Viceroy, and Christopher himself was born in Peshawar (which was then a part of British India) and taken to England at the age of one!

I learned from his letters that shortly after I left Addis, he met Lucy, an Englishwoman who was also a professor of English Literature and like him, teaching at foreign universities.

They got married and Christopher lived the life that he was meant to live. He became a paterfamilias and together they brought up two beautiful children and are now proud grandparents. The wife of his heart is beside him and they are spending their golden years in love, peace, and contentment.

In conclusion, I would only like to say that Christopher informed me that Lucy was as surprised when he heard from me after fifty-two years, as he himself was. He had told her about my year in Addis and our music-making and recitals, and in 1976 he also informed her that I had become Farah.

Now, in Lucy, I have one more dear friend in the world, and Christopher occasionally reads excerpts from my memoir to her sometimes, as they have tea together in their garden.

When I returned to Bombay after a year in Ethiopia and, thanks to the kindness of Mr. Krishnan, started teaching French at the Indo-American Society as well, one of my French students, Kushala Salian, wrote me an appreciative letter. (I was Farah by then). I had been religiously following Mr. Krishnan's noble advice, and immediately wrote her a warm thank you letter.

Kushala emigrated to England and I to America, and early in this century, she found me through the internet.

To my astonishment and joy, Kushala attached a photocopy of the letter that I had written to her in 1977!

She actually took it with her to England!

What have I done to receive such love?

It is as though a kind Providence sends me love from where I least expect it, to compensate for the absence of love from the three people I most wanted it - my father, my mother, and my brother.

14 - Falling In Love With India, The Eccentric Bapsy Sabavala, Simla

When I returned from Ethiopia, I was welcomed at the airport not only by my parents but by my dear boss Mr. Krishnan and by Jer Jussawala and Bapsy Sabavala (more about this eccentric woman later). We took a group photo outside the airport, and I remember those beloved happy faces as though it was yesterday.

Unfortunately, in the first flush of euphoria I felt after I became Farah, I locked up all my photos as Farokh in a trap drawer in our nineteenth-century carved teak wood cupboard and did not bring any of them with me to America.

I wanted to pretend that Farokh had never existed. I disowned "him" entirely.

Poor Farokh!

It was the Bollywood actress Deepti Naval who corrected me. Once, when I began a sentence with, "When I was a little girl," she said, "Farah, we all love and accept you as who you are. We accept you as the woman you are today. We accept you totally as Farah. But when you say, 'when I was a little girl,' we think "Who is she trying to fool'?"

I could have replied that inside I was always Farah. But she would have (rightly) replied that " Farah was trapped inside you and we could not see her."

Ever since, I have always said, simply "When I was little" or "When I was a child."

The first few years after I returned from Ethiopia were among my happiest in India. Compared to Ethiopia and Ethiopians, India and Indians seemed like paradise.

The first thing I did was to rent a room with a view of the harbour, just half a mile from my house, and live semi-independently from my parents.

It was a ground-floor room with a porch, and I could enter it directly from the porch without having to pass through my landlord's flat (apartment). It had a view of the harbour and the beautiful Sahyadri hills that lined the West coast of India, on the other side, six miles across the water. Sometimes, fishing boats would sail by very close to shore, and at night, as I lay in bed, I could hear the waves lapping against the rocky shore.

It felt like another world from my dilapidated building just half a mile away. Once again, the good Lord sent me compensation to make life worth living.

In the morning I would walk home, and as my room had no kitchen, have my first cup of tea, read the newspaper, and use our phone. So, I had the best of both worlds.

The second thing I did was to explore Bombay, starting with my immediate neighbourhood. On one side of my building was Cuffe Parade, and behind it was Sassoon Dock, where the fishermen would dock their boats and sail them laden with delicious, diamond-shaped silvery fish called pomfret and during the monsoon, a soft fleshed fish which the British named Bombay Duck, and in winter loads of sparkling "bangda" or mackerel. Yet I had never been inside Sassoon Dock! So, this was the first on my agenda. I enjoyed the fishing boats, their sails filled with the sea breeze, their fish nets laden with silver fish, the bounty of the Arabian Sea, and the fisherwomen filling their baskets to the brim with them.

My soul was refreshed by getting to see my own neck of the woods for the first time.

I also climbed to the top of the university clock tower and saw the seas on both sides of the island at the same time, for the island of Bombay is long and narrow, with one of the world's deepest and most beautiful natural harbours in the six-mile stretch of sea between the island and mainland India, and on the east, the Arabian sea stretching all the way to Dubai on the west.

One of my English students, Ashok Dalal, was from a prosperous Gujarati family and he loved driving. We would drive to Borivali National Park and go bird watching, in which I had developed an interest. I was surprised to discover how many different birds there were in Bombay besides the ubiquitous crows, sparrows, and pigeons. There were kingfishers and bee-eaters and crimson-breasted barbets, and by the sea, there were sandpipers and stilts, and whimbrels with their distinctive beaks, and at distant Thana creek there were even flamingos!

I also discovered what a variety of trees there were in my own neighbourhood besides the coconut palm and mango tree (home to a flock of joyous, screeching parrots) in front of my house.

Particularly in the cantonment area, there were ancient banyans and peepuls (huge fig trees where flying foxes roosted during the day and flew past my second-floor balcony at dusk), and the African baobab that stores water in its fat trunk, and gulmohars that burst into orange blossoms when the heat was at its worst in May, and cottonwood trees that attracted the tiny coppersmiths, and oleander bushes with their tiny blossoms - to name just a few.

I bought books on trees and flowers and birds from Strand Book Stall and felt alive and excited as never before. Ashok suffered from depression and even took medication for it, and so, me sharing my interests with him made him feel more eager and alive too.

But I will not dwell in detail on my Discovery of Bombay.

Instead, I will write about my travels in India and about people, including Bapsy Sabavala, the most eccentric woman in Bombay.

(2)

Bapsy S. was descended from the illustrious Parsi family of Sir Cowasjee Jehangir.

They had made their fortune in sugar and cotton. During the American Civil War, while the Yankees blockaded southern seaports, they sent cotton to keep the cotton mills in Lancashire running. In the eighteenth century, when Bombay was threatened by a nearby Maratha prince, the East India Company did not have enough money to hire trained mercenaries to defend the island. When Cowasjee Jehangir heard of it, he informed the Governor of Bombay that he would be happy to give the Company an interest-free loan to defend Bombay until the money was sanctioned from London (it would take a year at least, as ships carrying mail went round the south tip of Africa). The Suez Canal was still a hundred years in the future!

He supplied the Company with cartloads of silver rupees, and Bombay was saved. The Governor of Bombay recommended Cowasjee Jehangir for a baronetcy.

But his name was difficult for the English, so they called the family the Readymoneys.

Down the generations, the Cowasjee Jehangirs financed the neo-Gothic Elphinstone College building, the Institute of Science, the Cowasjee Jehangir Hall, the Prince of Wales Museum, and the

Jehangir Art Gallery.

One day, after I returned from Ethiopia, the phone rang, and what sounded like a male voice said, "This is Bapsy Sabavala speaking."

"Oh yes," I replied, "and I am Marilyn Munroe."

Bapsy Sabavala was well known, and the Parsi community were in awe, both of her eccentric and powerful personality, as well as her charitable works. So, I could not see her calling me.

"No, no, I am really Bapsy Sabavala! We want you to play the piano part in Bach's Concerto in D Minor, which the Bombay Chamber Orchestra would like to play for a fundraiser for the beggar's home. Lady Duggan gave me your phone number, which someone gave to her."

I immediately got the score, and my friend Jangoo Seervai (a student of Olga) got the LP from London, of Sviatoslav Richter playing the Bach Concerto, and I plunged into practicing it every spare minute of the night and day. So much so, that our teenage house boys (servants) started to whistle it!

The concert in Cowasjee Jehangir Hall went off without a hitch and I heaved a sigh of relief, as I had been given only one month in which to learn and memorize all three movements.

But now to the fun part!

Bapsy was wildly eccentric and did as she pleased.

Then in her seventies, she was short and fat and wore chunky jewelry, except that the huge stones were all real.

"The Maharanis were highly litigious, and they sold some jewels every time they needed money. The jewellers would bring them to Readymoney House and sell them to my mother, my grandmother, and my great-grandmother."

She also had a huge collection of dolls from all over the world.

She took a shine to me and here are some anecdotes about her:

"I pity you!" she said one day.

"Why?"

"Because you will never be able to go on a cruise around the world."

"Oh!"

"When I was in Japan, I went to a doll shop. There were all kinds of dolls, including porcelain ones, and I fell in love with them all."

"Which ones do you want?" asked the shopkeeper.

"I want them all!" I replied, "Ship them all to Readymoney House in Bombay!"

Sure enough, when I went for lunch to her house on Malabar Hill (not Readymoney House, this house was a wedding gift from her father - one of the last surviving ones that was not demolished to make way for luxury high-rise apartments, and which was formerly the palace of to the Begum of Palanpur), she showed me her gigantic marble bathroom with a sunken tub, surrounded by some of those Japanese porcelain dolls.

The lunch started with dessert.

"I always have dessert first," she said calmly.

She invited me to a film premier at the Metro theatre to finance one of her charities.

I arrived to find her standing in the foyer, talking to the British Deputy High Commissioner, holding a large doll under each arm. He kept a stiff upper lip and acted as though there was nothing unusual about what she was doing.

One New Year's Eve in the early Seventies she decided that she would take me to dinner at the Taj Mahal Hotel (she did not give invitations, she just issued commands, "I am taking you out to dinner on New Year's Eve!"). When I gratefully showed up, I found that she had got there before me, and the smiling waiters showed me to her table. On it were two dolls.

Once, when I told her on the phone that I had a sore throat, she sent her chauffeur over with a beautiful doll, and a note saying, "My name is Mary Lou. I am the best cure for a sore throat, and I have come to spend the day with you."

I made her sit on the sofa all day, and in the evening the chauffeur came to pick her up.

Once, my dear boss, Mr. Krishnan, told me over tea that he had never been to a hill station. So I recommended Matheran as the nearest and least expensive. Knowing that Bapsy had a bungalow there (she had talked about it more than once) I called Bapsy and asked if my boss Mr. Krishnan and his family could stay there for a couple of days.

"Of course," she said. "They can stay there as long as they want."

He and his family arrived at her bungalow to find the garden filled with porcelain dolls sitting on tiny rocks among the flowers.

I still have a huge amethyst ring that she gave me. I pride myself on having a ring from the Readymoney jewel collection.

But enough about imperious Bapsy. I Live Though Three Wars, Degree In Law, The American Women 's Club

(3)

Simla is situated at an altitude of seven thousand feet in the foothills of the Himalayas, and they are called foothills only because of what towers above them for hundreds of miles - the mighty Himalayan ranges with hundreds of peaks soaring over twenty thousand feet and stretching from west to east all the way from Pakistan to China.

I fell madly in love with this legendary hill station redolent of the Raj Era and with its pine trees and bracing cold. The locals all had rosy cheeks, unlike us haggard visitors from the plains. There were cheerful Tibetan women carrying loads, smiling, and bowing, and Lepchas from Sikkim and Bhutias from Bhutan. I swore to return one day in winter when Simla would be under a mantle of snow.

That day came seven years later, in January 1969.

It was one year and three months since my return from Ethiopia, and I had just turned 25. I was still in love with India, and eager to explore it and get to know it.

Before my trip, I went to Chor Bazar (Thieves Market) in Bombay and bought a hold-all (an Indian sleeping bag used during long-distance train journeys), a warm blanket and a woollen overcoat.

As I boarded the historic Frontier Mail, my spine quivered with ecstasy as it began to slowly move out of Bombay Central Station. It was only when the station platform appeared to be slowly moving backwards that I realised that my long-awaited journey had begun!

As a child, I had always travelled second class with my parents when they went to my mother's hometown, Bhusawal, or to visit my brother in boarding school in Poona.

Second-class rail travel in India is a nightmare, all shove and push to get into the compartment, bed bugs in the wooden seats, convoys of beggars, and standing passengers creating a claustrophobic atmosphere.

Now, for the first time in my life, I travelled first class, and it was Heaven!

When I found my reserved coupe and paid off the coolie who had carried my luggage, I settled on my berth opposite a stern-looking, middle-aged man.

He stretched out his hand and said, "Justice Agarwal, Delhi High Court."

I shook hands and told him my name (with no title) and I told him I was going to Simla.

"Oh, then you will be taking the Delhi-Kalka Mail from Delhi."

"Yes, sir."

"Is this your first visit to Simla?"

"No, sir, my second. But this time I'm going to see the snow."

"Oh yes, it will be very cold over there, and it has probably snowed already."

"Have you ever been to Simla, sir?"

"Oh yes, my wife and I go every year. But in summer."

What a cordial beginning to my first journey by first class, compared to the push and shove and "survival of the fittest" second class journeys I had experienced so far!

At Baroda in Gujarat, just before midnight, I snuggled under my blanket for the first time (alas, it is never cool enough for a blanket in Bombay!) and the next morning I awoke in central India and saw antelope from the window of the train, blindfolded ostriches walking around wells, turning wheels that brought up buckets filled with precious water for the winter crop.

The judge asked me if I would mind if he smoked and I said, not at all.

A waiter came from the dining car and asked if would like breakfast and we both ordered breakfast. It was all part of the magic of first-class train travel in India and I wanted to have the whole experience, denying myself no part of it. I was not going to skimp when I had saved all year for this trip!

As we left Agra station I saw the dome of the Taj Mahal from the train, in the distance, half hidden by trees. And at sunset when we stopped at Mathura, the birthplace of Lord Krishna, I watched the red sun disappear behind the plains of north India.

We reached Delhi at 9 p.m. and the Judge shook my hand and said goodbye.

"Enjoy your trip to Simla," he said with a smile.

With the help of a porter, I found the platform from which the Delhi-Kalka mail would be leaving late that night and sat on a bench and waited. Upon boarding the train, there was nothing to do but roll out my bedding and go to sleep.

This time I was alone in my coupe. Early the next morning the train stopped at historic stations like Panipat where the British won their first great victory in 1761 and became rulers of Bengal, though they were still nominally the East India Company. But in effect, the British Raj had begun.

And Kurukshetra, where Lord Krishna had sung the Bhagavad Gita (The Song of God) to Arjuna, a thousand years before Jesus walked the earth.

As we approached Kalka, where I would have to change to the narrow gauge train up the mountain, I saw the snow-covered peaks of the mighty Sivalik range, named after Lord Shiva, who had wandered these foothills and meditated there for thousands of years before man walked the earth.

As we drew nearer, the peaks disappeared behind the foothills that rose steeply before me.

At the tiny station of Kalka, I got on the train to Simla, known fondly as the "toy train." The climb up the mountain is a masterpiece of British engineering, passing through dozens of tunnels and over arched stone bridges. Halfway up, we stopped at the picturesque little station of Barog, resembling a Swiss chalet, where we had a quick breakfast of omelette, bread and butter, and tea. As we approached Simla I was overjoyed to see small patches of snow under the pines, until the ground was completely covered by snow by the time we arrived.

Guided by a porter who carried my bags (no cars or taxis are allowed in Simla, the only exception being the Viceroy's Rolls Royce). I climbed up to the Grand Hotel which had once been the baroque Bentick Castle.

It being the off-season, the hotel was deserted, and I was told that I could have any room I wanted. I chose a room on the top floor, and after going up three flights of large and spacious stairs, I was surprised to find that my "room" consisted of a large, covered balcony with windows, a sitting room, a bedroom, a dressing room, and a bathroom.

All rather dilapidated and dusty, and nothing grand, but as spacious as a comfortable apartment!

And it was unbelievably affordable.

The sun was setting, and I wanted to experience sitting by a fireplace for the first time after leaving Ethiopia, even though I realised that this time I would be all alone. So, I asked the man who had carried my bags if I could have a fire.

He said it would cost me ten rupees, which I gave him, and a few minutes later he returned carrying a bucket of coal and soon got a very pleasant little fire going.

As it grew dark, I began to feel isolated and alone up there, all by myself among those empty rooms, far from the people at the reception several floors below, and even a little afraid as my imagination went into overdrive and I started fearing spirits and ghosts in those abandoned rooms. So, I jumped into bed, pulled the blankets up to my chin, and awoke to a glorious morning, with the coals having turned to ashes in the fireplace.

I spent the day walking on the ridge with its historic Church and its library designed to look like a cross-timbered Tudor house, and past old English cottages, making snowballs and throwing them at trees and discovered a simple restaurant in the Native Town after going down several stone steps, which served the most delicious chicken biryani I have ever tasted. It was served on a silver platter (or what looked like silver to me) and was garnished with silver foil. As I had not had breakfast and was ravenously hungry after my rambles in the snow, I did full justice to it.

That evening I went to the ice-skating rink where a loudspeaker blared the ghazal composed by the last Mughal Emperor, Bahadur Sha Zafar, who died in exile in Burma after the Indian Mutiny of 1857.

"So unfortunate is Zafar, that he cannot even find two yards of earth for his burial in a friend's backyard."

It enchanted me and was a new experience as I never listened to Indian songs.

There was a restaurant beside the rink, and I ordered tea and sandwiches as I watched the skaters.

"Have you come to Simla to see the snow?" asked a voice from the table behind me, and I turned my head to see the sweetest young man with roses in his cheeks, wearing a sweater and a tweed coat.

"Why yes!" I smiled. "How did you know?"

"Everybody does."

He offered to teach me to ice skate and suffice it to say that I clung desperately to his gloved hands and crawled across the ice for a few minutes before I had enough.

We returned our rented ice skates, and I invited him to dinner at my hotel in return for his kindness.

With the swiftly and easily formed friendships of youth, he accepted.

I ordered a delicious chicken curry and chapatis up to my "suite" and we ate in the "living room."

I noticed that he was uncomfortable eating with a fork and knife, so I said, "Let's eat with our fingers. Who needs a fork and knife!"

Now it was he who was comfortable.

As I am left-handed, he begged me not to eat with my left hand, which only made it more difficult. Indians regard the left hand as unclean.

He told me that he lived in the village of Kotgarh, three miles from Simla where there were apple orchards. An Englishman had introduced apple orchards among the villages around Simla in the nineteenth century and they are marketed all over India.

He also offered to take me to the top of Jakhu Hill which looks down on the ridge in Simla, the next day.

I joyfully accepted. It was difficult going up the slithery, icy slopes, clinging to the railing by the side of the steep slopes, and seeing how inexperienced I was, the poor fellow (his name was Suresh) often held on to my coat to save me from a fall, especially on the way down.

After parting with him, I returned to the little restaurant in Chota Simla (Little Simla, as the native town is called) and once again enjoyed the fabulous biryani. This time I decided to be hoity-toity and compliment the chef. So, I told the waiter I would like to see the chef. Unfortunately, the waiter went into the kitchen and told the cook, "A customer wants to see you."

The terrified fellow came to my table and asked, "Is anything wrong with the food?" "Oh no! On the contrary, this is the best biryani I have ever had in my life, and I wanted to compliment you!"

"Oh, thank God! I thought you were going to complain!"

I learned not to put on airs and realised that "complimenting the chef" was not for the likes of me who patronised humble restaurants that served delicious food!

The next day was to be my last day in Simla and Suresh had given me the good news that it was likely to snow.

"The clouds have already started to gather and it is getting colder."

Sure enough, the next morning when I got up, it was snowing heavily.

I was overjoyed. It was the finishing touch to my long-awaited winter trip to Simla to experience snow for the first time in my life. I had agreed to meet Suresh at 10 a.m. at Scandal Point on the Mall (so called because it was the rendezvous for an elopement between a Maharajah and an English girl during the Raj) but seeing the snow coming down so hard and so fast I convinced myself that he would not show up. as he would have to walk three miles to Simla from his village.

At 11 a.m. there was a knock on my door, and it was poor Suresh!

"What yaar (friend)! I waited for you at Scandal Point for almost one hour in the snow!"

I was overwhelmed with guilt and shame.

I embraced him and felt his warm cheek against mine and realised how precious is a human being as compared to the hard, cold feel of gold or a diamond.

I made him sit on the worn, old sofa and threw a blanket over him and ordered tea and bread and butter, and also a fire in the fireplace. With the fire cheerfully burning in the fireplace and the tea and nourishment, he was restored to his normal self in half an hour. We decided not to go out that day but to just enjoy the snow from the warmth and comfort of the hotel.

The next morning, I caught the train down to Kalka with a grateful heart that God had answered my prayer to see Simla under the snow beyond my wildest dreams.

I was also taking back with me a beautiful little rabbit-fur purse that I had bought from a Tibetan woman for my mother. My mother accepted it with pleasure and the very next day she told me that she had given it to Dolly Aunty.

"But why? I bought it for you, I wanted to see you carrying the lovely, little purse!" I cried, bitterly disappointed.

She just shrugged with complete nonchalance.

15 - I Live Through Three Wars, Obtain a Degree In Law, The American Women's Club

Even though I was born during the Second World War, I have no personal memory of it, as I was only a year and a half old when it ended.

In April 1944, with the war still going on, and I was but five months old, Bombayites feared that their worst fears had been realised.

A British warship, the SS Fort Stikine, which was carrying large bombs to the eastern war front was docked in Bombay. A fire started in its hold, which the local fire brigade could not extinguish, and a whole load of bombs exploded.

The bomb blast was deafening, flames consumed half the docks, hundreds of lives were lost, sugar melted in the godowns (warehouses) in the docks and, as the Stikine had also been carrying bars of gold, a startled resident found a large bar of gold crash through the window of his third-floor apartment.

The High Court went into recess, and the Judges climbed up to the Neo-Gothic building's top balcony to gaze awestruck at the Bombay dockyard in flames.

Even though our building was two miles from the explosion, some of our windowpanes shattered, and Daddy grabbed my older brother, who was then five and a half and crossed the street because people were shouting that they could see thick, black smoke gushing from the vicinity of the docks.

This has gone down in history as The Great Bombay Dockyard Explosion.

In 1947, the newly formed Pakistan sent Afghan fighters to forcibly take over Kashmir, while its Maharaja, reluctant to give up his state to either India or Pakistan, sat on the fence, refusing to sign the Instrument of Accession to hand over his state to either country. When the Afghan fighters entered northern Kashmir, the Maharaja, who was a Hindu, hastily signed over Kashmir to India and India sent the army into Kashmir.

The southern half of Kashmir was saved, and after an armistice brokered by the UN, India was allowed to keep the southern half of Kashmir, and Pakistan was allowed to hold on to northern Kashmir which the Afghan fighters had occupied and which the Pakistanis call Azad Kashmir or Free Kashmir.

The stalemate remains to this day, and it has so far resulted in two more wars between India and Pakistan, and countless skirmishes on the heavily guarded border between the two enemies, ever since.

But before the Indo-Pakistan War of 1964, I lived through the Indo-Chinese War of 1962.

If it can be called a war at all!

The Chinese literally walked into India, almost taking Calcutta.

Ever since Independence in 1947, Nehru had desperately tried to make China an ally.

And for a while he almost succeeded, despite the fact that as soon as the British left India, the Chinese invaded Tibet and took over that vast and peaceful country, the size of Alaska and California combined.

The Tibetans desperately appealed to the world for help, but even the UN did not intervene. India was too weak to help.

But when Nehru gave asylum to the young Dalai Lama in 1959, after his heroic escape over forbidding twenty thousand foot passes to reach the eastern border of India, the Chinese got their excuse.

They claimed that a lot of territories that the British had ceded to India had really belonged to China for centuries before the British conquered India. They now claimed thousands of miles of that Himalayan territory.

Indian regiments fought in tennis shoes at those icy altitudes, the southern regiments in particular, never having experienced cold in their lives.

India had neither the weapons nor the training in high-altitude warfare and it was a rout!

Panic spread in the cities in the plains as far away as Bombay, and women donated their precious gold ornaments to save the country.

It was only when Nehru appealed to President Kennedy, who idolised Nehru, and the American fleet entered Indian naval waters, that China suddenly agreed to a truce!

Not only that, but it also even ceded most of the Himalayan territory it had conquered, while at the same time not relinquishing its claim to them.

The stalemate remains to this day!

The Indian armed forces have made great progress since then, and both countries are now armed with nuclear weapons.

So is Pakistan!

The situation is dire.

I fear that when the Third World War comes (and it will - it is not a question of if it comes, but only when it comes) it will start in South Asia.

I was in Elphinstone College during the Chinese invasion of India and was seized with passionate patriotism mixed with fear.

Then, in 1964, came the second war with Pakistan (over Kashmir). Blackouts were declared and I spent those dark evenings on a bench at Cuffe Parade, just five minutes from my house, by the sea. A group of college students from the neighbourhood, including Third Pasta Lane, most of them Sindhis, had gathered at a bench and as I was walking by just before sunset, they invited me to join them, with the easy familiarity of youth.

As I looked like a boy and I was supposed to be a boy, I joined them "in disguise", just as when I had spent my years growing up in a boys' boys' school.

They shared jokes and sang bawdy songs, and I spent a pleasant hour looking at the stars which were now much clearer before we all headed home for dinner with our parents.

The war ended with a peace conference held in Simla, India, facilitated by Russian peacemakers. Bhutto, the then president of Pakistan was hanged a few months later on charges of corruption and a few years later his daughter Benazir Bhutto became president. When I was in New York, the Pakistanis there said that I looked like her. I took it as a compliment, as they considered her beautiful because of her light complexion. This was because her mother was a Zoroastrian Parsi.

Many years later she died from an assassin's bullet as she popped her head out of an armoured truck to wave to her voters one more time. That was when I was in settled in the US where I now live.

Then came the third war with Pakistan in 1972, and this was over what became the new nation of Bangladesh. For many years, East Pakistan, which was separated from West Pakistan by nearly a thousand miles of Indian territory, as well as by language, culture, food, and history, had wanted to separate from Pakistan.

West Pakistan sent its army into East Pakistan and tens of thousands of refugees started pouring into Calcutta and its environs.

India was poised for war, but General Manekshaw, a Parsi, kept advising Indira Gandhi to wait.

At last, India declared war on Pakistan.

When the war started, I was on the upper deck of a bus, returning home from teaching a French class at the Indo-American Society.

Suddenly all the lights went out!

The streetlights, the shop lights, the headlights of cars, and then the lights in our bus.

It looked very beautiful.

And I also realised that we were now once again at war with our neighbour.

Thanks to a naval officer friend, Lieutenant K.K. Jaiswal, I had become fond of beer and even rum and coke!

So, every day I would get those large Indian bottles of Kingfisher beer (infinitely superior to America's most popular beer, Budweiser, which a German girl succinctly said, "tastes like piss!") and my parents and I would sit in the back room of our flat by the light of a kerosene lamp when the air raid siren went off, and drink beer.

The window panes were already covered with black paper and the curtains were drawn. The servants would bring their tea mugs and I would fill those also with beer.

As we all sat together in the dark, enjoying the buzz that the beer gave us, we could hear the anti-aircraft guns firing from the warships in the harbour behind our house.

Our hearts thumped, and we all thought only one thing:

"Is this it? Is this the end? Will a bomb drop on us any second?"

But none of us said anything, except for my mother who vehemently cursed the Pakistanis.

At last, the "all clear" siren would go off, to our great relief!

This happened several times during the two weeks that the war lasted, and each time the air raid sirens went off, my mother would begin cursing, while we all knew it was time to pop the beer bottles (including Mummy who was as fond of her drink as the rest of us).

Daddy quietly enjoyed his beer - no doubt, with a beating heart.

Pakistan was routed by India and the new nation of Bangladesh was born. To this day Pakistanis hate India for this, as also for being bigger, freer, and more prosperous.

General Manekshaw was elevated to the rank of Field Marshal and Indira Gandhi became the beloved "Empress of India." Anglophile Indians proposed a toast to Indira Gandhi as the English propose a toast to "The Queen!"

A few short years later she died in a hail of bullets for sending the army into the Golden Temple where the Akali Sikhs were preparing to secede from India.

While my friend Lieutenant Jaiswal returned safely from the war (he had had training in missiles in Russia, and his missile boat belonged to the "killer squadron" which played an active role in the war), another friend was not so lucky.

Lieutenant Commander Suri's ship sank to the bottom of the sea. I had met him on board India's aircraft carrier "INS Vikrant", which had earlier been a British aircraft carrier. I had been invited for drinks on its deck by Mrs. Grewal, who was in my French class, and whose husband, Captain Grewal, was the ship's commanding officer. This was just before the third Indo-Pakistan war. Commander Suri was a gentleman to the very tips of his fingers - shy, soft-spoken, polite, tall, and handsome as most Punjabis are.

I had looked forward to getting to know him better. But it was not to be. Now, decades later, let me pay tribute to his memory and to his ultimate sacrifice for his country.

(2)

In 1970 I joined Government Law College to get a degree in law. This was the result of a taunt from my mother.

I was the first college graduate in our family, and in the course of a conversation I mentioned it to her and asked, "Aren't you proud of me, Mummy?"

"Humph!" she scoffed, "Every bus driver has a college degree these days."

This wounded me to the core. That I was also a gold medallist Fellow of the Trinity College of Music, London, a pioneer in European classical music appreciation courses in India, and a veteran of several concerts wasn't even mentioned.

Even though I was 27, I continued to crave my mother's approval. But I was trying to get blood from a stone. I would be 42 before I was finally able to free myself from my mother's lifelong rejection and abuse.

So, I decided to get one more degree, and that would be a law degree.

I enjoyed my three years in law college. Memorizing and reasoning came easily to me. I liked Roman jurisprudence and Latin maxims, the law of Torts, the rules of criminal and civil procedure, and even won a prize in drafting, pleading and conveyancing.

But I did not take my three years in law college seriously, even though I was in the best law college in India.

For instance, when Professor Ranganath Rao, who had the face of a pit bull, asked the class, "Should a man be punished when he is sober for that which he did when he was drunk?", up went my hand while the rest of the class was cautiously processing the question.

"Yes?" asked Professor Rao.

I stood up (in India we never spoke to a professor sitting down!).

"No sir, because he was intoxicated and had no control over his actions," I said compassionately.

"Very good, very good," said Professor Rao slowly and his eyes narrowed.

I knew I was doomed as I remained standing.

"I hate my neighbour," he continued, "so this evening I will drink a bottle of whisky and kill him."

I realised how wrong I was!

"No, sir, a man must be punished when he is sober for that which he does when he is drunk," I said with my tail between my legs.

"Sit down!" he yelled, and I sat down, chastened, head bowed, and the class snickered.

Other experiences were more positive.

Professor Taskar, who was blind, called me to his office and asked me to correct his pronunciation.

(He knew that I taught English at the Indo-American Society).

I was abashed and said, "Your pronunciation is just fine, sir."

"Don't flatter me. I know it isn't. I want you to correct me every time I mispronounce a word."

Of course, I was going to do no such thing. I would have felt too presumptuous.

But one day, when he lectured on the law of Mortgages and pronounced the "t" in mortgage every single time, I felt it my duty to go to his office and tell him.

I went to his office:

"Sir, you had asked me to correct your pronunciation."

"Oh, yes!" he cried eagerly.

"Sir, I just thought I'd tell you that one doesn't pronounce the "t" in mortgage."

I even made him work on the second syllable which he pronounced as "guage."

And we practiced saying 'maw-guhj' a few times.

He got it down to perfection and we were both delighted.

After a couple of days, he invited me to his office and said, "You know, I delivered a lecture to another class on mortgage yesterday, and at the end of it, a student came up to me and asked, "Sir, what is this Mawguhj?"

"So tomorrow I will deliver the lecture all over again and say "Today we will talk about MorT - Guage!"

Professor Balsara, who taught us the Law of Contracts, asked me if I would coach his adorable ten-year-old son for his school's elocution competition, which I did, and Professor Wallywalkar (the only lady professor in the college) enrolled for my music appreciation course at the Indo-American Society.

I felt honoured to see her sitting there, listening to me.

I did get a degree in law, but after a one-year stint in Bombay High Court devilling (working for experience at reduced pay) for the State Advocate General, H.M Seervai (whose wife attended my concerts and talked him into trying me out as a devil in his chambers) I gave up in disgust at the hair-splitting and the lies.

"You know, you are too moral to be a good lawyer," Mr. Seervai told me. "You would have made a great judge, but unfortunately, you can't be appointed a judge unless you are a successful lawyer first!"

And so ended my flirtation with the law.

(3)

Returning to music, the American Women's Club wanted me to do a course in music history and appreciation, especially for them. About twenty ladies enrolled and the chairperson of the club, Linda Morrison, offered to host the lectures in her huge living room atop Cumballa Hill.

She also served refreshments during the break as it was a course of sixteen two-hour lectures, illustrated with long-playing records. If only we'd had YouTube in those days - they would not only have heard but also seen the greatest performances on earth, including Opera!

I was allowed to keep the entire fee as Linda was hosting my lectures in her home for free.

"So," I said during a refreshment break (lavish silver tea service, pastries, scones etc., rolled in on trolleys by servants in uniform), "Linda, not only are you hosting my lectures for free, but you are spending your own money on refreshments. It's not fair!"

"A woman can darn well decide what she does in her own house," she replied with hearty Texan forthrightness.

And when I kept talking about music during the break, Mrs. Virginia Braddock, the wife of the American Consul-General, and a warm-hearted, motherly type, told me, "Now you stop talking and enjoy your tea!"

Those were happy days indeed.

I happened to be in Law College at the time and had mentioned Principal Tope a couple of times.

One morning, the Times of India, wrote something about him on the front page, and the American ladies chorused, "You know even the newspaper called him Principal Tope!"

I hadn't known that they had been struck by how I referred to him.

They were also tickled pink that I started my lectures with "Good afternoon, Ladies!"

I remember, once, Linda said, "Ladies! May I please have your attention!" All the ladies laughed.

It was only then that I realised that they weren't accustomed to being called ladies and that British formality was new and fun for them.

Mrs. Braddock was already elderly in 1970 and I am sure that she is in a much better world than this, as I write.

But Linda was still young, and so was her very handsome husband, Richard Morrison, who was the manager of the Bank of America in Bombay.

As I was also giving their five-year-old daughter, Melissa, piano lessons, I got to know him too.

Whenever Melissa played well, I would exclaim, "Brava!"

One day she said, "Mommy, what's brava?"

"It means very good!" said Linda.

I googled Richard and Linda Morrison to let them know where I was living, but they did not show up (a host of other Morrisons did).

Then there was the Indo-US club which was a club where rich Indian women met American women.

One of them was Mrs. Pushpa Nagpal, who came to me for English lessons.

She told me that when she saw Linda Morrison's living room, she was so disgusted with the job that the interior decorator had done with hers that she had it re-done!

She was a beautiful woman and would come for her lessons in chiffon saris and pearls and in an aura of delicate French perfume.

But even though I wrote everything down in her notebook - pronunciation, vocabulary, correct grammar, etc. - she didn't pay attention to any of it.

So, one day, when we were having tea during her lesson (this was at my place) I told her, "Mrs. Nagpal, I am so happy to have you as a student, but you are not seriously learning, you know, and I feel guilty to take your money."

"Oh don't worry about the money," she said, "I am taking these lessons only to get out of the house! You see, my husband has told the chauffeur to report to him every day where I go."

Then one day, she asked me, "I've given a man 22-carat gold cuff links with real diamonds, but he doesn't know. I'm afraid that he might lose them, thinking that they are fake. How do I tell him that they are real?"

"Oh, just say - 'I just want you to know that the cuff links are real - the gold, the diamonds - so you don't throw them away.'"

No wonder her husband wanted to know where she went.

16 - Rajasthan With the Somanis, My Brother's Visit With His Family

My English students at the Indo-American Society were a motley crew.

One young man arrived consistently late for class, though I had made it clear that I loved punctuality. One day when he arrived more than half an hour late, I reprimanded him for disturbing the class with his late arrival. At the end of the class, he invited me for a cup of tea at the simple teashop next door and told me over a cup of tea that he lived in a distant suburb, that he came in an overcrowded suburban train, and that he lived in a "chawl" where there were only two bathrooms on each floor for twelve one room units and that often there were queues outside the bathrooms.

I felt deeply ashamed and apologised and told him that he could always come late to my classes, and I would never reprimand him again.

On the other end of the spectrum were two brothers from the family of Tribhovandas Bhimji Jhaveri, the famous jewellers, who arrived in a chauffeur-driven car, wearing diamond cuff links and rings that flashed whenever they moved their hands.

There were also the Somani ladies who arrived covered in jewels from head to toe. earrings, nose rings, necklaces, bangles, anklets et al, jingling whenever they moved. In fact, I could hear their arrival even before they opened the classroom door and entered.

"Here come the Somani ladies," I would tell the class with a smile, and their faces would light up.

The Somani ladies were Mrs. Leela Devi Somani, barely forty, and her daughter-in-law. The daughter-in-law was quiet and self-possessed, but Mrs. Leela Devi Somani was extremely shy, often drawing her sari over her head, and she had the most enchanting smile.

The Somanis were a well-known industrialist family with factories and mills all over the state of Rajasthan, with its legendary forts and palaces and romantic history.

One day Mrs. Somani said to me after class, "Respected Teacher

("Teacherji"), you always talk about Rajasthan (I had mentioned Colonel Todd's great book: "Annals and Antiquities of Rajasthan"). My husband is going on a tour of our factories and will be driving all over the state. We would like you to join us."

Wow!

I immediately told my boss, Mr. N. Krishnan, as I would need a week's absence.

"Of course," he replied. (May his soul be in a very beautiful place! He died too young because of his smoking.)

"It is an honour that they have invited you. You must go."

We were supposed to take a train up to Jaipur, after which we would travel by car.

I insisted that I be allowed to pay my first-class fare at least.

Mrs. Somani looked uncertain, but being very shy did not argue.

I arrived at the station only to find that we were not only travelling first class, but by air-conditioned first class, which is three times more expensive than first class and is much more spacious, private, and luxurious.

I wasn't carrying enough money and didn't know what to do.

Mrs. Somani proudly introduced me to her husband, Mr. V. O. Somani, who turned out to be just as young as her, and very outgoing and relaxed.

When I expressed my embarrassment to Mr. Somani for not having brought enough money, he looked at me and smiled and said, "You didn't think that we would take money from you, did you?"

I was awestruck, and more honoured and grateful than ever to be their guest on this trip."

We talked late into the night (the journey began at 8 P.M.) and Mrs. Somani relaxed and waxed eloquent (in a mixture of English and Hindi) on the custom of "Sati" - women who immolated themselves on their husband's funeral pyre.

Fortunately, Lord William Bentinck, the then Governor General of India, banned the practice of sati in the early 19th century.

It has been illegal ever since (not all cases of sati were voluntary), but sadly, occasional cases are reported even today.

Mr. Somani said, "You know I was just seventeen when we got married and she was fifteen."

They both laughed when he said how terrified she was of her mother-in-law, and I could see that they both loved each other very much.

God bless them both. My heart aches with love when I think of them!

The next day we stayed at the Rambagh Palace Hotel in Jaipur, where the marble bathroom attached to my room was bigger than my spacious living room in Bombay.

Under the doctrine of Paramountcy, the British had signed treaties with the great rulers, allowing them to keep their kingdoms while acknowledging the paramountcy of the King of England. One-third of British India consisted of princely states, some large, some small, and it saved the British endless battles that they would have had to fight to take over these states.

Among the great princely states were Kashmir, Hyderabad, Jaipur, Udaipur, Baroda, Bikaner, and Mysore.

The Maharajas were fabulously wealthy and owned huge palaces filled with treasures, fleets of Rolls Royces, and fabulous jewels, but after Independence, they were forced to sign over their states to India in exchange for privy purses which were about a tenth of their previous income.

The Maharajas had huge establishments and supported hundreds of servants and staff and retainers and their families, which they could no longer afford to maintain.

So they turned some of their palaces into five-star hotels.

A chauffeur-driven car was left at my disposal to see the sights, while Mr. Somani and Mrs. Somani drove off in another to inspect his factory. I felt more than a little overwhelmed.

The next day we went to Udaipur where we stayed at the Lake Palace Hotel - a fairy tale palace in the middle of a lake - the lake itself being a miracle in Rajasthan, the desert state.

We drove to the legendary citadel of Chittor, a fortress built on a rock soaring hundreds of feet above the surrounding plain, where the legendary princess-saint, Mirabai, beloved for her hymns to Krishna, who is one of the incarnations of God in Hindu philosophy. When the Christian missionaries came to India and told them about Jesus, the Hindus did not reject His divinity. Of course, he was one of the ten incarnations of God. We have been looking for the tenth incarnation for centuries. Jesus was the tenth and final incarnation!

Mirabai gave up the palace to live and worship in the fortress' temple. Her brother, the king, felt that she brought shame on the royal house with her simple lifestyle, clad only in a plain cotton sari and devoid of all jewellery, and tried to kill her more than once. When he sent her a poisoned drink, she told the people in the temple, "Look, my brother has sent me poison to drink. I will drink it in the name of Krishna."

She did, and it turned to nectar.

Another time he sent her a cobra in a basket of flowers. She held the poisonous serpent to her throat, but it refused to bite her.

We had arrived just before sunset and the tourists had left. There was a profound hush over the temple and the plains far below, and I was overcome by a profound sense of sadness. To this day I don't know why.

I also saw the place where hundreds of princesses and court ladies plunged into a huge sacrificial fire one night when the Mughal Emperor Akbar laid siege to the impregnable fort for months.

The emperor saw the fires in the fort from hundreds of feet below and said, "Look! Chittor is burning!"

"No, my lord," said his general, "the women are committing sati. Be prepared for a terrible battle tomorrow."

Sure enough, the next morning at dawn, the gates of the fortress opened and the rajput warriors, high on opium and crazed with grief, came down on their caparisoned chargers, wearing ceremonial robes under their armour, and the marks of their high caste on their foreheads, and fought to the death - every last one of them.

Akbar ordered honourable cremations for them and made peace with Chittor, which acknowledged his supremacy.

It was overwhelming to be in the presence of so much history.

In Jodhpur I saw the hands of the satis on one of the great gates of the fort and some of them were so small, I wept.

It was explained to me that before they immolated themselves (rather than fall into the hands of the Muslim enemy), they dipped their hands into a bowl of red powder called "kumkum" (used to paint religious marks on the forehead) and left their hand impressions on the gate of the fort. They were subsequently carved into the gate.

Mrs. Somani was from Jodhpur, and they took me to her ancestral home. The whole joint family trooped out to meet me, among them children ranging from the age of four to fourteen.

"Guruji ka pranam karo," said Mrs. Somani ("Touch the feet of the guru").

And they came up one by one and touched my feet.

I was excruciatingly embarrassed because I was no guru (spiritual teacher) but just an English teacher, but I humbly accepted the great honour she did me and held my peace, putting my right hand on the head of each child, by way of blessing, as I was expected to do.

I enjoyed every moment of my tour of Rajasthan thanks to the kindness of the Somanis, but the best moment came in Ajmer when we visited their two sons who were in boarding school at the famed Mayo College which was originally founded by an Englishman for the education of Rajput princes.

Their dorms were named after their kingdoms (Jaipur House, Udaipur House, Jodhpur House, Jaisalmer House, and so on) and the princes arrived on elephants with large retinues of servants.

The principal of Mayo College, who was an Englishman, gave the Somanis permission to take their boys out to lunch, and as we were enjoying the food in Ajmer's best restaurant, the boys spoke to me in fluent English as I asked them about their school and their interests and their daily routine. They were both very handsome, and also very courteous, products of the finest education, and their parents glowed with pride!

After we drove them back to school, even the ever-lively and cheerful Mr. Somani fell silent, and Mrs. Somani sobbed.

"Oh teacherji, I cannot bear to leave my boys!"

But still, it was a happy reunion with their sons, and it is with this memory that I will take leave of that beautiful couple!

I returned to Bombay greatly enriched in my knowledge of India, and with unforgettable memories which I am grateful for being able to share with you.

Memories of a distant past long since gone, and of great and good people.

(2)

Not all my memories are so pleasant.

1972 was not a good year.

Our dilapidated old building (built in 1870) was being repaired, and the tottering old wooden balcony was torn down, depriving us of the passage across our neighbour's balcony to our door, after we came up the stairs.

Our neighbour, Piroja Aunty, very kindly agreed to let us walk through her apartment after we came up the stairs (her door opened directly on the stairs) and then access our apartment through the back entrance which, like the torn-down balcony, also connected our two flats.

She did this despite the fact that my mother was not on speaking terms with her.

The repairs lasted several months, and Piroja Aunty was patient and kind and I felt great affection for her.

Television had just come to India - just one black-and-white channel! - and as I had bought one, I invited her every evening to watch TV with us. The servants were crazy about it!

As the cinema was the greatest enjoyment in their lives (melodramatic Bollywood films replete with villains, fist fights, songs, and dances), TV was the next best thing in their eyes.

Programs were aired only in the evenings, and the most boring of all was "Aamch Maati, Aamche Maanse" (Our Soil, Our People) which provided tips on farming. Being city kids, they hated it.

The most popular show was "I Love Lucy" which aired once a week, and they loved it. Such was the genius of Lucy, that these kids, who spoke little English, died laughing!

But evenings were also the time when water was released for two hours from the reservoir. Everybody was busy frantically filling large aluminium tubs with water, to last us for the next 24 hours.

Worse yet, there was not enough force in the water to come up to the second floor, so the poor servants had to operate a hand pump to bring it up. They would run dripping wet from the bathroom to the living room to watch snatches of TV.

As I type this, I am reminded of the flip side of my life in Bombay, which so far read almost like a fairy tale!

And I am grateful for my life here, wherever though I miss my darling servants terribly, and the sea of humanity in which I lived (nobody is lonely in India), where I have hot and cold running water 24 hours a day.

At the same time, the passage behind our flat, which connected it to the toilets and the servants' quarters, was also torn down, as it was on the verge of collapsing.

So, we had to use thunder boxes and a poor "untouchable" came each day to empty them. It was a windfall for him, as the whole building needed his services, and he charged a "take it or leave it" rate. Good for him!

The tearing down of the balcony and the rear passageway was accomplished in no time, but the rebuilding took months! As is the way with contractors in India.

I, at least, had my room with a view of the harbour, just half a mile from my house, so I could get away from my home at least for the night, and sleep in pleasant surroundings, listening to the waves lapping against the rocky shore and unable to close my eyes sometimes because of the moonlight shimmering peacefully on the water.

It was at this very time that a letter arrived from my brother saying that he and his family would be coming to visit us!

We received this news with mixed feelings.

On the one hand, we were overjoyed that he was, at last, coming to visit us after an eleven-year absence.

On the other hand, one thought, "What on earth are we going to do?" How will we make them comfortable?"

Daddy and I waited below our house at 5 A.M. in the morning for the taxi that would bring them from the airport. Out stepped my tall and handsome brother with his beautiful family, and after greeting Daddy, said to me: "Hello Rohinton."

Rohinton?

But Rohinton was our downstairs neighbour, slightly older than Mel, and they had never been friends. Why would he think that Rohinton would be standing beside our father at 5 A.M. in the morning to welcome him?

"I am Farokh," I smiled.

"Oh!"

It was only decades later that I realised that he had deliberately said this. Not for a second had he thought I was Rohinton!

But the wound cut deep - as it was meant to.

Why such deep hatred?

Why so much unnecessary venom?

I feel as sorry for him now as I did for myself then, that he has carried so much hatred for me in his heart all his life.

My brother had left solo and was returning with a wife and three little children.

In fact, he pointed this out to me himself! As he never spoke to me, I felt happy and honoured when he said to me "Look what I left with and look what I have returned with!"

I nodded with joy because the children were adorable and his Irish American wife, Mary-Anne was beautiful and poised.

Somehow, they all fit in. The children loved the thunder boxes and asked for peanut butter and tuna sandwiches. Since no one ate peanut butter in India, it was a huge relief to find that Rustom and Co. across the street carried it.

At the time, my eldest niece, Debbie, was 7, my nephew, Dennis, was 6, and my youngest niece, Shireen, was 5.

Debbie was poised and quiet like her mother. Dennis was the most adorable little American boy you ever saw, and Shireen was sweet and lively and played the opening notes of Fur Elise on my piano.

Daddy took his grandson for a ride on the upper deck of a BEST bus immediately after breakfast and I rather overdid it by arranging visits to the homes of my elegant friends and showing them the best parts of Bombay, taking them to lunch at the Taj Mahal Hotel (darling little Shireen kept asking, "Is this the Taj Mahal?!") and even a movie (on the life of the composer Grieg).

My poor brother, carrying Shireen in his arms, said "We've come to be with the family - not to meet everybody!" though they were treated like visiting royalty by all my friends.

Mea Culpa!

Speaking of royalty, among those I invited to meet my brother and his family was the beautiful and elegant Maharani of Sangli. Before she arrived, I explained to Dennis that she was a queen.

Her Highness arrived in a pastel-coloured French chiffon sari, and a string of pearls.

Dennis was hugely disappointed.

"Why wasn't she wearing a crown?" he asked after she left.

He had expected her to sweep in wearing a crown and an ermine cloak and carrying a sceptre!

Mary-Anne said that Malabar Hill reminded her of San Francisco.

All was going well, until one morning, when I walked into my house after sleeping in my little room by the sea, only to find Mel and his family gone!

What happened?

Mummy was grim and Daddy's face was crestfallen.

To cut a long story short, my mother had a huge fight with them after I left to sleep in my room.

Among the things she said (to my father), in the presence of her daughter-in-law and the children, "You can fuck her in New York, but not in my house."

For shame!!!

Mary-Anne said that she would not spend another second under her roof and my brother took his family to the Sea Green Hotel.

My heart sank to my feet, and I despised my mother.

I rushed to the Sea Green Hotel to see them, and Mary-Anne said, "If I ever see her again, I'll spit on her."

My poor brother, who loved our parents as I did, came to see them.

The visit was ruined, as well as my mother's relationship with Mary-Anne for the rest of her life.

My mother, being who she was, gave my brother a beautiful gold necklace (that she had bought for my Navjote, and which I loved, and had asked her to leave to me) to give to Mary-Anne.

I was speechless and kept mum.

My brother said, "We don't want material things from you. We want your love."

What love?

She had none to give.

Only spite and venom.

My poor brother had to assume the hero's role in the family, and I, who was born the scapegoat, continued in that role.

What my parents really wanted from my brother was money.

They had been proud of his looks and hoped he would make a big "catch" by marrying a rich, Parsi girl.

Once he left and married an American, they lost the little love they had for him.

They knew that he had left them forever and never forgave him.

He had been sending them thirty dollars a month, which went a long way in Bombay.

They were now afraid he would stop sending them the money.

He didn't.

After they left, and our building was finally repaired, I dug into my savings and gave my mother everything she wanted - a tiled bathroom, an electric water pump, a tank, placed on a marble slab, to store water in, a bathroom sink with running water, as it was connected to the tank, and also had our flat (apartment) oil painted for the first time.

I bought her a fridge, which she'd always wanted, and spent thousands of rupees on installing windows and tiles on our balcony and turning it into a cosy, little room.

She gave me no credit for any of this. Both my brother and I were starved for her love.

17 - Dolphin Days, Kersi Uncle

Even as 1971 was one of the worst years of my life, 1973 was one of the happiest.

I prefer to rush past the bad experiences and linger and dwell on the beautiful ones.

So, in this chapter, I shall re-live my happy days and nights in my "Rain Room" atop Dolphin apartments from 1973 to 1978. But for that, it is necessary to give some background.

The British always built cantonments beside the major Indian cities that had developed helter-skelter over the centuries and were chaotic and noisy. Indians have a crowd-creating tendency, so they were crowded and noisy, and along with that came slums and smells and sickness - fascinating and exotic though the cities were, with bazaars that contained the most beautiful textiles and jewellery in the world, and an astonishing variety of goods.

So, the British built cantonments alongside these cities, which were exclusively for the British. They were divided into civil and military cantonments, the latter being for the armed forces, and the former for senior civil servants like magistrates and judges and senior members of the government who belonged to the prestigious I.C.S (Indian Civil Service).

Here there were spacious bungalows with gardens, laid out along broad avenues lined with shade trees.

Our building in Bombay, dilapidated though it was, was only half a mile from the military cantonment at the southern tip of the island, that melts into the Indian Ocean.

Bombay itself, unlike other Indian cities, was a creation of the British, starting with a Fort in downtown Bombay, which is still known as the Fort area. (The fort itself, which was built to defend the harbour is now the naval base, INS Angre).

Bombay also has one of the finest and most beautiful natural harbours in the world, which is a deep, six-mile stretch of the sea between the island and mainland India lined with the blue hills known as the Sahyadris. The most prized locations in Bombay are those which have a view of the harbour. Though the harbour was also just half a mile behind our building, even a glimpse of it was completely blocked by several rows of buildings and by the bustling Sassoon Dock.

That is why I rented my little room with a view of the harbour behind my house when I returned from Ethiopia.

But even long before that, going as far back as my school days, I used to love walking in the cantonment. With its ancient trees and spacious bungalows, it was an oasis of peace and beauty compared to the noise and the traffic where I lived, just outside the cantonment.

The army officers' bungalows had beautiful gardens in front, with shade trees and flowering bushes of jasmine and magnolia trees, and behind them were the kitchen and the servants' quarters, where the servants and their families created a rural atmosphere with chickens running around, a cow tethered to a pole, and a vegetable garden.

By the time I was in college, the Navy had pretty much eliminated the Army from there, Bombay being a major naval base. The beautiful old colonels' bungalows were torn down and replaced with high-rise apartments and concrete parking lots under them, where once there had been gardens.

Still, many of the old trees remained, and there was still comparative peace and quiet, and a north Indian atmosphere, as most officers were from the martial castes in north India - tall, handsome Punjabis, and Jats from Haryana, on their scooters and motorbikes.

At the very tip of the cantonment was a graveyard with old English graves and heartbreaking dates on the tombstones.

"Mary Bennet, beloved wife of.. and mother of..

1832 - 1864."

Just before I left for Ethiopia in 1967, I noticed a high rise being built right on the very edge of the harbour (a concrete wall had been built to keep the waves back at high tide). When I returned, there was a twelve-story building called Dolphin Apartments which was inhabited by retired senior officers - Admirals, Brigadiers, and the like.

I envied those who lived there!

I envied them for the stunning view of the harbour that they had, which eclipsed the harbour view from the Taj Mahal Hotel two miles to the north.

Then, one day, a dignified, middle-aged woman called Mrs. Karmarkar joined my French class at the Indo-American Society. I discovered we were both going in the same direction when I called a taxi after class, and I invited her to join me on my ride home.

It turned out that she lived in Dolphin Apartments!

I insisted on dropping her off first and then driving half a mile back to my building which seemed to be in another world from hers.

Though she protested at first for not being allowed to pay her share of the fare, we enjoyed our ride together, and it soon became a comfortable routine for both of us. I confided in her how lucky I thought she was to live in Dolphin and how much I adored the location.

"I live on the twelfth floor," she said. "We have a room on the terrace that I could rent to you if you love the view so much."

I could hardly believe my ears!

The day I first opened the door to the terrace with my key and walked across it to my room, must rank as the happiest day of my life.

The moment one stepped onto the terrace; one was in another world.

Before me stretched the harbour all the way to the distant Sahyadri hills. Behind me stretched the cantonment with its ancient trees, all the way to yet another glimpse of the Arabian Sea (The northern part of the Indian Ocean), this time stretching all the way to Africa and Dubai.

As though all this were not enough, on the southern side of the terrace, I could see the island of Bombay vanish into the sea.

In a word, the sea was on three sides of me!

The room itself was simple, furnished only with a bed, a desk, and two chairs.

One of the reasons why Mrs. Karmarkar agreed to rent the room to me was because I explained to her that I would only be sleeping there and moving in with nothing more than my toothbrush.

The room was what is called a "barsati" in India, which means "Rain Room."

It is a room on the terrace of the house, where one can enjoy the three heavenly months of the monsoon, in a land that has drought for nine months in the year.

But what a "barsati" this was!

I would come home from teaching, have dinner, and then walk to Dolphin.

When I stepped onto the terrace, the warships were twinkling with lights on the sea spread out before me.

Full moon nights were sheer magic!

The black tiles of the terrace reflected the moonlight and its silvery radiance shimmered on the sea.

The sun rose behind the Sahyadri hills, but that was never a good time because it meant the beginning of blinding sunshine and searing heat for the rest of the day.

On the evenings when I was not teaching, I went early and watched the red sun melt into the Indian Ocean on the other side of the terrace.

On full moon nights, the koel, or the Indian cuckoo, mistaking the moonlight for dawn, would call through the night in its dulcet voice, and the enchantment was complete!

During the monsoon, migratory sea birds arrived. A whimbrel with its downward curving beak flew right by my window, and far below, the sandpipers and stilts scavenged among the pools of water between the rocks at low tide.

A brahmini kite soared high over the harbour with its huge bronze and white wings, and sometimes a hawk swooped down its prey like a bolt of lightning.

The gulls were there all year round. In the cool months that followed the monsoon, wagtails would arrive and forage on the terrace - running, and not hopping, because they put one foot in front of the other.

Dear Jer Jussawala must make a reappearance in this one.

I would occasionally invite Mrs. Karmarkar to join me for a drink on the terrace, and being the wife of an Admiral, she was no stranger to rum and coke.

One evening, Mrs. Karmarkar told me that a portion of the terrace that was sunken and separated from the rest of the terrace by a concrete step was reserved for a roof garden, and she was now ready to start one. She said that a truckload of soil would be deposited behind the building, and she needed someone to shovel it into gunny bags and bring it up in the elevator before dawn so as not to inconvenience the other residents of the building.

My mother had once hired a pock-marked little boy, who belonged to the caste of rag pickers, to work for us. When he grew into a strong teenager he started to work as a day labourer. I tracked him down, and he agreed to do the job. I paid him handsomely. Mrs. Karmarkar was delighted.

When Jer Jussawala first visited the terrace of Dolphin, she was enchanted by the panoramic view of the harbour, so entirely different from the view of the sea from her bungalow on Juhu beach. She pointed out how lucky and blessed I was, and I assured her that I knew and was more grateful than could ever say.

Now she was excited by the garden project. She drove up with seedlings - petunias antirrhinums, nasturtiums, dahlias, and balsams - and a watering can and a spade. She taught me how to plant them, and how to deadhead the flowers after they died, to stimulate more growth. These thrived during the cool winter months and the marigolds during the Monsoon. My job was to water the garden, and I loved it!

Mrs. Karmarkar got the "mali" (gardener) of the United Services Club to plant a small lawn which was surrounded by a border of flowers. The mali also brought a couple of magnolia trees which bore white and gold blossoms during the hottest months. So, I had flowers all year round.

Even though the roof garden was Mrs. Karmarkar's dream and she occasionally brought friends to see it (she was President of the Women Graduates' Union), it was really I who got to enjoy it, and watering it every morning and nurturing it added to the pleasure it gave me.

What I learned from that garden has stood me in good stead for the last thirty-six years, in creating and maintaining my balcony garden each summer where I live. The neighbours occasionally say, "I love seeing your flowers," and that doubles the joy they give me.

Soon after I got my terrace room, I took my parents to see it, and Daddy loved it, saying that it was well worth the additional rent (as I also paid the rent on our old flat at Wodehouse Road).

Mummy said, "Waste of money."

"But, Mummy, this is for my soul!"

Those were still my drinking days, and one evening I had an epiphany as I sat in a cane chair on the terrace and gazed at the beautiful harbour where the ships were lighting up one by one, sipping my rum and coke. It was utterly still and peaceful - the hardest thing to find in Bombay - and suddenly my soul was filled with ecstasy. I felt a joy such as I had never felt in my life. It was as though I had become one with the beauty all around me - the sea, the sky, the twilight, and utter stillness.

I forgot who I was, and the moment fused with eternity.

It was a quiet ecstasy that I imagine the souls in heaven must enjoy, and it lasted only a few moments.

But was, and is, unforgettable.

It was during my Dolphin years that I transitioned from Farokh to Farah, but that must wait for a later chapter.

It was also here that I had my first and only great romantic relationship, but I shall not dwell on my love life in this chapter. He shall remain anonymous, to protect his identity, and I shall just call him "Prem" in this memoir.

So let me just say that he was a dashing, drop-dead, gorgeous young Sub-Lieutenant with a dazzling smile, whom I met at the Western Naval Command Mess, which rose above the trees, not far from Dolphin, and which I could see from the western end of my terrace. The first rain had just fallen, and the dust of the dry months was washed off the leaves and they were a dazzling green.

It was the beginning of the most wonderful time of year in India, celebrated in song and in poetry.

Unlike my previous crushes, this love was consummated, and it was to him that I lost my virginity, two months after my surgery.

Of course, there was no question of marriage. He later married a girl from his caste, chosen by his parents, and we both agreed that our relationship would end once he got married, and we would remain just friends. I gave his wife piano lessons as she said that it was her dream to play the piano.

The years turned into decades, and he retired in the upper echelons of the Indian Navy, after a distinguished career.

He is now a grandfather. We still email each other occasionally, and he is always kind and supportive and encouraging.

So, this too is a memory of my Dolphin days.

(2)

My mother had a younger brother, and when they were old enough, my grandmother sent them both to boarding schools. My mother told me that the reason for this was that she feared for their lives.

I don't know what to make of the account that follows. All I can do is share with you what she told me.

As I had mentioned, my great-grandfather was an engine driver with the British Railways that connected the length and breadth of India after the 1857 mutiny.

It was a strategic job, entrusted only to Anglo-Indians and Parsis, who were known to be loyal to the British.

My great-grandfather built a house in Bhusawal, which is in central India, near Bhopal (remember the notorious poison gas leak in 1985 which killed thousands of the poor workers who lived in flimsy shelters around the Union Carbide factory, through whom the American military tested the poison gas).

He had a loving and happy wife who enjoyed making homemade wine with grapes from Kabul (I remember sipping Hall's Winer from her little wine glass). They also had their own well and a water buffalo with a man to look after it. He also kept buying parcels of land and became a small landowner.

They had two sons and my mother's father was the older one who would inherit the bulk of his father's estate ("fortune" would be too pompous a word, though my mother grossly exaggerated his wealth, claiming that my father lost her "large" dowry on the racecourse).

My maternal grandmother lost her first four babies to crib deaths. She had a loyal Muslim maid, who told her during the annual Shia Moharram procession, "One of the men becomes possessed during the procession. Please let me bring him to you, and perhaps he will know why your children keep dying."

My grandmother agreed.

The neighbours, Hindu, Muslim and Parsi, all gathered in her ground-floor living room, as this man was considered very holy.

He came and was told my grandmother's plight.

He went into a trance, and rolling his head violently, he said, "Bring me a knife."

My grandmother whispered,

"Oh, my, he will kill us."

But the maid, whose name was Putlibai, said, "Don't be afraid. Just do as he says."

The man began frantically digging the mud floor and pulled out a doll pierced with needles, owls' bones, and hyena bones, along with children's hair.

Then he spoke, and said, "Tell your mistress that the next time she is with the child she must travel as far as she can from this house, and not return to it until the child is one year old."

As my grandmother was already expecting, she left the very next morning for Ahmadabad, which was hundreds of miles away and stayed with relatives.

And so, my mother was born in Ahmadabad, the capital of Gujarat, on 2nd January 1916.

She died on 2nd January 1992.

My grandmother stayed with her in Ahmadabad till she was one year old before returning home.

My mother lived.

So did her younger brother, with whom my grandmother followed the same routine.

My mother went on to say, that the culprit in what clearly appears to have been a case of black magic, was my grandmother's sister-in-law who had access to the house and wanted my great-grandfather's estate for her own children.

I don't know what to make of this story!

But it does explain why my grandmother feared for her children's lives and put them in boarding school so that they would continue to be far from Bhusawal.

My uncle was put in the prestigious Barnes School in Deolali for Anglo-Indian boys.

My mother was sent to the humbler Dastoor School in Poona, where, coincidentally, my father grew up!

They never met, of course, as she was in a girls' school.

My mother also used an excuse to put my brother in boarding school. She said that by the time he was seven he used to run out of the house, and she feared that he would get run over by the chaotic Bombay traffic.

Whether there was any truth in this, we shall never know. The fact is that she didn't want to be bothered with children, and she had my brother admitted to the boy's section of Dastoor School.

So why didn't she do the same with me?

Because boarding schools are expensive, and my parents had very little money.

My brother was devastated that they sent him away while keeping me with them, and in his innocent childhood mind, they preferred me to him.

He never forgave me.

Not to this day, though he is in his eighties, and a grandfather.

When I was in New York and I called his house on Long Island he said, "Don't ever call my house!"

Nor did he answer my letters.

He did not allow me to have a relationship with my nephew and nieces, but by Googling him and the children I have learned that he is comfortably retired in Florida, my nephew is a paediatrician, and one of my nieces is a schoolteacher, while the other is a gynaecologist.

So, the children have done well.

None of them have any contact with me, as he forbade them to.

And as for their children, they don't even know that I exist.

So be it.

They are his children and grandchildren, and it is for him to decide.

It doesn't hurt me any longer.

It doesn't even matter any longer, as I am surrounded by the love of students and friends.

But returning to my mother's younger brother's story, (his name was Kersi Uncle) he became penniless when he was fifty, having squandered his modest inheritance.

He had stayed on in Bhusawal, in the three-story house that my grandmother built on Station Road after she was widowed. I seem to have inherited her passion for travelling, because after being widowed, she paid extended visits to her brothers in distant Karachi (now in Pakistan), Rangoon (Burma, now Myanmar), Calcutta and the beautiful hill station of Darjeeling. She took her children with her and gave her sisters-in-law gifts of gold jewellery to compensate them for her stay.

When Kersi Uncle became destitute, he wrote to my parents that all he wanted was a small room in which to quietly spend the rest of his days.

We lived in an apartment with two large rooms and had no spare room.

Of course, my father felt extremely resentful of his brother-in-law!

Kersi Uncle had never worked a day in his life, while Daddy had worked since the age of eighteen.

Our large back room was divided by a screen and there Kersi

Uncle slept, while I slept on a sofa-bed in the front room, which was the living room (called "drawing room" in India, just as business cards are still called "visiting cards", Victorian English elegances preserved forever in India).

I had just returned from my stint in Ethiopia and was 24 years old and understood my father's feelings about Kersi Uncle.

Imagine my surprise when I met him!

He was gentle, soft-spoken, and extremely courteous - a gentleman to the very tips of his fingers!

Every evening he went for long walks, so as to be out of our way. He sat silently in an old armchair and listened while I gave lessons - English lessons, Piano lessons, French lessons. Looking back, I think that he must have "gotten" to know me pretty well.

He never spoke unless he was spoken to, and asked for nothing, and during the two years that he spent with us before he died at the age of 52, I had to ask him at least twice to come to the table for every meal. He would hesitate before he got up from our weather-beaten old armchair.

My father never stopped telling anyone who would listen, that Kersi Uncle ate a whole plate of rice! I am mortified to this day when I think of it!

At his very first meal with us, my mother kept provoking me with remarks that she knew I would not like, and I took the bait. I was beginning to get agitated when Kersi Uncle quietly said to her, "Jer, please don't ruin everything!"

It was then that I realised what she was doing! Trying to show me in a bad light to Kersi Uncle from day one!

But Kersi Uncle knew her game. In hindsight, it is easy to see that she had been playing such games all her life, even in her mother's house, while she was still single!

I am desperately trying to think of at least one good thing that I can write about my mother but cannot come up with anything. She seems to have been an unmitigated troublemaker all her life.

While I am at it, I may as well tell you that not only had she quarrelled with all our neighbours, thus isolating me too from them, but she delighted in provoking a beautiful Punjabi woman called Padma who lived opposite our house. She would show the sole of her flip-flop to poor Padma, causing her visible distress.

But what does this mean? Showing Padma, the sole of her flip-flop!

I must explain that in India, to strike someone with one's shoe is the worst possible insult.

That is why an Iraqi man threw his shoe at George W. Bush during a press conference in Iraq.

The goal was not to injure the American President but to express utter contempt for him.

It is delightful that Bush ducked when he saw the shoe flying at him, and it missed him altogether.

Ah, the benefits of playing baseball as a kid!

The shoe would have hit an Iraqi politician squarely in the face.

So now you see, that by showing Padma the sole of her flip-flop, Mummy was telling her that she would beat her with it!

When I became Farah and all my neighbours accepted me for who I was with such grace, I stopped my mother when she was doing this, and in front of Padma, pointed to the interior of the house and asked my mother to go in.

She did.

From that day, Padma started smiling at me, and I gave her a friendly wave always.

One by one, I started greeting my neighbours and made friends with all of them.

Mummy needled Daddy by nagging him into buying clothes for Kersi Uncle, thus provoking fights that Kersi Uncle could hear, to his excruciating embarrassment. Looking back, I can see why she never asked me. It was because she knew that I would gladly have bought him a shirt. What she wanted was not the shirt, but the fight.

Once she bought him a shirt and told him, "But I will not give it to you now."

"Then when?" asked Kersi Uncle, taking the bait.

"At Christmas!"

Kersi Uncle never lived to see that Christmas.

But fortunately, before he died, he met his son a few times.

Here is how it happened.

After Kersi Uncle's divorce from my father's niece, my cousin Sam lived with his mother in Poona.

One evening, when Kersi Uncle had gone as usual for his evening walk by the sea, the doorbell rang.

A young man I had never seen before stood in the doorway.

"I am Kersi Uncle's son, Sammy," he said softly and politely, just like his father.

"Sammy!" I cried, "Come in! Come in!"

I told him that his father had gone for a walk and would soon return.

We sat on the sofa and talked, slowly getting acquainted.

Then the doorbell rang, and I told Kersi Uncle as quietly as I could, "Kersi Uncle, there is someone who's come to see you."

"To see me?"

He walked into the drawing room and instantly recognised his grown son.

"Sammy!"

"Papa!"

They hugged, and there were tears in their eyes.

From then on, Sammy came frequently to see his father, travelling hours each way by train from Poona.

My mother ignored him, but he and I slowly got to know each other better.

Then, one day, my mother again provoked my father, and they had another fight over Kersi Uncle.

Kersi Uncle had had enough.

He had Type Two diabetes and had been taking diabetes medication since he was a teenager.

He quietly stopped taking his pills. A few days, later, as he was leaving for his evening walk, he said, a polite "Bye Bye" as always. I was with a student, and cordially replied, "Bye, bye, Kersi Uncle," as I always did.

That was the last time we saw each other.

He never returned.

The next morning, after calling a few hospitals, my father found him in the morgue.

He had died of a diabetic coma in a tiny tea shop near our house. He ordered a cup of tea and then rested his head on his arms on the table. When the poor waiter brought the tea, he found that Kersi Uncle was dead.

My mother was overcome by grief, resulting from guilt and shame about how she had treated him all his life.

His son Sammy and I wept together at his funeral.

And so, ends the sad story of dear Kersi Uncle.

Though he was with us for only a brief two years, I remember him with extreme tenderness and respect.

His son Sammy never came to our house again, and I did not have his contact info.

He was a little younger than I and is probably in his early seventies now.

I shall end this episode with one more family memory, - this time about my brother's first phone call from New York.

It was 1970 just after Kersi Uncle's death, and it was still the days when long-distance calls ("trunk calls") were scheduled through an operator - two telephone operators, in fact - one in America and the other in India.

It was a big deal, as there was no direct dialling yet, and we waited on tenterhooks for over 24 hours before the call finally came through.

An operator had called us the day before and told us that my brother had booked a trunk call.

Of course, my parents and I were thrilled!

To my surprise, my mother started to drink glass after glass of iced water, which, of course, gave her a sore throat.

So, when my mother was speaking to my brother, he thought that she was crying - which was exactly what she wanted!

"Please don't cry, mom!" my poor brother kept saying, feeling rotten and guilty.

But the children were a delight!

This was less than two years before my brother's visit to us with his family, after an absence of eleven years, about which I have already written.

It was my nephew's birthday, and Daddy, in his formal British way, said, "Many Happy returns of the day!"

"What?"

"Many Happy returns of the day!"

"What?"

"Just say Happy Birthday, Daddy," I whispered.

"Happy Birthday!"

"Thank you" (after some prompting from his parents).

So at least this episode ends with a smile.

18 - My Transformation From Farokh To Farah

In January of 1976, when I had just turned 32, there was a book review in the Times of India. The book in question was Jan Morris' *Conundrum*.

In it, she describes her lifelong self-identification as a girl and her transformation from the well-known writer James Morris to Jan Morris.

While I had already heard of the first sex-change surgery in the world, that of the American Christine Jorgenson, (not really a Marine, she merely worked in the office), I had no hope that it would ever be possible for me, as I did not have the kind of money it would take to go to Europe to have the operation.

So, I resigned myself to living my whole life in the wrong body, as an effeminate gay - something that I made no attempt to hide.

At this point, I would like to pause to reflect on transgenderism. Doctors now say that the condition is caused in the womb when the wrong set of hormones bombard a baby's brain. Normally, a female foetus receives a large dose of oestrogen or female hormones, and a boy's brain receives a large dose of testosterone, the male hormone.

That is why little boys act as little boys and little girls act like little girls.

But when something goes terribly wrong, when mother nature makes a mistake, and bombards a male foetus' brain with female hormones, the little "boy" comes into the world with a "girl brain", feeling from earliest childhood that he is a girl trapped in a boy's body.

That is the cause of the mysterious condition - a lifelong compulsion to belong to the opposite sex.

In the 1970s the term transsexual was still in use, and it was a loaded word,because the word "Sex" was in it, and so there was a stigma attached to it.

When the correct term transgender came, it was a much better and much more accurate term. Being transgender is not about wanting to have sex with those of the sex into which one was born, but rather, wanting to *be* the opposite sex.

In other words, one's sexuality is whom you want to go to bed with.

One's gender identity is whom you want to go to bed as.

Homosexuals are perfectly happy with their bodies.

The trans-gendered hate their bodies and want to change them.

The difference is immense!

Anyway, as soon as I read the book review, I went to Strand Book Stall and bought *Conundrum*.

What she wrote about her childhood was familiar and common to all trans-gendered, but the chapters in which she described her transformation gripped me!

She described how within eighteen months of starting on a course of oestrogen (female hormones) her body was transformed. She developed small but respectable breasts, and her facial and body hair all but disappeared.

I wrote to Jan Morris, asking her the names of the pills she had taken, and she was gracious enough to reply by return of post. She wrote that she had taken Premarin, made in Canada from the urine of pregnant mares, 5mg. pills three times a day. She had also taken a synthetic oestrogen called Estinyl, and received 20 mg Progynon Depot injections, once every other week.

I couldn't wait!

I went to the nearest pharmacy and asked for the pills with a beating heart, fearing that I would need a prescription.

But to my great joy, the proprietor, who was at the counter, merely called out to the man within: "Are bhai, Premarin aur Estinyl lao."

"Oh, brother, bring Premarin and Estinyl."

When they arrived, I asked him how many bottles he had in stock and bought them all and requested him to order more.

He didn't bat an eyelash!

Never mind the cost!

That is what it is to be trans-gendered!

I took two doses that day and went to bed.

Nothing happened.

The next morning when I woke up and looked at my face eagerly in the bathroom mirror of my room atop Dolphin, I looked exactly the same.

But after four or five days, I did notice a change within myself.

I was no longer restless, but more at peace, content to sit on my terrace on the roof of Dolphin and gaze up at the stars, or at the twinkling lights of the ships at anchor in the harbour spread out before me.

I also started having dreams. All kinds of strange dreams that I can no longer recall. But they were pleasant and peaceful and after two weeks, just when I was beginning to give up hope, I noticed after my shower, when I looked at myself in the mirror (always above the waist, I could never bear to look at myself below the waist) that my nipples were getting darker and larger and starting to protrude.

I was overjoyed!

The transformation had begun!

I am now trying to convey to you medical and scientific information, and if you find anything I write in this chapter immodest, or in poor taste, I apologise in advance!

I also stopped shaving and tried bleaching my facial hair instead. But it continued to grow, and my bleached hair looked golden in the sunlight, but was still visible, and I knew that if I didn't do something, I would look like I was growing a blond beard! Argh!

You see, second only to the primary male characteristics, which are the male genitals, which a trans-gendered male loathes on "herself", she hates her secondary male characteristics - namely, facial and body hair.

I began to wax my arms and legs, and the little hair that grew on my chest (argh again!) and after a few times, it stopped growing back.

The facial hair was more difficult to rid myself of. I began to tweeze my facial hair one hair at a time each morning, and this required time and patience, though, as a result, it took much longer to grow back, and grew back finer, and I no longer had to tweeze my facial hair every day.

Still, I knew that there was no escape from electrolysis, which Jan Morris had also mentioned in her book.

So, I went to an electrologist who was exorbitantly expensive, but she did a great job, and I was finally rid of my facial hair, and my cheeks were smooth as ivory.

All this brought me ever-increasing happiness and peace, even though it was stripping me of every penny I earned, as well as depleting my meagre savings at an alarming rate.

I also went to our family doctor, Dr. Toprani, and confided in him, and asked him if he would give me Progynon Depot injections. He graciously consented, and I went to him once a week (instead of once every other week!) and he very kindly showed me how to inject myself in the hip, so I could save money.

Once I learned to do that, I started giving myself double doses and even triple doses, and yes, almost daily!

I had morning sickness, like a pregnant woman, and had dreams all night.

My hips broadened and became wider than my shoulders, and I unconsciously began to sway my hips as I walked.

For the first time in my life, I gained weight, and where once I had been a tall, skinning geek with glasses, I began to look more and more womanly, filling out in all the right places.

The green shadow on my cheeks which I had loathed, was gone. My breasts were clearly visible and my languorous walk with my newly broadened hips attracted attention from all quarters.

Everyone could see that something was happening to me. That I was turning into a woman.

I confided in my closest friends and even in some of my students.

They were amazed and awe-struck.

How did I have the courage?

I said I didn't care. I would rather die in the attempt or bankrupt myself even before that than ever be the wretched, skinny, geeky, Farokh that I had been for so long!

I was well aware that I was in very great danger of getting cancer, even breast cancer in my burgeoning breasts that I loved. I knew that I was playing with fire.

I knew that I was risking premature death.

But I didn't care.

This is what it means to be trans-gendered.

The compulsion to cross over is beyond all comprehension.

But still, I had no hope of having the surgery.

In other words, I had rid myself of all my secondary male characteristics. I never had the tertiary male characteristic - a deep male voice. My voice had never changed, so that was one cross I did not have to bear!

I began to grow my hair, and instead of going to the humble barber's shop around the corner from my dilapidated building, I went for the first time in my life to a hair salon.

In a ladies' beauty parlour, no less!

I fit right in and felt at home there, and the staff and the customers all accepted me as a matter of course.

The new, feminine haircuts she gave me, completed my transformation, as far as looks were concerned.

At that time, if had I decided to give up everything I had and start a new life in a distant place, wearing dresses and saris, and changing my name to Farah, no one could have suspected for even one fleeting second that "down there" I was not a female.

But *I* knew that I wasn't, and so I was not prepared to throw up everything and start a new life elsewhere.

By now I knew that I was transitioning and that I had transitioned remarkably well. Even my kind boss, Mr. Krishnan, knew and did not object, but accepted me for who I was.

My students thought that I was a novelty and a wonder, and everyone - friends, neighbours, students - marvelled at the awesome power of hormones.

Then providence took a hand!

One of my French students was a medical student and he told me that a plastic surgeon called Dr. Keswani, had just returned from America, having learned to perform transgender surgery there!

The very next day I made an appointment to see him, and at the consultation he told me that I was a prime candidate for the surgery, that I was completely ready for it and asked me if he could set a date.

I felt that I was in a walking dream, but instantly and joyously agreed.

I was ashamed that I was lower middle class and had almost no money to give him.

But he brushed it aside, saying that as long as I was prepared to pay for my hospital stay, the operating theatre and the anaesthesiologist, he would waive his fee altogether and perform the surgery for free.

"If I agreed to pose for before and after photos for articles about my surgery that he planned to write for medical journals, and also if I would be willing to go public."

"Of course, doctor! How could I keep it secret anyway? Nor do I want to! I can't tell you how extremely grateful I am to you."

A month later I went under the knife at the beautiful old Masina Hospital, which had once been the home of the millionaire philanthropist David Sasson, and which he donated in his will, to be used as a private hospital.

The wealthy Parsi Masina family endowed the hospital, making it affordable.

So, everything came together as if by a miracle, and if this was not the hand of God then I don't know what is!

I was admitted the night before the surgery and sitting in my private hospital room and gazing at the ancient trees that had adorned the garden of David Sasson, I felt ineffable peace.

I couldn't have been given a better setting to be released at last from my bodily prison in which I had been imprisoned for thirty-two wretched years, as if in a dark dungeon, from which there was no hope of release.

And suddenly, against all odds, God, to whom all things are possible, opened the door of my dungeon and allowed me to walk out of it.

Of course, some people had tried to talk me out of having the surgery, among them (understandably) my parents, and even dear, wonderful Jer Jussawala. I explained to my dear parents that what I was doing, I was doing to myself and not doing it to them.

That if there was any shame in what I was doing than the shame was on me, and only on me, and not on them.

As the whole transformation, starting with the hormones, was with my own money, they could not stop me, much as they would have liked to.

My mother even considered having me certified insane and locked up for life in a mental institution.

But considering that I was paying the rent and the utilities and the telephone bill and the servants' salaries, as well as buying her whatever she wanted (big ticket items like a refrigerator, TV, renovations on the bathroom etc.) she hesitated to act on it.

I had told Dr. Keswani what my mother was threatening to do, and he was livid!

"Transsexualism is a condition and not a mental illness!"

He immediately sent me for evaluation by a team of psychiatrists at the King Edward Memorial Hospital.

The Head of the Department of Psychiatry at Grant Medical College, which is affiliated with the Hospital, Dr. Doongaji, asked me if I would be willing to be interviewed in the presence of all his colleagues as well as his students and I agreed.

I had to take a preliminary IQ test in which I scored high enough to astonish the woman who administered it to me.

She then asked me a few simple questions as to why I wanted to become a woman, and at the end of our interview, she said, "I am going to refer to you as "she" and "her" in my report! You are mentally a woman."

And she wrote so in her report.

Bless her!

Then came the interviews in the presence of the entire psychiatry department.

Dr. Doongaji was ruthless in his mental examination of me.

"You do realise that you can never become a total woman, don't you? You will have a vagina, but you won't have a womb and ovaries. You'll never have periods."

"I don't want to become a woman in order to have periods."

"You won't be able to get pregnant either."

"That is indeed sad! But at least I'll be able to live authentically as a woman. Publicly declare my true gender and have the body to prove it. I will not be a complete woman, I know, but rather, like a post-menopausal woman or a woman who has had a total hysterectomy. I have no illusions and no false expectations.

Then he asked me the most brutal question of all, pausing significantly, and lowering his voice before he did: "Have you ever had an orgasm?"

I blushed to the very roots of my hair, and whispered with great difficulty, "Yes."

That did it for him.

He wrote a smashing report stating that on a scale of one to ten, I was a ten as a transgender and was the best possible candidate for the surgery. He also certified, along with the entire board of psychiatrists on the faculty, that I was sane, had an exceptionally high IQ, and was neither delusional nor schizophrenic.

I was now safe from what my mother had planned for me!

Dr. Keswani was overjoyed by the report, and said, "I am proud of you."

I called Dr. Doongaji and thanked him for his report.

But I could not resist adding, "Doctor, you were ruthless with me. I felt as though you were holding my intelligence against me."

"On the contrary! I think that your intelligence is the finest thing about you!"

Who would not be happy to hear that?

As I write this, all these great wonderful men and women are no more.

I called Dr. Toprani, our family doctor, from the US twenty years after my surgery and he said, "I've visited some places in the US and am now 76 years young."

May his soul be in a beautiful place.

As may the souls of my surgeon, Dr. Keswani, and the psychiatrist who evaluated me, Dr. Doongaji.

And so, my surgery took place in the light of day and before the eyes of all the world.

I hope this chapter helps you to understand better how much I had to go through to be the woman I am today after being trapped in the wrong body for thirty-two years before the surgery.

I thank God for the infinite mercy He has shown me by releasing me from my prison. How many millions have remained and will remain in their prisons all their lives!

My surgery lasted six and a half hours.

It need not have taken that long.

To surgically create a vagina is a fairly simple procedure, but Dr. Keswani was over-conscientious in working on the external aesthetic, which took a long time.

Perhaps it was because of the articles he wanted to write about my surgery in medical journals.

I bled a lot during the surgery, and towards the end, the anaesthesiologist pleaded with Dr. Keswani to hurry up because, "Her pulse is very low and dropping fast. I cannot keep her unconscious much longer. I must bring her back!"

My parents did come to see me in hospital that evening when I was back in my room after the surgery. I remember my father's voice saying, "The operation is over. It was a success."

My mind registered his words, I did not open my eyes and fell back into a deep sleep.

When I finally came to, it was late in the evening (the operation started early morning, at 7.30 AM), and it was getting dark. I felt tightly bandaged from the waist down, and a tube went into a bottle below my bed to collect drops of urine.

I was not in any kind of pain but felt tight and heavy below.

I learned later that Dr. Keswani had inserted a "mold" (resembling a dildo, which is about the easiest way I can describe it) into my vagina to keep it open, as the body automatically tries to close any opening it does not recognise.

The next morning, when Dr. Keswani came to change the dressings, he was cheery and said, "I did not know you were so famous! Everyone at the Willingdon Club asked me if I had performed a sex change operation on you!"

So, the city knew!

Or rather, everyone in the city of fifteen million who knew me, knew!

Good! I no longer had anything to hide and could step out of Masina Hospital as my new self.

A nurse came and gave me several pills twice a day.

I was kept on a liquid diet for ten days. I never felt hungry and did not miss food.

But on the fourth day I haemorrhaged and bed sheet after bed sheet drenched in my blood had to be changed.

The panic-stricken nurse called Dr. Keswani, who came as soon as he could. He removed the bandages and put some stitches under local anaesthetic, which stopped the bleeding. He then bandaged me tightly again.

"I'm sorry, I had not put enough stitches."

I had requested the nurse to call my parents when I realised how heavily I was bleeding because I wanted to see them one last time and not leave without thanking them for all that they had done for me.

My mother called a woman who had agreed with her before my surgery that I should be certified insane and locked up for life, and they both came wearing black saris, certain that I would be dead by the time they got to the hospital, and that they would go straight from there to the Tower of Silence, where my dead body would be sent.

But God had other plans for me, and I still had decades more of joy and sorrow and experiences left, both good and bad, and work to do.

The woods are lovely, dark, and deep,
But I have promises to keep,
And miles to go before I sleep,

And miles to go before I sleep.
-Robert Frost.

I once read somewhere: "Is your work finished? If not, you cannot die."

On the tenth day Dr. Keswani removed the tube and I tried to walk to the bathroom.

As soon as I stood up, my blood pressure plunged, and I almost fainted. I lay down again and after a while, got up more slowly and sat up in bed for some time, before walking to the bathroom and peed for the first time as Farah. There was no pain.

I am sorry for this intimate detail, but it was a significant moment for me, because I knew that everything was all right, and I could begin my new life in a new body, as Farah.

Indeed, I feel that I have two birthdays:

14th November 1943 as Farokh.

And 30th October 1976, as Farah.

A couple of days later, Dr. Keswani gave me permission to take a cab home, and as soon as I got home, I sat at my desk and picked up the phone and started talking to my friends.

Our servant made a delicious chicken curry and my parents, and I sat at the table together and enjoyed our dinner.

They had given me a cold reception when I returned home.

But I understood.

They would have thrown me out of the house if they could, but they needed my financial contribution and also needed me as insurance for their old age, which was not too far off.

But I still had to wear that wretched "mold" in my freshly created vagina another six weeks!

It was most uncomfortable, to say the least.

My high-spirited gay friends teased me, saying, "Oh, how wonderful to have a penis inside you all day and all night!"

Like Queen Victoria, I was not amused!

After spending a whole day at home, I started working again - not just tutoring at home, but also resuming my French classes at the Indo-American Society and my lectures on music appreciation.

My work was more important than ever, now.

I wish I could have said that I showed up in a sari on my first day!

But, alas, that was not the case.

Things had moved too swiftly.

My transformation had occurred in less than a single year, and my mother talked me not only into retaining the name Farokh but also to continue to dress in a shirt and pant.

As those were the days when many women dressed that way, I persuaded myself that I could do so, though I hated it, now that I had had the surgery.

And so, I lost five precious years as Farah!

What I did not know was that, as a consequence of my listening to my mother, everyone thought that my operation had been a failure!

They were bitterly disappointed.

They thought that I had performed a miracle, and they felt let down!

But I didn't know!

This was exactly what my mother wanted.

Yet another triumph for her.

And all because of my love for her and my desire to please her, which remained unchanged.

I kept hoping, and hoping, and hoping against hope, to win her love.......

Then, one day, a boy who was doing a Radio Officers' course at the naval base next to our building, told me that all the boys at the college believed that my operation had been a failure.

Yet, during the previous five years, when Dr. Keswani finally gave me permission to stop wearing the mold, I had had a normal sex life with "Prem" (he must remain anonymous).

I was enraged!

I now clearly saw the lie that my mother had spread!

That same evening, I went and bought a beautiful, black dress from a shop on Colaba Causeway, putting it on in the trial room of the store, and I walked home in it.

There was a happy smile on my face, and I was flooded with joy.

A poor woman who saw me, remarked in Marathi, "She is wearing a dress to-day!"

I smiled at her, and she smiled back.

From that day my mother knew that she was defeated, though she had one more victory to win.

She persuaded me to give up my sublime terrace room atop Dolphin. My private heaven!

Once again, I was fool enough to listen to her, and the Karmarkars were sorry to see me to go.

If there are two things that I regret doing in my life to this day, it is not majoring in English Literature (if I had, I would have long been a retired professor at Elphinstone College and still living at 61 Wodehouse Road, growing old among all the people I knew and loved), and the second is giving up my paradise atop Dolphin!

A tree is known by its fruit, and the fact that during the last four decades I have never regretted becoming Farah for one fleeting second, is proof enough of how right that decision was for me!

On the other hand, if I hadn't given up my private paradise atop Dolphin, I would never have been able to leave Bombay to start a new life in the west.

So, God works in mysterious ways.

Still, I wish that I had never given up Dolphin, and stayed on in Bombay, which was my home, and where I was known and respected and loved......

Anyway, leaving regrets aside, here's to happy memories.

I soon learned to wear a sari, and because of the grace and beauty of that garment, my happiness was now complete!

I went to Zaveri Bazar (Jeweller's Market) and sold Farokh's heavy, gold cuff links and gold buttons and bought a gold chain for Farah and some gold bangles, which every Indian woman cherishes.

I put a gold dot on my forehead and jingled with a glass bracelet and "payal', (anklets).

I literally had bells on my feet!

I had my nose pierced and wore a diamond stud as Indian women do, and chandelier earrings that suited my long, thin neck.

I wore perfume, and lipstick.

My transformation was complete!

"I wish I could be glamorous like you," said young girls to me.

"But you can be too" I cried!

Everyone was charmed by my femininity and modesty and conventional attire, and I radiated happiness and peace.

I interacted more easily and joyously with people.

I could kiss people on the cheek and cradle babies in my arms.

People loved it that I wasn't trying to be "sexy", but that I was being traditional and modest, and looked like a happy, young Parsi lady instead.

They were relieved that I wasn't conducting myself as a sex object, as so many unfortunate transgendered do, ending up as cabaret dancers or in Las Vegas, or - worst of all - as prostitutes in order to keep body and soul together.

Once again, I was blessed, and the hand of God was on me.

God has been very kind to me.

Afterwards, people told me, even Consuls of foreign countries, that they had observed how decorously I walked home from the Indo-American Society after dark, and past the streets behind the Taj Mahal Hotel, where foreign and as well as expensive Indian prostitutes plied their trade, and how they saw me being solicited and how I quietly continued walking, ignoring the Johns.

I learned that this was another side to being a woman in India - that is if you were a young woman walking unescorted after dark.

Men also treated me differently. They brought me gifts of perfume and flowers and opened doors for me and treated me like a lady and took me out to dinner. Decent, respectable bachelors, (I would never allow a married man to do so unless his wife came along too) and I enjoyed being treated at last as the woman that I was.

But money was running seriously short, and I had to start saving all over again from scratch.

So, though I had been approached by several magazines to write about my "sex change" (as it was called in those days, rather than transgender surgery) I finally picked "Imprint", India's most serious literary magazine. They were kind enough to pay me two thousand rupees - a sizable sum in those days for a magazine article.

I was surprised by how many people read that article!

It was an all-India magazine, and that issue was sold out.

Years later, when I was already settled in the US, a distinguished music lover, music critic and journalist, and a scion of the aristocratic Parsi family the Wadias, who were ship builders for the East India Company, wrote and told me that he had read the article when he was twenty.

And so did a very dear French student, Kushala Salian, who now lives and works in England.

As a result of the article, the editor received a large stash of letters, which kept coming.

They were from people in a similar plight (including born women who could not have periods and therefore their families could not find husbands for them) and I replied conscientiously and caringly to each and every one of them and regarded it as my sacred duty, just as I regard my teaching.

It took me months.

The letters kept coming.

They were addressed to the editor of "Imprint" with a request to forward them to me.

They were letters begging for more information and help and were not "letters to the editor."

The editor kept calling me every few weeks, asking me to pick up another batch of letters.

As a result of my article in "Imprint" I received hundreds of letters begging for help. I scrupulously answered each and every one of them, and I also preserved the letters.

But I left home in 1986, and the flat at 61 Wodehouse Road reverted to the landlord in 1991 when my mother died.

My brother went to Bombay and took whatever he wanted and left the rest to go to the landfill - the letters I had saved, along with hundreds of books (including music books), memorabilia, my journalistic writings, my certificates, and photographs, for none of which he cared.

Even the black dust to which they turned is long since gone.

So, I will have to write this entirely from memory.

One of the letters was from the brother of a girl in north India. The family had not been able to find a husband for her because she was 20 and had still not had a period, nor had she developed breasts.

I suggested that they take her to a gynaecologist who could put her on a course of hormone therapy.

A few months later I received a letter from her grateful brother who informed me that she had started to menstruate, and her breasts were developing.

A success story!

Needless to say, in all such cases their profuse expressions of gratitude and thanks, calling me everything from a lifesaver to an angel.

But I knew only too well that I was none of these things!

All I was doing was giving back to life what life had given to me.

Or, to word it differently, I was trying to repay in a small measure my debt to God.

Another letter was from a young woman who had always felt that she was really a boy.

As she was from Bombay, I invited her to come and see me.

As she was telling me about herself, I couldn't help noticing that all her gestures were totally male - stiff and manly.

She told me how much she hated her breasts, how she wished that she could have had a hairy chest, and leave her top two shirt buttons open, to proudly show her hairy chest.

I felt the whole time that I was in the presence of a boy and not a girl. The ambience around her was completely and authentically male, even though she had a girl's voice, small breasts, and smooth cheeks.

I told her about testosterone injections (unlike estrogen, testosterone cannot be taken orally as well).

They would, in a matter of months, give her facial hair. And if she shaved, it would grow back thicker, and she would develop a greenish shadow on her chin and her cheeks, as men have.

Her voice would deepen and sound male.

I warned her that this change would be irreversible, and if she wanted to go back to living as a woman, her vocal cords would not change even if she took oestrogen.

I gave her the good news that she would soon also develop chest hair and hair on her arms and legs.

In other words, she would acquire all the attributes and undergo all the swift changes that boys undergo within one year of entering puberty.

Her breasts would shrink, and if she wished, she could have a mastectomy to have them removed and have a totally flat chest. She could also undergo a total hysterectomy, so she would stop having periods (a mark of femininity that she hated in herself). But of course, she would then never be able to get pregnant.

"Motherhood is the ultimate expression of femininity," she laughed. "Getting pregnant is the very last thing I want!"

She was overjoyed by the information that I gave her.

Then I gave her the bad news.

Unlike male-to-female surgery, where a vagina is fairly easy to create, the creation of an erectile penis is well-nigh impossible.

She reacted just as I had hoped she would: "It's not about sex! It's about living as a man! Living my life as the man that I really am inside."

Before he left, I honestly told him that in my mind he was totally a boy and that was how I perceived him.

He thanked me warmly, but I never heard from him again, so I cannot say if his story had a happy ending or not. I did not think about it then because I was so happy living my new life as Farah.

But one cannot help wondering about and feeling sad about this strange and incurable condition called transgenderism.

Trans gendered are on a scale of one to ten, and I was a ten. But those much lower down on the scale (I am now speaking only of male to female) even manage to marry (a woman) and beget a child! Those cases are, frankly, totally beyond my comprehension.

But it was explained to me that gender issues are not always in black and white, as it was in my case.

I was one of the more fortunate ones.

Today they talk of a "spectrum" of gender identity.

Nor are all transitions as successful as mine.

Ever since my surgery, I have been able to live my life totally as a woman, and unless I told people, they never guessed my past.

But there are tragic instances where their maleness is all too obvious, and they speak with a male voice, and these cases are heartbreaking.

I will say it once again - God has been very kind to me!

Then there was an Anglo-Indian boy - so light-skinned that he looked European - who I also guided, and after a year on hormone therapy, she went to Dr. Keswani and completed his transition.

I even visited her in Masina Hospital after her surgery.

She would come to see me from time to time.

Unfortunately, she had a male voice, which could not change, and when another friend dropped in while she was at my place, she did not open her mouth from the moment I introduced her till the moment she left.

Later, when I asked her about it, she said, "As soon as I speak, it is a dead giveaway."

How very sad is that!

One of the weirdest, and surely the saddest, cases of all, was that of a Gujarati journalist.

He did not want to transition. He came to see me only because he needed to tell his story to someone, and he felt that I was the one person in the world he could tell it to, and that I would not judge him.

He had a wife and children and was a freelance film journalist.

"But I am not like you, Miss Farah," he said with a shy smile.

"You are totally honest, but I get paid a small monthly stipend by the Bollywood actors and actresses to keep them in the news and write about them as often as possible. So, I just make up stories about them."

This came as news to me!

But I did not judge him!

I understood that he had to do what he did in order to support himself and his family.

But this was not what he had come to tell me.

He told me that from time to time he had this uncontrollable urge to dress as a woman and go and work in the "hijra" section of Bombay's Red Light district, which is hell on earth.

There are poor Nepali and Indian girls in what are called "cages" because they are forced to work in brothels in pain of death.

And the darkest section is where "hijras" or eunuchs work.

Obviously, the clientele here must be homosexual. But they are the poorest of the poor.

I was aghast as to why he would want to humiliate and mortify himself like that. It was clearly an extreme case of masochism and self-hate.

But I hid my feelings from him and kept quiet, nodded with my head bowed, and absorbed the pain that he had shared with me.

He added that when he was working in a brothel, he called himself Radha (his real name was Rakesh).

Before he left, he thanked me, and said, "I needed to tell someone. I knew you would not judge me."

"Who am I to judge anyone?" I asked him sincerely.

People had accepted me for who I was. Then who was I to judge anyone who was different?

A few weeks later, the phone rang, and a voice said, "Miss Farah, I am calling from a pay phone just to let you know that I am Radha just now."

"Be careful Radha. Be safe. God bless you."

This must surely be one of the saddest stories in the world!

I will end with the story of a young Parsi boy called Adi Banaji - alias "Aida."

He included a photo of himself, and he was very personable.

He had dropped out of Cathedral School, the most expensive school in Bombay.

His father was India's most famous eye surgeon and oculist and had been flown to Delhi to perform cataract surgery on the President.

Adi lived with his parents on Worli Hill - one of the most exclusive neighbourhoods in Bombay.

I replied to his letter, and he wrote back saying, "Thank God there are Good Samaritans like you who extend a helping hand to those who have fallen by the wayside."

I invited him to come and see me.

After receiving my reply to his letter, he had already started on a course of hormone treatment and tweezed his eyebrows. He came in high heels and tight jeans.

Piroja Aunty next door (the same dear Piroja Aunty who had allowed us to walk through her flat for a year, to access ours, when our common balcony had been torn down and who had run her fingers tenderly through my hair as I lay in bed with measles at the age of seven) was standing on her balcony when he rang our doorbell and was amused.

When I told her who he was she said, "Dr. Banaji's son?"

The next time he came to see me, I introduced Adi (high heels, tight jeans, eye shadow, feather boa and all) to her, and she was delighted.

Adi's transition was swift, as like me, he was naturally feminine.

But unlike me, he was very high-spirited and flamboyant.

So, it was embarrassing when she sometimes encountered me on the street and came running across the road, calling, "Faroo! Faroo!" (her pet name for me) to my modestly clad self-wrapped in a conventional sari.

She still hadn't had the surgery when I left India but wrote to me years later that Dr. Keswani had performed the surgery on her, and her transition was complete.

I was very, very happy for her.

A distinguished filmmaker, Riyad Wadia, grandson of the founder of the famous Wadia Studios, and scion of the great shipbuilding family, made a documentary on Aida before her surgery, titled, "A Mermaid Called Aida."

This catapulted her to world fame, and after her surgery, she received several proposals for marriage, including one from a tall, handsome Dane.

They got married and she lived in Denmark for two years, before returning to India because she was homesick.

Thanks to the internet, I found her phone number in Goa, a hippy paradise on the west coast of India, where she bought herself a large flat with her inheritance after her father's death.

She was as high-spirited as ever!

"I lived for two years in Denmark with my Danish husband, and I did not learn a word of Danish!" she told me triumphantly.

Now if that is not a mind-blowing record, I don't know what is!

She died of hepatitis C at the tragically young age of fifty.

This is just a sample of the hundreds of suffering souls who reached out to me and whom I did my best to help.

19 - My Three Trips to Kashmir

Having written about the central event in my life - my transformation - please go back with me in time to my last six years as Farokh.

I skipped those intervening years because I experienced so much in my 32 years as Farokh that I felt that I would never get to my transformation, which meant so much to me, and which, I felt, that you too must have been getting impatient to read about! So, I took the liberty of skipping ahead. But now I must fill in the blanks. So come, take my hand, and let us wander peacefully together through India in the early 1970's.

Among the many things I did after returning from Ethiopia, to explore the city of my birth more fully, was to become a member of the Royal Asiatic Society. It was housed in what had once been the Town Hall, built in the late 1700s in the Roman style, with a long flight of steps leading up to it, and a stately pillared front, and it was located next to the original fort of Bombay which is now the naval base I.N.S. Angre.

I remember, once, when I came out of this august building and needed to open my first automatic umbrella to protect myself from the hot sun, I noticed an out-of-work young man idling on the top step, and as we made eye contact, I stretched out my arm and pressed the button on my umbrella. As it flew open, he said "wah!" (wow!) and we both laughed.

Inside, the Asiatic Library was all twenty-foot ceilings and marble statues of the Englishmen who founded it, but its real treasures lay in the basement which contained thousands of rare and precious out-of-print books donated by Englishmen from their private collections. It was a privilege indeed to be allowed to borrow them and take them home! One of them was a book on Kashmir by the great Himalayan explorer, Sir Francis Younghusband, who had also been the Resident at the court of the Maharaja of Kashmir in the early 1900s. The book was lavishly illustrated with beautiful water colours and each one was protected by tissue paper which made my bibliophile heart ache for the great bygone days when these vintage books were printed.

The book, in which Sir Francis described his large garden in every season and meticulously recorded day-by-day temperatures in all the seasons, and Kashmir's flora and fauna, and its priceless shawls and papier-mache work, captivated me, and I longed to go to the fabled Vale of Cashmere (as the Victorians spelt it).

Unlike the rest of India, Kashmir has four seasons, just like Europe.

My trip to Simla in January 1969 to see and experience it for the first time, did not satisfy my appetite for snow, it only whetted it.

So I set off for Kashmir in January 1970. As always, I not only enjoyed the destination but also getting there. First, the historic Frontier Mail to Pathankot on the Pakistan border. (This legendary train used to continue on to Lahore and end at Peshawar at the foot of the Khyber Pass during the days of the Raj, until the partition of India cut its journey short at Pathankot.) Then a bus up the mountains from Pathankot to Srinagar.

The thirty-six-hour train journey by first class was bracing in the winter cold of north India, but the bus ride from Pathankot to Srinagar took two days and one night as we went higher and higher up the foothills of the Pir Panjal range till we reached the Banihal Pass at ten thousand feet. There we had to spend the night in a travellers' stop in a dorm-type situation, sleeping in our sleeping bags (beddings or hold-alls, as they were called in India) because there had been a heavy snowfall that the snow ploughs had not yet been able to clear.

When the caravan of the Mughal emperors approached this pass each summer with their horses and elephants and convoys of soldiers and all the paraphernalia of a great court moving from the plains to the mountains, the hermits who lived on these great heights cautioned silence, for fear of triggering avalanches.

At Srinagar the bus was surrounded by clamouring touts, but fortunately, I was taken to the Nedou's Hotel - a grand old hotel built by an Austrian hotelier during the Raj.

But the very next morning I was eager to leave for Gulmarg because Srinagar is at 5,000 feet, and there was no snow. Gulmarg, at 8,500 feet was being developed into a ski resort, and I had read that it got anywhere from five to fifteen feet of snow each winter.

I took a bus from Srinagar to Tangmarg, which is at the foot of Gulmarg (Meadow of Flowers, as the Mughal emperors named it, because that is what it becomes in Spring), along an avenue of ancient poplars planted by empress Nur Jehan (Light of the World).

There I was surrounded by horsemen who took tourists up to Gulmarg on their horses. I picked a sweet boy, barely eighteen, called Gulam (Slave) and his horse was called Duty Boy.

All the way up, he spoke to me in his "native woodnotes wild."

"Have you come here to siki?" (which is how he pronounced ski).

"No. I have come to see the mountains and the trees and the snow."

"But what is there in the mountains and the trees? As for the snow, we used to hate it, because it is so cold, but now we love it because it will bring tourists from all over the world, who want to siki. I wish I could see a big city like Bombay!"

Gulmarg did not disappoint! It was buried in snow. There were two hotels of which only one was open. The newly built Hotel Highlands Park was designed like a Swiss chalet with a huge scenic window in the lounge with a stunning view of Apharwat which soared a thousand feet above Gulmarg.

I had arrived at dusk, and I was taken to a cozy room that the receptionist had assigned me.

As I was unpacking my clothes, a hotel employee of the hotel came and said, "You cannot stay here!"

"Why?"

"You cannot stay here because the owner, Major Benji, wants you to stay in a suite of rooms."

"But I don't want a suite of rooms! I can't afford a suite of rooms."

"No, no, Major Benji will charge you the same as for this room. The hotel is empty."

Wow!

The next morning, I met Major Benji in the lounge and thanked him warmly. He had studied at Sandhurst, sported a military moustache, and spoke with a posh British accent. He was the grandson of Mr. Nedou, the Austrian founder of Nedou's Hotel where I had spent a night in Srinagar, and his mother was Kashmiri.

He grew convivial over a glass of brandy: "Punjabi women come here in their diamonds. Who shows off one's diamonds at a ski resort? Ha! Ha!"

The "bearer" assigned to look after me was a tall and very

handsome Kashmiri, and not at all like the typical beaked-nosed, ugly, avaricious one. His name was Gulam (Slave - what else?) and when he was helping me to unpack my bag the previous night in the suite of rooms assigned to me (actually, it was a detached log cabin) he told me, "When you wake up, just call my name from the door of your room and I will bring you your morning tea. I live in the servants' quarters directly up from your room."

It snowed heavily that night and I woke up to a winter wonderland with the pines buried in snow.

I was transfixed!

I was so happy that I had an out-of-body experience.

I forgot where I was or who I was, and my whole soul was in my eyes.

I became one with the landscape before me!

But soon I began to tremble from the cold and my soul returned to my body. The thought of that piping hot tea and biscuits now felt really good, and I called, "Gulam! Gulam!"

I felt stupid standing at my door and shouting "Slave! Slave!" first thing in the morning.

He came running and said that he would bring me my tea in a jiffy, which he did.

He also had a fire lit in the fireplace.

"How much will I have to pay for the fire?"

"You don't have to pay for the fire. Major Benji never charges for a fire. You can have a fire in your room whenever you want."

Whee!

I went to the dining room for breakfast (very English - porridge, eggs, toast, butter, and the finest raw, unfiltered Himalayan honey), and the bearer proudly pointed out to me that he had warmed my plate. Oh, dear! If he could only see my lower-middle-class self in my dilapidated building at 61 Wodehouse Road, would he still treat me with so much respect?

I shared a brandy with Major Benji, (brandy after breakfast - sheer decadence! - but I was on vacation, and had the temerity to ask him to join me, which he graciously did, without batting an eyelid. That is what aristocrats do. They never shame you.

I wrote a letter to Jer Jussawala - Dear Jer Jussawala, that magnificent woman with whom I have already acquainted you. I wrote to her that I was so happy after what I saw when I woke up that morning, that if I were informed that I had lost all my savings I would not feel the least sadness.

When I returned to Bombay, Jer told me, "Do you realise that you were having an epiphany that morning when you wrote that letter to me in Gulmarg?"

I have had an epiphany only twice after that. Once, when I was sitting in the twilight on the twelfth-floor terrace of Dolphin, gazing at the panorama spread out before me - the moonlight glimmering on the sea, the lights of ships at anchor twinkling on the water, and the utter peace and stillness!

And the third and the last one in New York as Robert Clere, with whom I was then in love, and I were walking after attending a concert in Carnegie Hall, past Christmas lights and decorations on Fifth Avenue, after having shared a glass of wine and a baked potato together.

But epiphanies are like the "hour of splendour in the grass, glory in the flower," and we can never bring them back. One can only "take comfort in what is left behind."

So let us move on. Around mid-morning I set out for a walk and as I was tramping through the snow, two soldiers on skis, came up to me, just at the foot of a low bluff and said, "You cannot walk here!"

"Why not?"

"Because you are headed straight for an icy stream that is buried under the snow."

Oops!

"Oh, thank you!"

"Our officer, Major Chauhan invites you for a cup of tea on the ski slope."

Wow!

I followed them to where Major Chauhan and his colleagues were enjoying hot tea from chipped white cups (my Indian readers can easily visualise them because they are ubiquitous in India).

Major Chauhan turned out to be the head of the High Altitude Warfare School (it was 1971, just nine years since the Indo-Chinese war of 1962, which was fought- and lost - at high altitudes) and was instructing his fellow officers and jawans (soldiers) in skiing.

He offered to race me down the ski slope on his skis while I ran down and offered me the advantage of starting halfway down the slope.

"Ready, get set, go!" he shouted, and I started running like mad and reached the bottom of the slope with no sign of him. I looked up and saw him still standing at the top of the slope, slapping his thigh, and laughing, along with his colleagues!

He invited me to visit them at the Officer's Club that evening.

Writing about this fifty years later, I can't believe how incredibly lucky I was!

All these wonderful people! Let me never bemoan my unloving mother because God sent me so many other compensations! The love that should have come to me from my father, mother, and brother, came instead, from "the kindness of strangers."

There was an old upright piano (no doubt dating back to the Raj era) in the Officer's Club, and I played for Major Chauhan and a couple of young Captains who were the only other people there, besides the soldiers who waited on us. More brandy, of course, this time on the house.

They then offered to teach me to ice skate on the skating rink next to the club. I put on my skates, and with an officer supporting me on each side, hobbled to the centre of the rink where they suddenly left me and said "Bye!" They roared with laughter as I crawled back on my hands and knees.

When I returned to Bombay, Major Chauhan sent me a little plaque in the form of a pyramid, saying "with compliments from the High Altitude Warfare School."

I was so proud of it, and considered it such a great honour, that I put it on my piano, where it stayed for fifteen years till until I left home in 1986.

Now every atom of it is gone after it landed in a landfill in Bombay after I was gone.

"Sic transit gloria mundi." (Thus passes the glory of this world.)

On my last evening in Gulmarg, as I was following the coolie who was carrying my bag, a long line of Himalayan peaks - the highest peaks of the Pir Panjal range, all over twenty thousand feet, with the highest, Nanga Parbat, at the centre - all of which had remained hidden behind clouds during my entire five days in Gulmarg, suddenly appeared, glittering white, red, and golden in the light of the setting sun. The suddenness and the surprise of it took my breath away! I stood transfixed, while the coolie marched on.

"Behold us!" they seemed to be saying in all their majesty, like an assembly of gods.

It was Gulmarg's parting gift to me on that magical trip.

(2)

I returned to Kashmir eighteen months later, in May of 1971, to experience it in spring, and again in November of the same year, to see the autumn colours, which I had never seen except in books and Swiss calendars.

After my winter trip to Gulmarg, which cast a spell on me with its beauty, I figured that if I went back to Kashmir in May, I could experience both late spring and early summer.

Oh, how wrong I was!

Because of its lower latitude (thirty degrees north), spring is short and swift in Kashmir.

The crocuses and daffodils arrive in March, and the tulips in April, and are gone by the end of the month.

So, when I arrived in Srinagar in mid-May, it was full-blown summer.

The Chinars (the great Kashmir Plane trees whose leaves resemble the Maple) were in full leaf, and it was surprisingly hot - about 25 to 28 degrees Celsius. (Srinagar is at an altitude of five thousand feet.)

At the bus terminal, I was mobbed by hotel touts who received a commission for every customer they brought to the hotel. They even grabbed my arm and tried to make me go with them. I was frightened but remained firm. I had made a reservation at the vintage Nedou's Hotel, redolent of the Raj, where I had spent one night in January of the previous year.

Now the empty flowerpots that had lined the broad steps that led up to the large entrance hall and reception desk, with a grand oak staircase leading to the second floor, were filled with flowering plants.

The hotel was so large, that despite the summer tourist rush, it didn't feel at all crowded.

I was given a large room with access to the broad veranda which wrapped the hotel on both floors.

There I fed sugar cubes that came with my morning tea to the perky little "bulbuls" (a finch-like bird, beloved in Persian poetry for its rhapsodic spring song) who came and pecked at them fearlessly as I put them on the white tablecloth.

After that, I went for a long walk on the Bund, along Dal Lake, with the thousand-foot Solomon's Peak towering above it. The lake was so still that all the surrounding hills and poplars were reflected in it.

There was a dock where one rented "shikaras" - the humble Kashmiri "gondola" in which one reclined and gazed at the sky and the clouds and the mountains and let one's fingers trail in the cool water.

On my way back to the hotel, I stopped at the dock to experience a short shikara ride. They had names like, "Honeymoon Delight, With Springs" whatever that means. As usual, I was mobbed by shikarawalas who assailed me with typical Kashmiri ferocity. I chose a clean-shaven young man whose name was - you guessed it! - Gulam (Slave).

He was pleasant enough, and as the oars created gentle ripples in the still surface, he started talking about what huge tips he had received. To lower his great expectations, I told him that I was a humble teacher who had saved all year to make this trip. He couldn't care less. In his mind, if I could visit Kashmir, I had money!

I gave him a small tip when I disembarked but engaged him for the next day at his request.

When I arrived at the dock, he came running up the steps shouting, "That is my customer!"

Dal Lake is surprisingly large and has different sections. There are floating vegetable gardens, and on closer inspection, there are underwater plants gently waving as the shikara goes by.

Along its further banks are anchored large "boat houses" where the tourists on the highest budget stay with their families. They have decks with lounge chairs, and I could just imagine what it would be like to watch the sunset behind Solomon's Peak while sipping a "sundowner", as the English called them.

But even on tranquil Dal Lake, one cannot escape the bane of Kashmir. Shopkeepers hastily rowed up to my shikara and offered me carpets and shawls at astronomical prices. In vain did I tell them that I wasn't on the lake to shop. All I wanted was some peace and quiet! All I wanted was to be left alone!

Finally, Gulam yelled at them in Kashmiri, in which I recognised a couple of choice obscenities, and they left.

Peace and tranquillity returned.

In the middle of the lake was a tiny island with four great "Chinar" trees on it.

It was called "Chaar Chinar" (Four Chinars).

But the interesting thing about it was that Gulam told me that Jesus (who he called "Eesa") had preached on the island.

I had read in Sir Francis Younghusband's book on Kashmir that during the "hidden years" of Jesus' life - that is, the years between when he was twelve years old and surprised the scholars in the Temple by arguing with them, and the age of thirty, when he started his Ministry, he had come to Kashmir and even gone as far as Tibet where he had studied ancient Hindu and Buddhist texts in remote monasteries.

This was a pleasant fantasy that Theosophists loved, and that dear Jer Jussawala quite readily believed, but as much as I loved and respected her, I couldn't share this belief.

I believe that nothing is written about Jesus in the Gospels about what he did between the ages of twelve and thirty is because he was quietly practicing his trade as a carpenter during those years, until, at thirty, he felt that it was time to begin his Ministry

But the secluded little island beckoned, and I asked Gulam if he could row us up to it. "Of course," he replied, "we can even visit the island!"

In the centre of the island was a tiny pavilion where we sat and ate the delicious lunch of mutton and cheese sandwiches that the hotel had wrapped for me at my request.

From one of the Chinars, a cuckoo called, deepening the silence. Unfortunately, even in that hallowed place all that Gulam could talk about was money.

On our way back, the wind picked up, and the large but shallow and tranquil lake was suddenly covered with waves. They didn't look so ominous to me, as I had grown up by the sea and seen its monsoon fury every year. But Gulam knew the lake that he had grown up on and was visibly frightened. He stood up and used his pole to stabilise the shikara and battled the waves.

"Please stay still, and don't move!" he cried.

We reached the dock safely thanks to his skill and I tipped him handsomely - though, I am sure, not measuring up to his lofty expectations.

I remember him fondly because he too spoke with "native

woodnotes wild."

The next morning, I met a cheerful old French lady in the lobby.

She looked up at the grand staircase and said, "One imagines women in ball gowns coming down those stairs (the hotel did have a large but by now dilapidated ballroom), and officers in uniform."

At that very moment, Major Chauhan called from the landing, "Farookh!"

"There's your army officer," I told the astonished French lady.

Though Major Chauhan was in khaki, and not in scarlet and gold as she must have surely imagined the officers to be back then.

We were both very happy to see each other again and I introduced the old French lady to him.

Just then a fire truck arrived, and Veeru (Major Chauhan) and I watched anxiously as they attached a hose to the fire hydrant. But the French lady was surprisingly insouciant and laughed and cheered: "Here come the pompiers!"

Luckily, the fire, which was in the kitchen, was quickly extinguished.

With Major Chauhan was a Sikh officer and the two of them went trout fishing and came back with some trout. Veeru gallantly presented it to the French lady (I was still Farokh, alas!) and she asked, "Ow do I do with this truite?"

"You can give it to the chef and he will cook it for you," explained Major Chauhan courteously.

But Gulmarg beckoned. It was uncomfortably warm in Srinagar (though nothing like the ferocious heat in the plains at that time of year) and I wanted to see Gulmarg's summer face.

Once again, Gulmarg did not disappoint.

On the way up, on horseback, the groom asked me to dismount when he we halfway up, so he could take his horse to a sparkling stream of melted snow.

But the horse just stood there, refusing to lower his head and drink as the groom expected him to.

"He is not thirsty," said the groom, and we continued climbing.

I understood with full force the meaning of "you can take a horse to water, but you can't make it drink."

(As every parent and teacher knows.)

Gulmarg was covered with emerald, green grass and a variety of wildflowers - lupins, artist's paint brush, bluebells, and a host of others whose names I did not know.

I walked by the old bungalows where British families had spent their summers.

Years later I saw the bungalows again at the end of that great film about India before and after Independence, in the final scene where we see a posthumous image of Shashi Kapoor listening to his English mistress playing Schumann, through the window of one of these bungalows.

My heart ached for times gone by and I took my face in my hands and I wept!

I stayed for four days at the old Nedou's Hotel (a smaller, mountain version of the grand old Nedou's in Srinagar) as Hotel Highlands Park was full.

The Nedou's was much older, and belonged to Major Benji's older brother, Colonel Nedou.

Though just as English as his younger brother, Colonel Nedou was gentler and more mellow.

On my second morning, I decided to climb the thousand-foot Apharwat that towered over Gulmarg, so Colonel Nedou very kindly sent one of his men with me.

On the way up we passed small snow fields, and I watched entranced as a little fawn pranced on one of them.

But on the way down, storm clouds gathered out of nowhere, and there was a fierce hailstorm.

"You must be very brave now!" said my companion, and held my hand to stabilise me as we ran downhill as fast as possible. There were no trees and no shelter, and I took a real beating from the hail.

I was shivering from the cold, but we made it safely back to the meadow, and the sun came out and shone sweetly as though nothing had happened!

I developed a new respect for mountain weather.

I have seen it replicated several times where I now live, but, fortunately I have been able to watch it from the safety of my covered balcony.

I tipped my companion, and taking his hand in both of mine, thanked him warmly.

"I'm glad you are safe," he said with a big smile and left with the sense of a duty well done.

I changed into dry clothes and a snug sweater and felt that a brandy was in order. (Gulmarg seems to be the place to sip brandy!)

I found Colonel Nedou sitting at a table on the lawn and asked him if I could join him.

He was relieved to see me and said, "I was worried about you when that hailstorm came!"

I thanked him for having given me such an excellent guide without whom I would have been very frightened indeed and asked him if he would join me in enjoying a brandy.

He readily accepted and we chatted amicably.

"You know, my grandfather always said, 'There are only three things that a hotel needs: Location, Location Location!'"

Like his brother Benji, he too complained about "the nouveau rich Punjabis who come to Gulmarg these days, and prefer my brother's flashy new hotel, Highlands Park, to good old Nedou's."

I refrained from telling him that I too had stayed at Highlands two winters ago. But then the Nedou's Hotel had been closed for the winter and Highlands Park was the only hotel that was open, and I was its only guest!

That evening I played for him on the old upright piano in the lounge, on which I am sure that many an Englishman and Englishwoman had played in better days. I played a couple of waltzes by Chopin, and he asked me if I could play "Besame Mucho", a song that was very popular back then. I too like the song and had learned to play it by ear.

He had tears in his eyes when I finished playing it.

And on that note, I shall take leave of Gulmarg for the last and final time.

(3)

In November of the following year, I went back to Srinagar to see the autumn colours in Kashmir. The Poplars and the Chinars were almost bare, and the Chinars just had a few, dead, brown leaves clinging to their branches. So, after two days, I decided to leave.

20 - The Saga of Little Akbar

Less than a year after my operation, a little boy came into my life, and he became my son.

While I was still Farokh, I was living with any number of suppressed emotions, including my strong maternal feelings, but now there was no obstacle to my feeling them.

He was ten years old. His name was Akbar, and he was from a small village in Gujarat.

My mother was always in a perpetual search for servants as the turnover was high because of her treatment of them. Akbar's uncle was a "chowkidar" (watchman) of a building near ours and he brought little Akbar to my mother.

He was the most innocent and adorable little ten-year-old you ever saw!

After two or three days, he had learned to make a cup of tea.

So, as I was writing a film review at my desk, I called, "Akbar!"

He came running and asked, "Ji, memsahibji?" ("Yes, madam?")

I smiled at him and said softly, "Tea, please."

"Hain?" he asked.

So, I told him in Hindi to please bring me a cup of tea.

"Ji, memsahibji," he said eagerly.

It was then that I loved him for life.

Till today, when someone makes a mistake while playing a piece, I say "Hain?" in homage to little Akbar.

He had been a good child to his parents. When his mother cried that she had nothing to cook for the evening meal, he would run into the small adjacent forest of thorny acacias and thorn bushes, gather firewood, sell it in the bazaar, and with the money, buy some rice for his mother to cook.

One evening he saw a shadow, and it frightened him because he thought it was a ghost (no doubt he had heard more than one ghost story).

He was terrified, and the village doctor decided that he was possessed and recommended that he should be beaten to drive the devil out.

I learned this in 1977 when he was ten years old, and my blood is still boiling as I type this!

Thank God, that forty- four years later (at the age of 54) he is a grandfather, and has two grown-up sons, (Icon and Asif) and a most wonderful daughter (Asma).

As a result of this experience, he had become a somnambulist, and my mother let him sleep in our back room, near her bed (instead of the distant servants' room where he would be afraid). He would get up in the middle of the night and stand next to her bed with his eyes closed, rocking from side to side, and mumble "Mmmmm....... I have to make tea........"

This just broke my heart!

I tried to teach him the English alphabet, but he told my mother, "Tell memsahibji to stop teaching me, or I'll run away."

Terrified, I started buying him toys instead.

He was full of mischief and told my mother the most obscene jokes (learned from elders in his village), but not to me, because I guess he respected me too much (he saw me teaching all day, playing the piano etc.).

When the monsoon came, he would run downstairs with a bucket, to catch the water dripping from the eaves, for the sheer joy of it!

When I told him he didn't have to do that, he made it clear that he wanted to.

So, I got him a plastic raincoat and hat.

Every evening he would operate the hand pump when water was released in our area for an hour, filling the huge tub, while running every few minutes to look at the black and white TV with only one channel, which also ran only in the evening!

One day I got a mannequin's head on which to put a waist-length wig that I had bought.

When he saw that he said softly "Boodha" (Ghost).

I immediately threw away the mannequin head and kept the wig as best I could without a stand for it.

I got him a transistor radio on which he listened to Bollywood songs while taking his afternoon nap in the servants' room. It was the only room left in the outhouse which did not have a ceiling fan, so I installed one there at last. Akbar loved it, so Mummy went and switched it off all the time.

It was sheer malice because I was paying the electricity bill, and I had a big fight with her over it.

But she did manage to make Akbar anorexic.

This is how she did it.

I used to put little pieces of goat meat in his plate of curry rice from my own plate. She made nasty comments about it, till one day Akbar stopped accepting them from me. He also started to eat less and less and became hollow-cheeked and skin and bone in his teens, when he had been a beautiful ten-year-old when he came to work for us. I hope her Karma caught up with her when she finally died.

Sometime during the next couple of years, his toothless father and mother came to see him, and I was overjoyed. A couple of years later he got a letter that his father had died. I offered to get him anything he wanted, and he asked for a parrot. I paid for it, of course, as well as Daddy's taxi fare to and from Crawford Market. Daddy made sure to get one that did not speak. He too shared in my mother's karma of abusing Akbar because I loved the child. Though he was far better than her, his hands were not entirely clean either. He joined her in malice against me after I became Farah and they hurt me in every possible way they could, day and night.

I wish I had gone myself to buy him the parrot!

Dear Piroja Aunty next door had become very old and started to fall. She would call out Akbar's name and he would go and lift her up.

At night it was my turn.

She would sit in her rocking chair by the balcony door and start calling, "Farah! Farah!" at around 10 P.M. Her only son, Hoshang Uncle, who was middle-aged, went out every evening and returned home late.

"Yes, Piroja Aunty?"

"Where is Hosi?"

"He has gone out."

"Will he come back?"

"Of course, he will come back!"

"Thank you," (with a grateful smile).

At about one in the morning, I would hear him come home and open the squeaky balcony door.

"What time is it?" Piroja Aunty would ask.

"It is nine-thirty."

"Don't you lie to me, or I will slap you and smash your teeth."

This is what she had said to him since he was a child, so as not to spoil him. She was widowed very young and was a single parent, but her much older husband had left her a nest egg, so she didn't have to work.

She was skin and bone, and Hoshang Uncle would bend down and lift her gently out of the rocking chair and carry her to her four-poster bed.

In his teens, Akbar developed a passion for Hindi films, so I would give him a couple of afternoons off every week, as well as money for movie tickets.

One day a policeman caught him because he suspected that Akbar was selling tickets in the black market.

Thank God, he let him go, or we would never have known what happened to Akbar!

I immediately sat down at my desk and wrote a letter, "To whomsoever it may concern: This is our loyal servant Akbar S. Sandhu. He has served us loyally for many years. Please call us at 212-376. Farah Rustom (followed by all my degrees), Jehangir Rustom, and Jer Rustom."

I told him to carry the letter with him wherever he went.

But soon he began to demand more and more pay raises.

I explained to him that I was a working woman, that we were middle-class people, and that I was already paying him as much as the rich people at Cuffe Parade were paying their servants.

He insisted on leaving.

I begged him not to.

When he took his meagre belongings (his clothes and his transistor radio) in a small metal trunk, I pleaded with him not to go! Nay, I begged! I told him that our door would always be open to him whenever he returned.

But he went.

And when I closed the door behind him, I went and sat on my sofa utterly defeated, empty and spent.

Weeks went by and I felt empty and worried about him day and night.

Then one evening the doorbell rang, and there stood Akbar!

I welcomed him as the father welcomed his prodigal Son in the Bible.

He sat and watched TV.

I served him tea and some food.

He was quiet and subdued.

I begged him to stay and not leave.

But he said he had to.

When I asked him where he lived and what he did, he was not forthcoming.

But he promised to return.

He returned once more, and the next time after that he stayed!

It was only then that he told me that a gang of drug dealers had been using him to carry drugs.

I realised then that it was nothing less than a miracle of God, that he was still alive - that he was not dead or in prison - but safely home!

He never demanded higher wages again.

He never threatened to leave again.

He must have been through hell.

And unimaginable fear!

He had gone from being a child to being a man - and not just a man, but a sad and wise one - in a matter of weeks and months.

To fast forward now, I left Bombay in May of 1986.

Before leaving for the airport, I touched my parents' feet and thanked them for everything that they had done for me.

I knew that I was never going to come back or ever see them again.

I had taken as much abuse from them as I could.

My father died in December of the same year.

He was knocked down by a car on Marine Drive and killed.

He had been suffering from Parkinson's and my heart ached when I saw his hands tremble.

When I told one of my students, a professor of Political Science at CU, about how he died, she said, "Perhaps just as well. He would have become bedridden and demented."

I would not wish such a death on my father.

He died in harness, without suffering from cancer or other long-drawn-out, painful, and debilitating illness, lying on his death bed for months.

He died within minutes, with blood pouring from his head.

I hope that I too die in harness, as he did!

I want to be a worthy daughter of my father.

He left his hometown, Poona, and made a life for himself in

Bombay.

I did not want to grow old in the apartment that he had found in 1938 and lived in till his death because of the Rent Control Act.

I wanted to make a life for myself just as he had.

And I did.

So did my brother.

He, in New York, and I, far away elsewhere in the same country.

In that, we are both worthy children of our father.

I sent my mother money every month just as my brother did.

I talked with her on the phone, including with Akbar.

She kept asking when I would return, and to placate her, I said, "Soon."

When I received the telegram that "Mr. J.M. Rustom expired on 6th December" from my father's employer, dear Mr. Agarwal, I was getting ready to play at the Duplex, Greenwich Village's premier cabaret bar.

Numb with shock and grief I walked to work and played.

But the tears kept flowing, and the patrons, who loved my playing, were startled, and one by one they came and asked how I was, and when I told them about the telegram, they said I didn't have to play. But I told them that "the show must go on."

I cried for my father for two years.

I couldn't imagine the world with him not in it.

I would go to the roof of my single-room occupancy, gaze at the not-too-distant Twin Towers, and cry.

All this time, Akbar and his wife Najma looked after my mother. He had married an eighteen-year-old girl from his village (he was nineteen) and she was wide-eyed and anxious when she met me for the first time. I embraced her and said, "You are my daughter-in-law" (Tu meri bahu hai) and she visibly relaxed.

My mother outlived my father by four years.

The last time I called, my boyfriend Robert Clere was with me, and I asked him to speak with her too. My mother started to cry immediately because she knew at once that the game was over.

If I had someone who loved me, I was not going back.

Robert kept saying "Please don't cry" and when he handed the phone back to me, I told my mother that I would call back soon and said, "Bye, bye, Mummy darling," as always.

To my amazement, she for the first time in my life said, "Bye, bye,

Farah darling," and continued to sob while I reluctantly hung up.

What amazed me was that she had never used an endearment while speaking to me ever!

Not ever!

Never!

And she had unexpectedly used the word "darling" to me.

Was this her way of saying goodbye?

Was there just one drop of love for me in her heart for me after all, that even she hadn't been aware of till the last?

I keep hoping against hope that there was!

From that day on my mother stopped eating and died a few weeks later in the Parsi General Hospital.

Dear Jer Jussawala wrote to inform me of her death.

My brother went to Bombay for her funeral at the Tower of Silence but did not write to inform me.

I had to find out from a beloved friend, after all!

He then took whatever he wanted from the flat and tried to "sell" the rented flat for a huge amount (called "pugree" or "key money").

But the landlord's lawyer informed him that the flat was inherited by both of us, and neither of us could prove that we would live in it!

So, lo and behold, I got a letter from my brother, asking me to go to a notary public and send him a certified letter that I was going to return to Bombay and live in my parent's flat.

Firstly, I had no intention of doing so.

I had made a life for myself at great personal cost and was not going to throw it away.

Secondly, he did not even begin the letter with "Dear Farah" - he did not address me at all.

And thirdly, he added, "Since I have been sending our parents money all these years, I will keep all the money from the sale of the flat."

And was there to be no acknowledgement of the fact that he had been able to enjoy his family and his life in America because I stayed with our parents and looked after them for twenty-five years after he left them!

So, I wrote back that I was not going to write an untruthful letter, as I had no intention of returning, and that the landlord had a right to have his flat back at last.

My brother never forgave me for it.

But then, he never forgave me for being born!

So, what difference does it make?

My mother had died without making any provision for Akbar and his wife and their three-year-old son, even though she knew that our rented flat would revert to the landlord, and they would become homeless.

My brother had asked Akbar and his family to stay on as long as possible, to protect the flat till he could sell it.

It is a shame that even Akbar did not send me a letter that my mother had died.

He could easily have had it written by someone.

In India, there are even professional letter writers outside the General Post Office.

When I opened the letter from dear Jer Jussawla saying that "your mother has passed away," I burst into tears!

To my utter amazement, a flood of tears poured down my face.

It must have been biological - a child crying for the loss of its mother.

Because I never cried for her again.

Piroja Aunty had died before I left, of a broken hip.

One evening, I came home at 8.30 P.M. and found an ambulance parked below our balcony. Worried that something had happened to my parents, I rushed up the steps to find paramedics in Piroja Aunty's flat.

I went in and saw her lying on her bed.

"What will happen now?" she asked me, her eyes filled with fear.

"What do you think will happen?! You will get well and return home, of course!"

She smiled and said, "Thank you."

That was the last time I saw her. She died in the Parsi General Hospital a week later.

But when Mummy died, Hoshang Uncle stepped up to the plate. He invited Akbar and his family to stay in his flat. Subsequently, they had two more children, and Hoshang Uncle sent them at his own expense to the Sir Cowasjee Jehangir High School, instead of a free municipal school, where they would have learned nothing.

A man who rented what had been our servants' room got our old 1937 Bell telephone by bribing the appropriate official, and to my great joy, I could call Hoshang Uncle on my own phone number and talk with him and with Akbar and the children, who were growing up fast.

I told Hoshang Uncle, that "there is a place waiting for you in the Seventh and highest Heaven for what you have done for Akbar and his family."

But he loved them all, and they brought light into his lonely life.

As a lonely bachelor, even when Piroja Aunty was alive, he would enter our flat by the back door and cry, "Jehangir Uncle! Jer Aunty! Indira Gandhi has been shot!!"

And Daddy would groan, "Here comes the news bulletin."

In one of the phone conversations when I asked Akbar what my brother had done with my things, he said he didn't know, and added that "there is a difference of day and night between you and him!"

Once, Akbar had called my brother, but since our flat had reverted to the landlord, my brother didn't show the least interest in him.

And no one knows how to be cold like my brother does!

Akbar was humiliated and shocked to the core.

Hoshang Uncle died on 8th November 2012, at the age of 80, surrounded by Akbar and his family, and went to his just reward.

Akbar's daughter Asma emailed me in panic, and we all even spoke on Skype.

But the landlord allowed them to stay!

So, if anyone ever tells you, "No good deed goes unpunished," - don't believe them!

This cynical statement is not true.

It is a just universe, and every good deed receives its just reward, if not in this world, then in the hereafter.

21 - If It's Tuesday, It Must Be Belgium

As long as my parents were alive, I honoured them and never spoke a word against them to anyone, so everyone thought that my mother was really this sweet little lady that she portrayed herself as, so that she could poison their ears against me if they came to see me and I wasn't home.

In New York, I discovered support groups for Adult Children of Dysfunctional Families, and after hearing others share, I was able to open up and talk about my own mother. As she was in Bombay, and no one knew her, I felt that I no longer had to protect her, but could tell my story.

Over the years I learned that there were mothers like mine the world over. To give just one example.

Tatyana, a talented and vibrant Croatian woman whose murals adorn public buildings in several States, and who was my piano student, told me that her mother always called her "ugly, stupid and useless."

"But that's exactly what my mother always called me!" I exclaimed in astonishment.

While my mother's taunts could not destroy my self-esteem as a human being, because I knew who I was, or my faith in my God-given gifts or in my work, thanks to the feedback from the best of people, she did succeed in making me think of myself as "ugly."

And "Useless?"

After all that I had done for her, gratifying her every wish, and after I had devoted the first forty years of my life to win one drop of love or recognition from her!

I used to love talking to my mother as she sat on her bed stuffing tobacco up her nose and asking Akbar to bring her a glass of water, but she always looked bored and uninterested.

One day, in desperation, I told her, "Mummy, the finest people in Bombay pay to listen to me speak!"

"That is because they have nothing better to do," she said, without missing a beat.

But In New York and elsewhere later I realised that I was not alone in having had a venomous mother.

Well, it is now three decades since she is gone, and my other abuser, my dear brother, refused all contact with me since he demanded that I help him to rip off our landlord.

So, at last, I was free of all three of my abusers, including the least of them. My father.

After visiting Kashmir, my travel bug turned my thoughts to Europe.

But I couldn't afford to go on my own, as I did to Kashmir, nor could I have booked international flights, hotels and drawn-up itineraries on my own.

It was completely beyond my means, my ken, and my capacity.

So, I did what all middle-class Parsis like me did, and joined a Lala Tour to Europe.

Because if you are a Parsi it is de rigueur to go to Europe.

Mr Lala's Tours was well known among the community, not only for their affordable tours to every nook and corner of India but also for their trips abroad.

We were given a printed itinerary with dates, and various "do's" and " don'ts" and I found myself on a plane to Rome with a small group of middle-class Parsis.

The first thing that struck me when we arrived at Rome airport was the sparkling floors, clean enough to see my face in, and realised at once that I had arrived in another world.

We stayed at a "pensione" - an Italian bed and breakfast - where our hosts were friendly, the fare homely. This was to be the pattern throughout the trip. The pensione became a pension in Paris.

Then we boarded a tour bus, and another set of surprises started.

But I am not talking about Rome!

The surprises came from the group!

They all started singing "Arrivederci Roma," a popular American song in 1973 (it was three years before my transition, so I was still skinny, geeky Farokh with glasses). "Goodbye, Goodbye to Rome" and we had only just arrived! Ha! Ha!

Throughout the tour of Europe, the singing on the bus was constant, as I was to learn.

Even "Que Sera Sera," was included!

So, when we got to Paris, I led them in singing Nat King Cole's "I Love Paris in the Springtime."

They sang each phrase after me, and it sounded very nice with the "echo effect."

The first stop was the Vatican.

There the group was let loose and told to return to the bus in three hours.

In the vast concourse of St. Peter's, I was able to separate myself from the rest of the group and wander around on my own. There were little groups of tourists scattered all over the Cathedral, with guides speaking to them in every major language known to man.

I stood before the Pieta, and the sweet, innocent face of the Virgin as she held her dead son on her lap, and seemed to be asking us all, "Why have you done this to me?"

I burst into uncontrollable sobs!

It was the fact that a terrible wound had been inflicted on a blameless soul that made me cry.

And the fact that she represented a mother's love - a love that I longed for and never received. It is only now that I am analysing the reason for my sobs.

At the time, I did not know what came over me, and just wiped my tears as soon as I could get hold of myself.

Let that be my tribute to the beautiful, incomparable, awesome Pieta.

I continued to wander around, but all the murals and statues meant little to me, as I am not an Art person.

That is my brother's realm. He is a wonderful artist.

Then suddenly the great Cathedral Organ began to play and all the murals - nay, the whole Cathedral - came alive for me! It was as though everything in it began to quiver and breathe with a soft radiance.

Jesus welcomed me through music because He knew that I would respond to that.

"Welcome to my home, you silly thing," he seemed to be saying with a gentle smile.

"I know that you are an unbaptized Catholic and a heretical one at that, but I am happy that you are here."

Oh, I felt so happy and grateful!

But the clock was ticking, and I set out in search of the Sistine Chapel.

It was at this point that a middle-aged lady who was a member of the group latched on to me.

"Where are you going?" she asked eagerly as she saw me speeding off.

"To see the Sistine Chapel."

"The Sistine Chapel?" she asked as she tried to keep pace with me in her sari and flip-flops.

"What's in the Sistine Chapel?"

"The frescoes of Michaelangelo."

"Michelangelo? Oh, yes, he just died!"

"He died five hundred years ago."

"No, no, he just died! It was in the newspaper!"

It was then that I realised that she was thinking of Picasso - he had just died!

We walked through marble corridors adorned with tapestries by Raphael etc. and she kept asking, "How far do we still have to go?"

When we finally did arrive and entered the Sistine Chapel, I looked up at the ceiling, and all around me at the walls, and was filled with awe.

It was much larger than I had imagined it would be, and altogether overpowering.

I sat on a bench to take in the vast symphony of frescoes all around and above me.

Before me stood The Last Judgment and above me was the white-bearded Jewish Jehovah bringing the beautiful Greek Adam to life with a touch of his forefinger.

After enduring my awe-struck silence for as long as she could, the lady fidgeted and said, "Is this all? You mean we walked all this way to see this?"

If looks could kill, her life would have ended in the Sistine Chapel in 1973.

I ran on the way out and went in search of the Tiber. I stood by a bridge and thought of Horatius about whom we had learned in St. Mary's from Macaulay's "Lays of Ancient Rome" and thought, "Wow! I'm actually in Rome! I never dreamed back then that I would be standing on the banks of the Tiber one day.

We were not taken to see the myriad other sights of Rome but started driving South towards Naples and Capri.

When we got there, the first thing I noticed was that the Mediterranean really was blue.

What a glorious contrast to the polluted, opaque waters of the sea around Bombay which looked like milky coffee.

At this point I would like to add that as we were flying over the Greek islands on our way to Rome, the Mediterranean was not only blue, but translucent, and I could see into the depths of the waters!

I loved Capri with its posh villas and bougainvillea spilling over their walls!

As for Naples, I failed to understand why Elizabeth Barret Browning said, "See Naples and die."

But I did love the view of the conical shape of Mount Vesuvius rising out of the sea.

"Are we still in Europe?" asked the Sistine Chapel lady.

I realised to my dismay the vast gulf between the middle-class Parsi and the aristocratic Parsis who had taken me under their wing because of my piano playing. I was one thoroughly spoiled and over-educated middle-class Parsi!

Even then, I am certain, that almost everyone in the group had more money than I did!

Low budget though this tour was, I had to clean out my bank account to pay for it.

In Venice, we stayed at a Pensione in a nearby suburb.

The gondola ride on the Grand Canal, past marble palaces sinking into the sea (yes, even back then, in 1973!) was memorable, and when I saw the Ponte Vecchio and the Rialto I dreamed of The Merchant of Venice and Shylock crying: "Oft on the Rialto you have called me dog!"

I felt lucky indeed to be there - a spot hallowed by Shakespeare himself!

Just off the Piazza San Marco I almost drowned.

I was walking by rows of fabulous boutiques, peering in through their glass fronts, when suddenly I found myself two feet from a deep and opaque (yes, opaque) sea, with wind-swept waves.

Two more steps and I would have been in it, never to return, because I couldn't swim.

I had requested my mother to let me take swimming lessons, but she refused, and as an adult, I felt like a Titan among the minnows when Mrs. Grewal, the wife of Commander Grewal got me a pass to the Naval swimming pool. There were all those little children holding on to a bar and kicking their legs, and there was I, three times their size, doing the same in the midst of them! Had I been Farah by then, I would have been comfortable in my body, but as Farokh, I hated to show my unwanted body. So, I just couldn't go back!

So, I could have died in Venice.

That would have been quite a Lala Tour!

A Parsi lady dying in the Sistine Chapel and Farokh Rustom, aged 29, drowning in Venice!

But it was as though a hand had yanked me back by my shirt collar.

Once again, my Guardian Angel saved me from death by drowning as he had thirteen years earlier, when I was sixteen, in my foolhardy attempt to walk to the Prong's Reef Lighthouse at low tide from Ducksbury Point.

I still have dreams that I am about to drown, even though where I am is completely landlocked, over a thousand miles both from the Atlantic to the East and the Pacific to the West.

Believe it or not - I miss the sea, having grown up in Bombay and even though the sea was twice thwarted from swallowing me up.

From Venice, we drove North to Milan, an affluent commercial city, with a North European feel, with mannequins in furs in the shop windows, and quite different from southern Italy and Florence.

I loved Florence!

Especially the domes of Florence as seen from the hill that overlooks the city.

And who would not think of Dante and Beatrice and the Divina Commedia when one sees Firenze from that hilltop?

And, of course, there was the Uffizi with all its treasures, and the Palazzo Vecchio.

I had an embarrassing moment outside the Palazzo Vecchio.

The men stood and gazed at the life-size reproduction of Michael Angelo's David marvelling at how tiny his penis was.

While they nudged each other and exchanged bawdy jokes, I tried not to look, though they had aroused my curiosity.

We continued to drive North, through the tunnel under Mont Blanc and then arrived at Innsbruck in Austria.

In October it did not feel like a ski resort.

The thing to see there was The Golden Balcony.

As we were loaded off the bus for one hour, I asked an elderly lady where the Golden Balcony was.

"The Golden Balcony!" she cried. "You want to see the Golden Balcony?" she asked excitedly.

She ran ahead of me and stopped before an old, cross-timbered house.

On the second floor was a small "Juliet" balcony with some wrought iron work in gold.

I suppose it must have been real gold.

"Here is the Golden Balcony!" she said proudly, beaming from ear to ear.

I tried to show as much enthusiasm as I could for her sake and thanked her profusely.

"Vielen Dank, meine Dame ! Herzlichen Dank!"

Vienna was not included in the tour, to my dismay. But I did visit Vienna on my own twelve years later, in 1985.

Only Munich was included in Germany (after landing at Rome, the whole tour was only by bus).

We went to the Marienplatz with its Rathaus ("What is a Rat House?" asked the Sistine Chapel lady) and stood below a medieval clock, waiting for it to strike twelve, when knights in armour and other medieval characters emerged from the space below it and went round and round.

I felt as though I were in the film, "If it's Tuesday, it must be Belgium."

It is about a group of Americans on a tour of Europe very much like ours, humorously illustrating the whirlwind nature of European tour schedules.

In Switzerland, we stopped in Geneva where I had tea with my friend Gerard Bouvier's mother in her immaculately clean house. If only she could have seen her beautiful young son walking barefoot through the crowded and filthy bazaars of Bombay, as happy as a child in a candy store!

We took the cog railway for a close-up look at Jungfrau, changing trains three times.

Arguments broke out among college students from all over Europe when someone tried to save a seat for a friend.

"Aber das ist Verboten!"

Decades later when I took a similar train to the peak of a mountain in the Rockies, it was much nicer, much less crowded, and more peaceful, with just a few American families with their children on the train.

While changing trains to the Jungfrau, we had to take an elevator to get to an ice tunnel. We found ourselves packed in with a group of Japanese tourists.

When the elevator doors opened, I was surprised and amused to find myself being poked in the back by the Japanese as we were filing out, just as I would have been in India.

In Brussels, we saw the Manneken Pis.

Then on to Paris!

We were dumped at the Eiffel Tower where I climbed up to the first landing, which was pretty high up.

Then we were dropped at the Louvre.

Not being an Art person, I walked through room after room of paintings till I reached the Mona Lisa and then listened to something with headphones as I stood in front of her plump, self-satisfied face.

The bus did not take us to Notre Dame, alas!

My best memory of Paris is standing on the Pont Neuf in the twilight and gazing at the domes and spires of Paris in the deepening twilight.

As I was trying to find my way back to my pension, and walking along the banks of the Seine, I asked a young couple how I could get to Rue - --. I spoke in French, and they said,

"Gee, we're sorry! We're American."

"Good, then we can speak in English."

And I repeated my question in English.

"Now that makes three of us who are lost," they laughed.

I liked their easy friendliness.

Then on to London.

But for that, we had to cross the Channel.

We crossed from Ostend to Folkstone.

A Romanian on the boat told me, "I have never seen the sunset in the sea before," as we gazed at the setting sun.

And I marvelled because I had done so all my life, from Cuffe Parade, and then from my twelfth-floor paradise atop Dolphin, where I saw the hot sunrise each morning over the Sahyadri Hills on the continent of India, on the other side of the harbour from me, and then, in the evening, watch the red sun melt into the Arabian Sea from the opposite end of the terrace.

I still dream that I am back on that terrace.

Then I sat at a table on the deck and ordered a beer. At the same table was an Englishman with whom I tried to make friendly conversation in a most un-English manner, and he tried politely to fend me off. But I persisted and finally, I noticed that he was doing his best not to smile.

We were each playing a role.

I, the friendly, loquacious Indian, and he the taciturn, reserved Englishman.

We were let loose in London, and I remember speaking to a Bobby who looked uncomfortable when I told him that I was so happy that I was in London!

At Buckingham Palace I took photos for the Japanese, with their cameras, of them with the guards.

They would run up to the tall guards and stand beside them.

After I took the photo, they each bowed to me first and then to the guard.

The guards stood without flickering an eyelash.

But then a Frenchman too bowed to the guard and said, "Thank you," and asked me, "Why didn't he reply?"

"He's not supposed to move."

And then I noticed just a flicker of a smile on the young guard's face.

In Park Lane, I saw Arabs going around in limousines, and on the tourist bus with the open upper deck, the Japanese were terribly excited as they kept pointing out the landmarks to one another and shouting, "Marble Arch! Marble Arch!"

As I was crossing a garden, I greeted what was almost the epitome of an Englishman with a tightly rolled-up umbrella and a top hat.

He was friendly.

He said to me, "Do you see these roses?"

"Yes?"

"It is from this very garden that a rose was picked after which the War of the Roses is named."

I thanked him warmly.

He reminded me of Christopher, my friend from Addis Ababa.

On the way back to the Continent we crossed the Channel from Dover to Calais, and I thought of the wartime song, "The White Cliffs of Dover."

We drove back to Rome, passing once again through the long

tunnel under Mont Blanc which transported us from the Austro-German world on one side, to Italy on the other.

To the man who processed my passport at Rome airport, I said a hearty, "Grazie, signore," to which he replied with an equally hearty "Bravo!"

And so, it was "Goodbye, Goodbye to Rome."

But by now the group was tired and they were all looking forward to being home and had stopped singing.

At Santa Cruz airport, while I was waiting for a taxi, a vintage chauffeur-driven Chevrolet drove up, and the Sistine Chapel got in and drove off without a backward glance.

I told you! Even the middle-class Parsis were better off than I was!

22 - My Five Years In Limbo, Totally Farah At Last

You will recall that after my surgery my mother talked me into continuing to live as Farokh, thus depriving me of five precious years of hard-earned happiness, as well as leading people to wrongly believe that my surgery had failed.

In this chapter, I will share with you some things about those lost years - 1977 to 1982.

In 1980, I contacted the editor of the popular afternoon daily, "Mid-Day," and he offered me a column as "western classical music critic."

From then on, I received two passes for every concert from the two main organisers of concerts in Bombay: the Time and Talents Club (run by rich and elegant Parsi ladies) and the Bombay Madrigal Singers Organisation (BMSO), run by Parsis and Anglo-Indians.

(Why "Madrigal Singers?" Did they ever sing a madrigal? I don't know because I never tried to find out.)

I proudly showed my reviews to "Prem" whenever he came to have tea with me when he got off his ship and pick up his wife from work afterwards.

He advised me to write under the name of F. Rustom, and not Farokh Rustom any longer, which I did (F. could also stand for Farah).

The two passes I received were among the front-row seats and a different experience altogether from the cheap seats at the back of the hall where I used to sit.

At one concert I was sitting behind a famous cardiologist and his wife.

At the end of the first movement of a Mozart sonata, the cardiologist, who had been dozing, woke up and started to clap. But no one else joined him.

His wife whispered, "Go back to sleep!"

The venue for some of these concerts was the grand Bhabha Auditorium, which was in the cantonment area, not far from my terrace atop Dolphin. And as I was always graciously sent two passes, I invited dear Jer Jussawala to join me. As her villa was in a distant suburb, this could not be done often.

She arrived early in order to enjoy the beauty of the terrace, the serenity, and the panoramic view. We sat next to the garden where she had both taught and helped me to grow a variety of flowers.

But my usual companions were male escorts (students/friends) who knew nothing about classical music. It was a new experience for them.

I had been promised one hundred rupees per review - a handsome sum for me.

But the actual cheques were only for twenty-five rupees. I kept mum.

One day, the editor, Behram Contactor, who had given me the column, and was well known under his nom de plume "Busybee" for his daily humorous column, said: "You write very well. How would you like to be the foreign film critic as well?"

"But I wouldn't know how to do it!"

"Just read as many reviews as you can, and get started."

Of course, I agreed. Who wouldn't?

The films were to be rated "Excellent, Good, Fair or Poor" at the end of each review.

Alas, my very first review was of a film by Clint Eastwood called "Any Which Way But Loose," about him and an orangutan.

Decades later Clint Eastwood became my hero after I saw "Gran Torino." (About a Hmong boy in the Upper Mid-West. Please see it if you haven't.)

But back then, I had never seen Westerns, etc. The only films I had seen and enjoyed were "My Fair Lady," "Dr. Zhivago" and the like.

My reaction was to rate it "Poor," but I felt that it would be a mean-spirited way to start my career as a foreign film critic, so I rated it "Fair."

In all future ratings, I was scrupulously honest.

There was one film about a Blue Grass Festival and after being forced to sit through one and a half hours of Country and Western music, I developed a lifelong hatred of country westerns, blue grass, and the sound of the electric guitar.

There were some wonderful films I reviewed like "Far from the Madding Crowd" (with Julie Christie) and "The Story of Adele H."

My reviews were emotional, and when I was distraught, I said so.

For one thing, I was amazed by the fame that these reviews brought me, as so far I had only been known among classical music lovers.

I suddenly found myself with tens of thousands of fans, some of whom were kind enough to write letters to the editor, which were published.

People said that they read my reviews because they were personal and emotional.

Of course, I read books on films and learned about cinematography and things like the "long shot" and "chiaroscuro" effect etc. which lent a touch of professionalism to my reviews.

I felt so happy!

There was only a small price to pay, which was having to sit through some really bad films.

I proudly clipped and pasted my reviews into a large scrapbook.

I did not take them with me when I left Bombay forever in 1986.

There was just that much I could carry on an international flight.

A year later, when I had a rent-controlled studio apartment in New York, I wrote to my mother, requesting her to send me the scrapbook with my film reviews, my certificates, and merit cards from St. Mary's etc. all of which I had kept in my large desk.

Of course, she would not have had to do this herself. Either Daddy or Akbar would have done it.

And, of course, I would have paid the cost!

She wrote back saying that the roof had leaked during the monsoon and that they had all been destroyed!

I knew that this was a lame excuse, and may not even have been true, but it was clear that this was her revenge against me for leaving, and that there was no way that she would ever grant my request.

It broke my heart.

One great film I reviewed was "36 Chowringhee Lane" (You can see it on You tube! Please do).

It starred the English actress Jennifer Kendal (sister of Felicity Kendal) who was married to Shashi Kapoor, who is the Nawab in "Heat and Dust."

The film is about a simple Anglo-Indian school teacher in post-Independent India, very like the teachers I had in elementary school in St. Mary's and Jennifer Kapoor gave a brilliant and unforgettable performance!

I raved!

My editor was sceptical and asked, "Is it really that good?"

"Yes, it is."

But he went and saw it himself, nevertheless, and told me, "You were right!"

A few months later the film opened to rave reviews in London.

I called to congratulate Jennifer Kapoor and she said, "But you were the first to recognise it."

I was, however, short-changed on the cheques, as I was with the music reviews.

I didn't mind.

I was used to never having enough money.

The other compensations were more than enough!

One saw a preview in a mini theatre, which was also a new experience for me.

I always took a friend or a neighbour along, which was also one of the compensations.

And I wrote my reviews in the Sea Lounge at the Taj (which swallowed up a quarter of my cheque, but it was worth it).

Those of you who are from Bombay, know how beautiful and elegant the Sea Lounge at the Taj Mahal Hotel is, with its beautiful view of the harbour (though not a patch on the panoramic and unforgettable view from the twelfth-floor terrace of Dolphin), which my mother had by now made me give up.

It was air-conditioned, and just a fifteen-minute walk from my house.

It was a cool and beautiful haven where I enjoyed writing my reviews while gazing at the harbour and sipping my tea.

Sometimes, the waiter who served me also stood by and chatted with me for a couple of minutes because he was my student.

How could that be?

Because I was also fortunate enough to be hired to tutor the waiters in English and good manners, thanks to the Indo-American Society, which the Taj Mahal Hotel contacted for a tutor.

As you see, my debt to my kind boss, Mr. N. Krishnan, is unending!

May his soul be in a very beautiful place!

I was required to teach at the Taj Mahal Hotel itself, and I had to teach in whatever room was available. Each time I had to inquire at the reception in which room I was to teach in.

Of course, the rooms were luxurious, and they all faced the harbour!

I would like to share a couple of humorous anecdotes with you.

A waiter who served in the Tanjore restaurant asked me how he could direct guests to the restroom.

"Would you like to tell me, first, how you do it now?"

"I say to them, 'First, get out!'"

"What?"

"Madam, the restrooms are far from the Tanjore and I tell them how to go there."

I hastened to explain that the words "get out!" have a terrible connotation, and suggested that he should begin with, "Sir, when you come out the door, please turn left, and then walk down the corridor. The restrooms will be your right."

Of course, I dictated all this and made them write it in their notebook.

In the "politeness" department, I told them to hold the door open as the guests were leaving and say, "Please come again, sir. Hope to see you again, sir/ma'am."

(It is the hardest thing to get an Indian to say "ma'am." They always say "madam")

Many of these nice young men had degrees in Commerce or Science (though they had not been to Catholic schools or the best colleges).

One of them said to me: "Madam, you are always teaching us to be so polite to them, but some of them are so rude to us!"

"How?"

"Well, they call us "boy" and snap their fingers at us. I told the man who did that, "Excuse me, sir, I am not a dog!"

"Good heavens! And what did the man say?"

"He said "I'm so sorry! I did not mean to offend you!"

I did realise how this would make him feel, and explained, "The guest was perhaps French. The French word for the waiter is "garçon" which translates into English as "boy." And in France, the normal way to summon a waiter is to raise your arm and snap your fingers. Anyway, the Taj Mahal Hotel is not a school to teach the guests politeness. Please don't be so sensitive. They mean no harm."

When there was a Quatorze Juillet (Fourteenth of July) reception in the Crystal Room, given by the French Consulate, my students, who were walking around with trays of champagne, were overjoyed to see me among the elegant guests, and kept plying me with champagne.

"My dear, thank you, but you will get me drunk!"

So, you see, all the happiness that I have experienced in my life has come from others - good, wonderful people. And all the unhappiness came only from three people, my mother, father, and brother (and yes, it has left scars).

Alas, one only has to look at the tragic life of Princess Diana, who had the whole world in love with her but was denied the love of her parents and her husband, to see what can happen. She was starved for love, and even the love of the whole world could not fill that void.

Poor Diana!

(2)

I will conclude with yet another pleasant memory.

Dear Jer Jussawala had arranged, through the Nalanda Cultural Club, for me to deliver a course of lectures at the Tanjore Restaurant (yes, the same one from where it was hard to access the restrooms).

Because of the beautiful and prestigious venue, large numbers of people attended, and I was at my best.

It was during these courses that I finally came out as FARAH, after having seen through my mother's cruel five-year victory.

The newspapers used to announce each of my lectures under "Today's Events" on Page Two.

They were always announced as "By F. Rustom."

But this time it said, "By Farah Rustom."

People noticed.

The Tanjore was filled to overflowing.

I did not disappoint.

I showed up in a beautiful sari (instead of in a shirt and pants), right down to a golden dot on my forehead, chandelier earrings, and lipstick.

There were smiles all around, and the happiest smile of all was on my face.

Bombay saw at last that my surgery had not failed!

One of the people who attended my first lecture as Farah at the Tanjore Restaurant at the Taj Mahal Hotel was the widow of a famous industrialist, Dhirubhai Khatau, head of the family of Khatau Textiles. Hildegard was Swiss-German, a beautiful woman in her late fifties. She complimented me on my talk and invited me to her penthouse in El Cid, atop Malabar Hill. The unique feature of this penthouse was that the living room ran the breadth of the apartment, with a large, covered balcony at either end. These were strewn with scattered couches and armchairs where one sat and had tea or a glass of wine, or even breakfast or dinner.

One balcony provided a panoramic view of the city, five hundred feet below, and beyond that, of the harbour and the Sahyadri Hills. The other side provided an uninterrupted view of the Arabian Sea (as that part of the Indian Ocean which washes the shores of Bombay is called - the same ocean that runs all the way South to Antarctica) all the way to the horizon.

It reminded me of my terrace atop Dolphin because one could see the sunrise from one of her balconies and sunset from the other.

She showed me her closet with dozens of dresses and gowns. She told me that once a year she gave away her dresses (except for her favourite ones) to her friends, so she could have new ones made. She asked me to pick any dress I wanted, and I chose a backless, black, floor-length gown.

The Austrian Consulate had planned a gala concert in commemoration of the two hundredth and fiftieth birth anniversary of Haydn, featuring a range of music, including Jean Kingdom who would sing some arias from "The Creation", a performance of one of his Symphonies by the Bombay Chamber Orchestra, and so on. They asked me if I would play something by Haydn on the piano. I chose his Sonata in E Flat, which I loved.

I decided to wear Hildegard's backless black gown for the concert, which was to be at the newly built National Centre for the Performing Arts. The auditorium seated a thousand people and, as I had already been to a few concerts there, I was aware that one entered the auditorium from above, after ascending a grand flight of stairs, and the seats were arranged in row after row, one below the other, all the way down to the stage, which was at the bottom.

I never expected that I would be called upon to play on that stage and was quite anxious.

As I walked onto the stage, the audience did not recognise me at first, even though my name was in the program. They had seen me in demure saris by now, but who was this European woman in a backless black gown? It took them a few seconds to realise that it was their very own Farah!

But as I started playing on the beautiful, new, Steinway concert grand, and Haydn's music unfolded, I lost all self-consciousness. There was warm applause at the end, and the next morning the critics particularly praised my "poetic and lyrical" rendering of the great slow movement.

Bombay's leading social columnist, Shobhaa Kilachand (now world-renowned as the novelist Shobhaa De) referred to my gown in her column: "Farah Rustom made a startling entry in a backless, black mini."

Since I had the pleasure of knowing her (Shobhaa is still a dear and loyal friend who still stays in touch despite her world celebrity status) I called her and said, "I'm flattered that you mentioned me in your column, Shobhaa, but I wasn't wearing a backless, black mini! It was a formal ball gown going all the way down to the floor!"

"I know, Farah, but I just wanted to make it more fun."

I didn't mind.

Shobhaa also happened to be one of the most beautiful women in the world. Writers and journalists, both Indian and foreign, raved about her beauty. She was also exceptionally talented, and a famous journalist and writer.

She started giving me tips about how to do my eyebrows and how to highlight my cheekbones etc.

So, I was lucky to be taken under their wings of beautiful and famous women.

23 - Aijaz Ahmed

In 1983 I met an exceptional man.

One morning, I read an article in the Sunday paper about a man called Aijaz Ahmed who helped homeless children just off the university campus. He looked very distinguished and handsome in the photograph that accompanied the article, and I was drawn not only by the work that he was doing, but also by his looks.

The article was written by my gifted journalist friend Rajendar Menen who was still only in his Twenties. He had also given me a weekly social column in his newspaper, The Daily, which I enjoyed writing. I called up Rajinder and thanked him for the article. He spoke warmly of Aijaz.

So I went to see him, and found him surrounded by barefoot, homeless children, both boys and girls, in humble, grubby clothing, between the ages of eight and fifteen.

I introduced myself and asked if I could be of any help. He had courtly manners, a Greek profile, salt and pepper hair and a deep, mellifluous voice. He spoke English with an aristocratic accent, and I was quite overwhelmed.

He thanked me and showed me the drawing books that the children were colouring.

The little ones surrounded me, calling me "Aunty, Aunty" and the teenagers stood back, feeling shy.

I sat on a rock and started teaching them the English alphabet under the welcome shade of a tree because it was quite hot even though it was November.

I was wearing a beautiful, white summer dress given to me by Hildegard and I asked Aijaz if he wouldn't mind taking a photograph of me with the children. He graciously did, and that photo stands on my desk in my living room to this day! It is one of my treasured possessions that I brought with me, and which my mother could not, therefore, destroy, or my brother throw away after she died.

I started showing up once a week (I still had to teach evening classes at the Indo-American Society), and after about an hour with the children, Aijaz started asking me to join him for a cup of tea at a nearby restaurant.

It was a humble Irani tea shop (like the one my paternal grandfather had owned in Poona), in one of the by-lanes behind Kala Ghoda ("Black Horse", meaning the equestrian statue of King Edward VII, the then Prince of Wales, which stood atop a high pedestal in the large square opposite Elphinstone College).

I asked for "tea in a tray" (milk and sugar served separately) much to his amusement. He opted for the cheaper "chai", which I did not like, as it was repeatedly boiled with milk and sugar.

I always insisted on paying for my tea, so he wouldn't feel that I was presuming on our acquaintance.

I cannot recollect our casual conversations, but I vividly remember my joy in being with him.

Yes, I was in love!

It was yet one more of my unconsummated, platonic loves, which began fifteen years earlier with my love for Christopher, in Ethiopia.

One afternoon Aijaz said, "I'm hungry. Let's get some Chinese. My treat!"

So off we went to a nearby air-conditioned Chinese restaurant.

"Would you like some chicken lo mein?' he asked.

"What's that?" I asked.

"You mean you haven't had chicken lo mein? You must! It's delicious!"

A few days later when we were back at the little tea shop and talking about the children, though I was elegantly dressed as always, he said, "And you too are struggling."

"How did you know?" I asked.

"Because you did not know what chicken lo mein was."

I was grateful because I realised that he thought of me even when I was not with him.

There was an elegant young woman, exuding wealth, who would occasionally come to see Aijaz. She came in chiffon saris and expensive pearls and court shoes and wearing an exquisite perfume. Aijaz would speak politely with her, as he did with everyone.

One day, after she left, he told me, "One day I will just disappear."

"Why?" I asked, my heart in my mouth.

"Because she has threatened to hunt me down no matter where I am."

It was obvious that he did not care about her, while she was mad about him.

Then Aijaz stopped coming and the children were forlorn. I comforted them as best I could, but I needed comforting myself. I called Rajendar Menen and told him about Aiyaz's disappearance.

"He is depressed and is refusing to come out of his room."

I asked Rajinder if he knew where Aijaz lived. He did, and we took a cab to his place, which turned out to be in a posh building on Malabar Hill. Along the way, Rajinder told me about Aiyaz's family.

He came from a rich business family. When his father died, he inherited the family business, but he ran it so badly that his younger brothers took over to save it from bankruptcy.

From time to time, Aijaz would have black moods during which he closed the curtains of his room and just did not come out. He lived with his widowed mother and his brothers. They all talked about him in whispers. His mother seemed particularly cold and indifferent to him, and reminded me of my own.

Aijaz refused to come out of his room even when he was told through the closed door that his journalist friend Rajinder and I had come to see him.

But the next day he showed up for the children.

It was after his brothers took over the family business that Aijaz started to do what he really loved to do - which was to help the poor.

He found homeless children, met their parents, organised games, and activities for them, and took them under his wing. He gave them prizes and treats.

When he drove in his vintage Cadillac to see them, he parked it blocks away, so the children did not know that he was a "burra Sahib" (a "Rich Man").

While I was well aware that he had had an expensive education, I had no idea that he was that rich.

He was perfectly at home in the little Irani tea shop he took to me to, where we sat with poor labourers who dipped their "bun maska" (buttered bun) into their tea as a special treat during their workday.

Then he started having blackouts.

He told me that the doctors suspected diabetes and would have to take more than one blood sample at the Bombay Hospital.

In India, people are always escorted by a family member when they go to see a doctor.

So, I asked him if I could accompany him, and to my joy, he

consented.

Even though I was 37, I was inexperienced, and my hunger for love was extreme.

So, when the doctor asked me how I was related to Aijaz, I stupidly blurted out my fantasy, and said, "I'm his wife."

I felt my ears burning and my heart pound as soon as I said that.

How would Aijaz react to such a preposterous lie!

I stared at the ground, but after a few seconds, shot a glance at his face.

He was smiling.

A week later he told me, "You know when I went for my test results, the doctor asked me,

"How is your wife?"

"My wife?"

"Yes, your wife. She has not come with you today?"

"Oh, my wife!"

Ha! Ha!

Try as I might, I could not get him to come to my place, so I could play the piano for him.

So, we walked to the Goethe Institute instead (called Max Muller Institute in India, after the great German Indologist) where I played Brahms for him on the grand piano.

The German Vice-Consul, Doris Hertrampf, who was an immensely obese woman, saw him and asked me about him.

She fell for him immediately and asked me to introduce her to him.

Aijaz accepted her invitation to both of us, to have tea at her place.

But he was silent and distant, and when I went to the balcony to see the extensive view (by now you are all familiar with my love of high balconies and terraces, and the view from them) he left her and came and stood by my side.

Still, she persisted. She gave a dinner party and invited Aijaz and me. She was wearing a specially tailored "salwar kameez." It was the first time I saw her in Indian attire.

But Aijaz did not show up.

When I called, he said that he was not well.

She gave me taxi fare to go and bring him myself.

Aijaz refused to come but saw me down to the taxi.

She finally got the message.

Once, when I was having a bad hair day and had combed my hair straight back from my forehead to disguise the fact, Aijaz suddenly said, "You look smashing."

Soon after that I left Bombay for ever to get away from my mother.

I believed that Aijaz did not love me, and would not miss me, and would soon forget me.

Twenty years later, I wrote to him and included a copy of the photo he had taken of me and the children on the day that I first met him.

He sent me a handwritten reply (my letter too had been hand written, and mailed to his address on Little Gibbs Road, Malabar Hill).

It is written in a beautiful hand, and in the formal, Indian Victorian style.

Here are some excerpts from his letter dated 8th September 2006:

"My Dear Farah,

I am so very happy after reading your letter and feel exhilarated that I am connected with you again.

Farah, we are kindred souls - wherever we are, and whichever part of the world we may live, yet we are connected.

Memories of the yore and of the bygone era kept coming back to my mind and reminding me of those lovely, beautiful days we spent together."

(Oh, Aijaz, why didn't you tell me then? I would never have left)!

"Never ever in my life can I forget you for the sterling qualities and grace with which you carried yourself with such dignity.

I shall always admire the exemplary courage you have shown in handling your life on your own terms.

You are indeed a brave woman who is blessed with great talents and a kind heart.

I am feeling overjoyed and feeling very happy writing this letter to you."

(Oh, Aijaz!)

"The children's photograph with you that I had taken, made me nostalgic.

All the faces of the children came alive in my memory.

I am now living by myself in a cottage in Lonavala, sixty miles from Bombay.

My phone number is......

I was delighted by your sweet letter, which you wrote with such warm feeling. Words cannot express the depth and intensity of my feelings. I am overwhelmed."

We spoke a couple of times on the phone after that.

Aijaz died two years later of a massive heart attack at the age of sixty, behind the wheel of his car, before he could start the car.

24 - My Brief Flirtation with Bollywood

Bombay is rightly called Bollywood because , like Los Angeles, it is home to a great film hub.

Co-incidentally, both Hollywood and Bollywood are on the west coast, and both are hot and in a city by the sea.

In the early 1980's, I received a phone call from a man called Mr. Subramanium who introduced himself as the Dean of the recently established Film and Television Institute of India.

He asked if I would be willing to spend a week in Poona to teach a course on "Western" classical music to the students.

"I inquired from a number of people about a suitable person to do so, and they all suggested your name!"

I was flattered and gladly accepted.

"We will provide you accommodation in our VIP living quarters (which turned out to be a modest, but cozy room) and we will pay you at our highest rate for visiting lecturers.

"But - can you lecture six hours a day?"

"I could lecture ten hours a day if you wanted me to," I replied honestly.

I took the train to Poona, 120 miles from Bombay, and the town where my father had grown up. I enjoyed the ride up the mountain (known as a "ghat"), with an additional engine pushing the train up from behind, while the one in front pulled it. The additional engine was attached at the junction of Karjat, at the foot of the ghat.

As always, I enjoyed this brief contact with nature, especially during the monsoon, when the mountains turned green. We passed through a number of tunnels before we reached the top of the Deccan Plateau, which is at 2000 feet. Compared to my trips to the Himalayan hill stations, this was nothing, but still, anything was preferable to steaming hot Bombay with its suffocating crowds.

The FTII campus, with old growth trees, was beautiful. It had once been the Shantaram film studio.

The next morning, I delivered my first three-hour lecture. The students were in their early Twenties, and I was in my late Thirties. I had taken along dozens of long playing records to illustrate the music

- symphonies, concertos, sonatas, chamber music, operas, operas, oratorios etc.

In the first lecture I gave them an overview of the different styles of European music over three centuries - Baroque, Classical, Romantic, Impressionist, and 20th century.

At the end of the lecture the students asked me to join them in the canteen (cafeteria) for the one-hour break.

They said, "We dreaded your arrival! We dreaded the thought of six hours of lectures on music for five consecutive days! Now we know that this will be the best week we will have in FTII!"

The Dean Films was delighted with the enthusiastic feedback from the students, and needless to say I was grateful.

They requested if I would start my day an hour earlier by letting them listen to my LP's. I was delighted, and so I spent seven hours a day with them.

But this was not all. In the evening they were supposed to watch films from the film archive.

They showed me films by Fassbinder and Kurosawa and others, which I would otherwise never have got to see.

The next morning, I would tell them my reaction to the film (I was already a film critic, but those were mostly Hollywood films).

"Your feedback was more interesting than the lectures from our film appreciation professor," they said.

I thanked God for whatever little talent He had given me, because my feedback had been gut level and not academic.

From then on, I was invited every semester to do these courses, and I loved my week at FTII every single time.

As I was well paid, I walked to a nearby Kwality's and had a grand chicken biryani dinner with a glass of beer.

By now you must have noticed my love of Indian food.

Unfortunately, when I taste the bland fare at my local Nepali restaurants here in the US, I could sob!

On one of my trips to FTII, my next door neighbour in the VIP rooms was the actress Deepti Naval.

I had seen and admired her brilliant performance in an "Art Film" called "Ek Baar Phir," (Once Again).

The art films movement had just begun in Hindi cinema with Kumar Shahani (my classmate in Elphinstone College who had come to my place for my very first sessions on classical music appreciation, along with Kaveh Munshi and Nitin Desai, both of whom later went to Oxford - and opened up for me a lifelong career in lecturing on music appreciation and teaching, right up to the present day.

Anyway, returning to Deepti Naval. I had heard of her arrival the previous evening from my students. The next morning, as I came out of my room, she was standing in the passage which doubled as a common balcony.

"Hello, I am Deepti Naval," she said. "I am an actress."

"I know who you are, Deepti! I greatly admired your performance in "Ek Baar Phir."

And so began a lifelong friendship.

We exchanged phone numbers, and upon returning to Bombay I called her, and she invited me over for lunch.

She was utterly and totally unpretentious, and natural.

A Punjabi beauty with large, expressive eyes, she was convent educated and had spent a few years in New York where her father was teaching. But her dream was to become an actress and make it in Hindi cinema. Not as a star, but as an actress.

She has fulfilled that dream.

The art film movement in Hindi cinema ended - alas! - soon after I left for New York.

When I requested a famous director to make more art films (which had a select and appreciative audience), he said, "Farah, if we all tried to please people like you, the film industry would go bankrupt!"

Sad, but true.

It does not cost anything to write a good book, but it costs a small fortune even to make an art film!

Deepti's and my journeys in life have been in opposite directions.

She came from New York to Bombay, where she created a life and a career for herself.

I went in the opposite direction, with much smaller ambitions, of course.

But reverting to when we were young - Deepti had a keen interest in learning about classical music and attended my introductions to Bolshoi Ballet films, at the House of Soviet Culture (Anna Karenina, Carmen, Spartacus, Swan Lake etc.). She would also come over to my place and curl up in an armchair with a glass of wine and listen to me playing, after I had briefly introduced the piece.

Like me, she was fond of her drink, so we would occasionally go to the Harbour Bar at the Taj Intercontinental Hotel.

I was an object of interest myself, but being with a well-known Hindi film actress meant that we were watched continually. Both of us pretended that we did not notice.

The only thing is that Deepti is short, and I am tall, so she wore her highest heels when she was with me.

Deepti also mentioned me in her interviews for film magazines.

"I am not going to spend my life stomping my foot over what the gossip columnists have to say about me. I would rather spend an evening with Farah Rustom at the House of Soviet Culture. There is so much to be learned from Farah!"

This led my dear friend, the famous Shobhaa Kilachand (now Shobhaa De) to tease Deepti, "Hey Deepti, what's going on between you and Farah?"

Deepti replied, "Both Farah and I are too well known for our love of men!"

Before one of these presentations of Bolshoi Ballet films, I got a call from the American Vice-Consul for Cultural Affairs, asking if he and his wife could attend.

"I don't see why not! I will speak to Mr. Smirnov and call you back as soon as possible!"

"Please tell him that we would be delighted if they come. They are most welcome!" said Mr. Smirnov.

This was just before Gorbachev and perestroika and Glasnost, and so I feel that Bombay can take a little credit for being among the earliest participants in the thaw in the cold war!

Anyway, through Deepti, I met other Bollywood stars. And I mean stars.

The actress Nutan and her actor son Mohnish Behl, and Mithun Chakraborty (the John Travolta of India) and others.

Let's begin with Nutan.

She was the only Hindi film star who lived in downtown Bombay, less than half a mile from my place, but in a Duplex penthouse on the thirty-second floor atop Sagar Sangeet (Song of the Sea).

It had a panoramic view of the harbour and was built where the garden of Heliopolis had once been.

Heliopolis was built in the 1920's, containing large, luxury flats where English magistrates and rich Indians lived. It had a garden in front where the sea waves rolled almost up to the lawn.

The towering Sagar Sangeet now stood where the seaside garden had once been, and dwarfed Heliopolis which looked like a poor relation.

Nutan had moved here from her distant suburban property in Thana, and now enjoyed all the amenities and conveniences of living in downtown Bombay, while at the same time enjoying the privacy of her ivory tower.

And there I went, as a social columnist, to interview her.

She was then fifty years old and as beautiful as ever.

There wasn't a line on her face, and she was tall and slender, convent educated, and gracious.

She offered me delicious refreshments which she herself did not touch.

As we got to know each other better, and I earned her trust through my accounts of our meetings, she became even more friendly. I was able to drop in on her unannounced, and she always received me when her young servant Kamal, from the Himalayan foothills of Pauri Ghadwal, told her that I was at the door.

One evening she offered me a drink. Her beautiful living room with glass walls providing an unobstructed view of the harbour, was gently lit with lamps scattered around the room, and in this soft glow she walked to and fro in a white chiffon sari, tall and slender as a lily. Her favourite drink was whisky and soda, and I opted for something milder.

I told her that it was a pity that she could not go to the Taj Mahal Hotel for a drink with a friend, if she felt like it.

"Everything comes with a price," she replied.

She even asked me to go along with her one morning as she drove herself in her little Fiat to see her tailor to pick up some sari blouses. During the drive I noticed that if we stopped at a red light and she was recognised, she immediately put a smile on her face, and, taking the cue from her, I did the same.

I also interviewed her handsome son Mohnish Behl, with her permission. He was aristocratic, and soft spoken and he reminded me of Aijaz. His career just would not take off, as he was too posh for the poor Indian film goer and could not sing and dance around trees or fight off ten men at the same time.

After I left India, a clever director cast him as a villain, and his career took off!

Nutan loved talking about him as he was her only child, and the apple of her eye.

"One night he came home very late. It was almost morning when he came home. I let him go to bed without saying a word. The next afternoon, when he got up, I made an omelette for him with my own hands and told him that I was worried sick about him and that he could at least have called me and let me know where he was. You see, it is not only important to say the right thing, but to say it at the right time, and in the right way."

I had taken my other teenage servant Anthony (who was now a good companion to Akbar) along when I went to see Mohnish so he could take photos of us together (I cherish those photos with Nutan, taken by her servant Kamal, and the photos with Mohnish taken by Anthony, who I knew would love seeing a film star in person).

When we returned home, Anthony told me, "Memsahibji, he is very handsome! But in the movies, they put all that white paint on his face, which ruins his looks."

Aha!

Mohnish was a chain smoker and was never without his packet of Marlboro cigarettes.

I also met Nutan's husband Commander Behl, who resigned from the Navy to manage his wife's career.

He spoke freely when Nutan was not home but left immediately as soon as she came.

One of the things he said was, "I told Nutan not to pluck her eyebrows as it gives a woman a hard look."

I'm glad Nutan listened to him because her natural eyebrows only enhanced her beauty.

I also spoke on the phone with Nutan's mother, Shobhana Samarth. I had seen photos of Shobhana Samarth taken in her heyday as a film actress, and she had been breath-takingly beautiful, frankly, even more beautiful than her famous daughter.

Unfortunately, mother and daughter had fallen out years ago, as Shobhana Samarth told me on the phone (I never met her, alas).

"I miss Mohnish so much! I love the boy, but Nutan won't let me see him!"

During my second year in New York, I learned that Nutan had died of lung cancer at the tragically early age of 54. I don't know if she smoked when she was alone, but she never did in front of me.

A few years later, their penthouse caught fire, and dear Commander Behl, died in the blaze. I hope and pray that he died of smoke asphyxiation. I cannot bear to think of any other way! Not him, not anyone!

Nutan was a Maharashtrian, and Maharashtrian women are the most feminine and beautiful that I have ever met. There were Shobhana Samarth and Nutan, and there is the spectacularly beautiful Shobhaa De, who is now in her seventies!

After them come South Indian actresses like Rekha.

The heroes are all Punjabis!

Or at least were, during my time, which was more than thirty-five years ago.

I will now write about the only famous Bollywood actor who was not handsome - Om Puri.

He was pock marked and had a bulging nose.

I met him at the Prithvi Theatre in Juhu, where he acted with gusto and abandon in a traditional Gujarati comedy. He exuded talent!

I went backstage to congratulate him, and his eyes lit up when he saw me. I requested an interview, and he agreed to meet me at the Sea Lounge (in the Taj Mahal Hotel) two days later.

I arrived first, and as soon as I saw him walking up to me, I knew that he had been told!

Told what?

Told about my transition, of course.

When he met me, he thought that he had met the woman of his dreams.

That was clear even to me when I saw his excitement and joy at meeting me.

So, I dreaded what was to follow.

You know what they say - if it's too good to be true, it always is.

He looked sad and dispirited and the sparkle had gone from his eyes.

We talked about the film and his training in acting at Alkazi's great drama school in Delhi (Alkazi was a close friend of dear Jer Jussawala, who also loved theatre!) and about his career so far in Hindi films.

He had shown that you don't have to be handsome to be a hero.

That his level of talent can achieve success with talent alone!

He had given a spectacular performance in "Ardha Satya" (Half-Truth) opposite the great actress Smita Patil, who died tragically in childbirth shortly afterwards. Not even the best gynaecologists in Bombay could save her as she haemorrhaged after giving birth and bled to death.

When I met him at a party a few weeks later, he gladly posed for a photo with me. And when I wrote to him from where I finally settled in the US, he promptly replied, rejoicing in my "happiness."

A lot of people thought that I lived "happily ever after" in the years after leaving India.

Oh, how wrong they were, though they wished me well, and I love them for it!

But since I intend to end this memoir in 1986, I shall not write about my life in the New World except that I still enjoy playing the piano, teaching, and making instructional piano videos for my You Tube channel. That should suffice for me. Nobody ever lives happily ever after.

Sadly, Om Puri is also no longer with us.

And this brings us to one of the greats - Dev Anand.

Dev Anand was not a great actor, and he was one of the usual, handsome Punjabi's.

But he had a certain charisma, an aura about him, that won the hearts of the sophisticated as well as the unsophisticated.

There was a saying in film circles:

"A film of Dev Anand can flop, but Dev Anand himself is never a flop."

Please see him in the iconic song sequence "Yeh Hai Bombay, Meri Jaan" (This is Bombay, my darling!) on You Tube, as he sings to the blushing heroine in an open horse carriage (ghoda gaari) going down Marine Drive! Daddy loved this song! Along with a few million other Indians, including myself.

Dev Anand was in his fifties when I met him.

After keeping me waiting for the required amount of time in his living room, he came in, looking as curiously at me as I did at him.

He had his trademark lock of hair on his forehead and his equally trademark shirt collar turned up.

The flurry that my transformation had created worked in my favour.

I was not just one more journalist that they were meeting.

They were as curious about me as I was about them.

Right away he told me, "You know, I slept on the sidewalks of Bombay when I came to Bombay from Amritsar."

"And look where you are now!"

His son, who had studied in America, was stuck up and unpopular and I told him, "Unfortunately, unlike you, he does not know what lies on the other side of that high, protective wall of your compound, as you do."

"How right you are!" he cried, with a sad look in his eyes.

I read to him what I was going to write about him over the phone, and he requested only one minor alteration in the wording.

The interview was published in the newspaper belonging to dear Mr. Ahmed (for once my memory fails me!), and a few months later he suggested that I do a second interview.

This time Dev Anand suggested that I meet him at a hotel in Juhu.

I thought nothing of it until Dr. Ahmed asked me, "Did he ask you to meet him at his house or at the Holiday Inn?"

"The Holiday Inn."

"Ah, then you have passed the test."

This raised a cautionary flag.

Dev Anand was as handsome and friendly and courteous as ever.

But at the end of the interview (I was wearing a sari as usual) he said, "I love your blouse."

I had just had breast implants, so it was boyishly transparent.

Though flattered (millions of his female fans would gladly have been in my shoes at that moment), I said, "Thank you" and smiled.

And that was the end of that.

After all, I was not in love with him, and being deeply in love was for me a prerequisite for physical intimacy.

Around this time, Eve's Weekly did a lengthy interview with me and put me on the cover.

I'll never forget the photo shoot for that cover.

I was made to sit under the blazing sun on the roof of the Jehangir Art Gallery.

There were light reflectors and assistants to the photographer who took any number of shots.

It was all very flattering.

The photos were one better than the other, and all that light made me look snow white.

I was wearing a red silk sari embroidered in white silk. It was a hundred-year-old "gara", made in China, which had belonged to my grandmother (yes, the same one whose funeral I attended at the Tower of Silence when I was seven).

The issue was sold out as soon as it hit the stands, and more copies were printed.

It was also translated and published in a number of Indian language magazines, so that people as far away as Assam got to know about me, turning me into an all-India figure, when all I wanted to do was to explain to people what had happened. I did not seek fame, but fame sought me.

It was best summed up by my journalist friend Rajinder Menen: "You've performed a miracle. You said to people 'I am Farah' and they accepted you for who you are."

"For one week you were more famous than any of us, you know," said Mithun Chakraborty when he met me at the Sun and Sand Hotel. (Thanks to my friend Deepti Naval who was in the scene that he was shooting. She called me to practice her French with me prior to leaving for the Cannes Film Festival.)

Mithun Chakraborty was the John Travolta of India and adored by his millions of fans as he was of humble origin and a great dancer.

He made no attempt to hide his humble origins or attempt to be anyone other than who he was.

Once I almost met the Dalai Lama who was due to inaugurate an exhibition of Tibetan handicrafts at the home of Bepsy Sabawala.

"Would you like to meet the Dalai Lama?" she asked over the phone.

"Like to meet the Dalai Lama! I would love to meet the Dalai Lama! But what will I say to him?"

"Don't be stupid! Just be yourself, and you can meet a king. Try to be somebody else, and you won't even fool a beggar!"

It was a lesson I never forgot!

As it turned out, I could not meet the Dalai Lama as he showed up two hours late (he was a guest of the Governor of Bombay and at the mercy of all the protocol surrounding him).

I had a class to teach at the Indo-American Society, and I felt that my duty to my students was more important than even meeting the Dalai Lama, who I loved and revered - and still do.

Mithun was known for his drinking, and he was in his late thirties when I met him.

I complimented him on maintaining his physique despite the calories added by the alcohol (we were both holding a drink when I said that).

"You know, Farah, that is because I don't eat when I drink."

Alas, he paid a heavy price for that.

Soon after I left New York for where I now live (I stayed in New York for four years) I heard that he was hospitalised in Switzerland with cirrhosis of the liver.

Fortunately, he survived!

This brings me to one of the less famous ones - Jitendra.

He had been a matinee idol in the sixties but had sunk into oblivion.

One day the phone rang, and he introduced himself.

He was asking me to interview him!

Oh, how have the mighty fallen!

What showed up was a fat, doubled-chinned, potbellied Jitendra.

I told him bluntly that he would have to lose weight to restore his career.

"I will lose weight with mind power" he declared.

"I think that you should also diet and exercise!"

A few weeks later we met for a follow-up interview at the Shamiana restaurant at the Taj.

This time he brought his Parsi wife with him.

She had been a model, but now she too was fat, like him.

Incidentally, she had grown up in Royal Terrace, opposite my dilapidated building - the same building in which my childhood playmate at checkers, Farrokh Bulsara, who later became Freddy Mercury.

Every time I asked Jitendra a question, she replied on his behalf.

I wrote my article in question-and-answer form, and it went like this:

Mid-Day, "What do you do etcetera."

Hutokshi, "We blah blah blah."

(Of course, I quoted her words).

Everybody had a good laugh.

But there is a very happy ending to this story.

Jitendra was seen jogging seriously on Juhu beach every morning and evening. He also went on a diet and regained his looks and got a role in a TV series which became very popular.

His career was restored!

I had a brief encounter with Rekha, who was then a superstar.

She had just made an audio tape on Yoga and held a press conference to launch it.

I took my servant Anthony along, because I knew that he would be thrilled to see her.

She was literally his poster girl, as he covered the walls of the servants' room with magazine cut-outs of her.

On the taxi ride back home I asked him, "Well Anthony! You've seen Rekha. What do you think?"

"Memsahibji, how many flashbulbs went off when she entered!"

To me she had looked fantastically beautiful, but to my surprise, Anthony said, "But she is dark skinned! On the screen, they show her looking snow white! It is the job of these women to make suckers of men! Why, even you look better than her!"

A dubious compliment indeed!

But I understood why he said that. Like all Indians, he equated a light complexion with beauty.

And my Parsi light complexion worked very much in my favour - never mind that I did not have large, lustrous eyes, glossy waist length black hair or perfect features, as Rekha did.

Farokh, the ugly duckling, had turned into Farah - not quite a swan, but ... at least a respectable white goose.

Just a week before boarding the plane to New York, I met Rekha in the ladies' room of the Tanjore Restaurant. To my amazement, she repeatedly splashed water on her face, bending over the sink, and her make-up remained untouched.

She was an artist and did her own make-up.

"I love the way you do your face, Rekha," I said.

"Do you? Would you like me to make up your face one day?" she smiled.

(Did she know who I was?)

"Would I! Why, Rekha, I would never wash my face again after that!"

We both laughed.

When I returned to the Tanjore, the manager came to see me and asked if I wanted anything.

Word had already reached his ears that Rekha had spoken to me in the ladies' room!

I thought bitterly that he had taken no notice of me all evening and was now fawning on me just because Rekha had exchanged a few words with me!

And that brings me to the greatest and the best of them all - Shashi Kapoor.

He combined in himself all the appeal of the matinee idol to all his millions of poor fans, as well as a great acting talent that delighted lovers of art films. Like a Colossus, he straddled both worlds.

Among his many art films are the films by that great Producer-Director Duo, Merchant and Ivory.

I had the pleasure of meeting Ismail Merchant who had a kind smile on his face the whole time and a twinkle in his eye, and when he noticed that I had not applied red nail polish to the sides of my nails to make them look longer, he looked straight into my eyes with undisguised delight and smiled from ear to ear.

His marvellous book on how to cook my favourite Indian dishes occupied pride of place in my kitchen.

One of Shashi Kapoor's earliest Merchant-Ivory films is "Shakespeare Wallah" based on the lives of his wife's parents, the Kendals. An absolute "must-see."

He is at his handsomest ever in this one, as he was very young when it was made.

Then followed "The Householder" and "Bombay Talkie", climaxing in "Heat and Dust."

In each of these, he gives a masterly performance!

But immediately after returning from Ethiopia, and during my "Discovery of India" period, I also saw him in a typical Bollywood film, with singing and dancing, as a typical matinee idol - and even there he shows some class!

He was unique in that he was able to straddle both worlds - the song and dance melodrama of the Hindi film, and the excellence of Indian art films.

All the art films in which he acts are in English.

Little did I dream in 1968 that before 1986 I would meet him a few times before leaving for the western hemisphere.

Born into the film world as the son of the actor Prithviraj Kapoor, and with the virile good looks and light complexion of a Punjabi

Pathan, he had everything going for him - extreme good looks, acting talent, an English education, love of life, and a brilliant mind.

I first saw Shashi Kapoor in person at a reception for Prince Charles during his visit to India just before he married Lady Diana Spencer.

Prince Charles stood in the centre of the room, shaking hands, and talking with people who were presented to him.

There were two kinds of guests: VIPs and artists.

We artists were included because the reception was at the National Centre for the Performing Arts after all.

The most prominent of these were actors like Shashi Kapoor and Rohini Hattangadi who played Gandhi's wife Kasturba in Richard Attenborough's "Gandhi."

I scrupulously avoided going anywhere near Prince Charles, terrified of speaking to him, and chose, instead, to enjoy my champagne and circulate among the guests, some of whom I knew.

I kept stealing glances at Shashi Kapoor and noticed more than once that he was looking at me with those large eyes fringed with curling eyelashes that only Indian men have.

Then suddenly the host, Dr. Homi Bhabha, came up to me, and, taking me by the hand, said, "Come, Farah, let me introduce you to His Royal Highness."

I held back, but he said, "Don't be afraid. It is his job to talk with people."

Prince Charles was then at the height of his rugged good looks and was considered to be the most eligible of bachelors in the world.

"Your Royal Highness, meet Farah Rustom, one of our leading pianists."

Prince Charles smiled at me and asked, "Do you like Chopin?"

"I love Chopin, your Royal Highness."

There was a pause, and to fill the silence, I asked, "And your Royal Highness, do you like Chopin?"

"I idealize Chopin," he replied with a big smile.

Just then Dr. Bhabha came up to us with a famed Indian classical dancer, and I quietly took a couple of steps backwards, making sure not to turn my back on him.

The next day, Shobhaa De got the last word on the evening: "It was an honour and a pleasure to meet Prince Charles," she wrote, "but the real prince in the room was Shashi Kapoor!"

I met Shashi Kapoor at his home a couple of years later, when I went to interview his son Kunal Kapoor.

Shashi Kapoor was married to the great actress Jennifer Kendal, and so Kunal had the looks of an Anglo-Indian, with his mother's blue eyes.

When I first called Kunal, he agreed to meet me at the Shamiana restaurant at the Taj.

When I suggested 11 A.M. he surprised me by asking,

"How about 10 A.M.?"

"Of course."

I got there before 10 A.M, but there was no trace of him even by 10:30.

I left a message with the restaurant manager, asking him to inform Kunal, in case he showed up looking for me, that I had waited half an hour and left.

The next day Kunal called and explained that he had been under the impression that our appointment had been for 11 A.M.

We made another appointment for 11 A.M the next day, and I deliberately showed up ten minutes late.

I found him waiting at a table for two and I started with, "I'm so sorry to keep you waiting, Kunal."

"You aren't sorry at all," he replied, "It was deliberate and intentional."

I burst out laughing. He was my kind of guy. We were well-matched.

He had just broken up with his starlet girlfriend and he said, "She gave me quite a run for my money."

I did a follow-up interview at his place on Malabar Hill (he was living with his parents, which is normal in India).

He conducted me to his room, where we would not be disturbed, but left the door open.

Just as we were about to conclude, Shashi Kapoor walked into the room in a white muslin kurta pajama and leather flip-flops. He was every inch - Shashi Kapoor! - the nawab in Heat and Dust, looking at me with his unforgettable eyes and smile.

Even though I was a woman, I stood up as a mark of respect and brought my palms together in the Indian greeting.

But Shashi extended his right hand and shook my hand warmly.

"I hope he hasn't given you too much trouble?" he asked, looking fondly at his son.

"Let me not disturb you," he added and left.

Then Jennifer came in and said hello. I had met her at the reception to launch 36 Chowringhee Lane, but by then my rave review in "Mid-Day" had already appeared. As always, she had the gentlest, most affectionate smile.

When the film opened to raves in London, I called her, and she laughed into the phone, "I knew I would hear from you today!"

Sadly, the world lost her to breast cancer while she was still in her fifties.

But when Kunal was seeing me to the door, Shashi was standing in the middle of the living room and saw me to the door himself. As is often the practice in India, he walked me all the way to the elevator. It was an old-fashioned lift, with chain doors that one opened and closed manually.

As the elevator went down, the last thing I saw was his toes peeping out of the flip-flops.

I thought I would see him again, planning to interview him when I returned from New York a couple of years later for the first of many visits to India.

But it was not to be.

I never saw Shashi Kapoor or India again.

After Jennifer passed away, Shashi sought solace in food and became obese, but continued to give great performances.

Shashi Kapoor passed into eternity in 2017, but his films are on You Tube for all of us to see.

I have watched the DVD of "Heat and Dust" many times, sharing it with friends, and also have all his other Merchant-Ivory films.

We have not lost Shashi Kapoor.

He is now ours forever.

And with that, I end my memoir of my years in India.

Thank you for reading it.

THE END

PHOTO GALLERY

My grandmother, with my mother, Surat, 1916

Daddy on the jetty at Cuffe Parade, 1939, with his Anglo-Indian friends. The little boy on his left was Ganpat, a servant, who sadly died a year later.

Daddy with his winning horse, 1941

Mummy after her second abortion, 1942

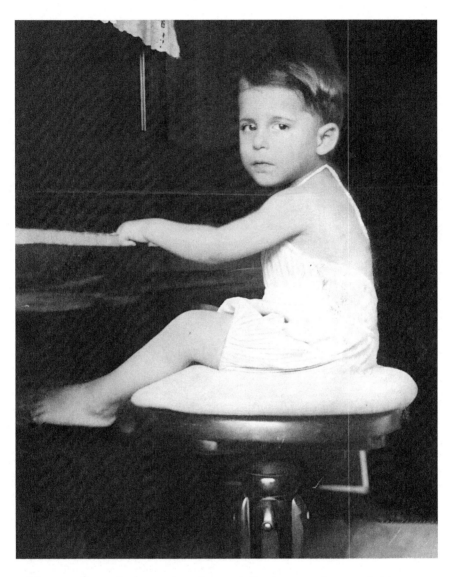

My very first photo at the piano at the home of my neighbours, the Borthwicks.

Photo by Jerry Borthwick, a passionate amateur photographer

At my Navjote in 1955, with my brother Mehli on my left and
my parents on my right

St. Mary's High School, Bombay

Mario De'Souza	Farrukh Rustom	V Desai	Emile Joshi	Aubrey Stanley	P Mehta	Akbar Currim	R Kamlani
K Zaveri	H Karani	Clark Gibbs	C Patel	M Dah	Issaks Bahar	Iqbal Begmohamed	N Silva
Bruce Allams	V Khanna	D Mathur	Francis Nunes	D De'Mello	R Rahmany	Richard Fernandes	V Idnani
J Jambusarwalla	R Sanjana	R Chinoy	J Dubash	K Mama	Clarence Rodrigues	L D'Monte	V Patwardhan
M Mastor	M Mistry	B Shroff	Y Godiwalla	A Madhani	Joseph Noronha	Winston Reuben	F Carvalho
N Dubash	M Kapadia	K Garebian	Keith Major	L Nawlands			

Senior Cambridge Graduation Class Of 1959

Above : St. Mary's (circa 1865): note the Neo-Gothic architecture.

Left : Class of 1959

At the House of Soviet Culture, while being
introduced to the audience by the Director,
Mr. Dimitri Smirnov, 1983

With Deepti Naval, serving me "palak" (Indian spinach) cooked
by herself, on the terrace of her house, 1983

Cover photo for a feature article on me, Eve's Weekly, 1984

With actor Sunil Dutt, 1984

At Home, 1984

With the Prince of Porbunder, 1985

At my piano , 1985. This piano now has a home
with Deepti Naval

At my desk in Bombay 1985, with our 1930s Alexander Graham Bell telephone

With Frank Weiss, Berlin, 1986

At the Charlottenburg Palace, Berlin, 1986

Akbar, aged 18, with his bride Najma, 1986

With Nutan on the terrace of her penthouse atop Sagar
Sangeet, not far from Dolphin

With actor Faroukh Sheikh

With Mithun Chakraborty, the John Travolta of India

Our servant Anthony with his brother, Peter, his
sister Rita, and mischievous Yellappa with his friend

Aijaz Ahmed

On the roof of my building, New York, 1987

On the Hudson River, Greenwich Village
West, with Kurt Martin from Berlin, 1988

Atop the World Trade Centre, 1990

ABOUT THE AUTHOR

Farah Rustom was born in Bombay in 1943, and currently lives in the US. She was born as Farokh Rustom but always felt that she was in the wrong body. In 1976 she underwent gender reassignment surgery at the Masina Hospital. The surgeon was Dr. M. H. Keswani. This created a sensation, as she was well known by then as a pioneering lecturer on western classical music appreciation, and also as a freelance journalist. She is a gold medallist Fellow of the Trinity College of Music, London. She blazed a trail for other transgendered souls trapped in the wrong body with her newspaper, magazine and television interviews and articles. This is her story, which includes her many passions in life, including travel, and portrays life as it was in Bombay in the Nineteen Fifties, Sixties, Seventies, and Eighties.

Other Books from JMHA Publishing

1st short story
collection

2nd short story
collection

Novel set in a Bombay
apartment building

3rd short story
collection

Decorative collection of
original German poetry

An epic
fantasy novel.

A novel of war
and time travel

4th short story
collection

Novel of WWII
and magic

Novel of time travel
and ancient Britain

Sequel novel to
Heaven's Above

Novel in the style
of Jane Austen

Printed in Great Britain
by Amazon

28516743R00145